Hours of Thought

ON

Sacred Things.

BY

JAMES MARTINEAU, LL.D., D.D.,

AUTHOR OF "ENDEAVORS AFTER THE CHRISTIAN LIFE," ETC.

Ψυχῆς ἁγνῆς τόπον οἰκειότερον ἐπὶ γῆς οὐκ ἔχει Θεός.
DEMOPHILI *Sent. Pythag.* 45.

Um Gott zu *haben*, muss man zuerst etwas sein, das Gott haben *kann*.
RICHARD ROTHE: *Stille Stunden*, 189.

BOSTON:
ROBERTS BROTHERS.
1876.

CAMBRIDGE:
PRESS OF JOHN WILSON AND SON.

PREFACE.

THE first duty, it has been said, of a retired preacher is to commit to the flames whatever he has prepared for the pulpit, and secure the world against further tedium from his labors. In the face of this canon of clerical duty, I have hesitated to rescue a few fragments from the process of destruction, and let them try for themselves whether their natural life has reached its term. If I have found courage for the experiment, it is chiefly because a previous collection, which thirty years ago I did not expect to reproduce, is apparently more true to the feeling of the present time than to that of the last generation. Those who have spent thought and zeal on the moral movements of their age may naturally dread, as their strength declines and their speed slackens, to be thrown out of the great march which they have long shared; and they may legitimately put it to the test, whether they have dropped off into loneliness, or whether their voice is still in harmony with the tones which meet the future. If the following pages should foster any high impulse in those who have the work of life before them, or shed any light on those who have the sorrows of life behind them, I shall be content not to have withheld it.

This volume represents, on the whole, a considerably later stage of feeling and experience than the "Endeavors after the Christian Life"; and doubtless bears traces, in parts, of the more recent aspects of religious speculation. But essentially the same view of life, the same conception of the order of the world, the same interpretation of the Christian mind, will still meet the reader; for they remain unaffected, so far as I can perceive, by the real discoveries, and are prejudiced only by the philosophical fictions of the last five and twenty years. The new lights of historical criticism certainly change, in no slight degree, our picture of the origin and growth of the Christian religion: but every larger comprehension of the universe only invests the principles of that religion with sublimer truth; and every added refinement of conscience the more attests their spiritual worth.

LONDON, October 6, 1876.

CONTENTS.

HOURS OF THOUGHT.

I.

The Tides of the Spirit.

LUKE iv. 16.

"And he came to Nazareth, where he had been brought up; and as his custom was, he went into the synagogue on the sabbath day, and stood up for to read."

WE cannot wonder that something in his look,—some visible flush of inward life,—fastened the eyes of all upon him. For to his human feeling, which could nowhere assert a greater right than there, the moment was overcharged with a certain sad intensity. Since last he stood upon that spot, a change had passed upon him: a light, long struggling with the clouds and often drowned in a golden haze of mystery, had cleared itself within him: he was no longer at his own disposal, or free to rest upon the trodden paths; but the sacred dove was ever on the wing before him, and now alighted on the synagogue of Nazareth, and there, where he naturally fell into the attitude of docility, left him to speak the word of supernatural power. Never is it so hard to follow and trust a higher inspiration, as amid the crowd of customary things; and in proportion as the heart is tender and gracious, clinging with fibres of reverent affection to the past, is it a sorrowful loyalty that takes us out to anything beyond. If ever Jesus could yield to misgivings of what was committed to him, it would be in that place; whose threshold he could not reach without passing the cottage and the workshop door, and overtaking the slow steps and bent forms of village elders, and being startled by the remembered laugh of many a child; whose walls were written all over with early memories; where bars of sunshine painted the floor with a meaning not to be erased; where the voices of familiars whispered round him; and the venerable features were turned upon him of the Levite who taught him to read the very scroll in his hand; and he felt the eye of Mary, and knew all the flutter of her heart. There, in presence of those at whose feet he used to sit,—there, where he first heard and pondered Israel's hope, and watched a holy light on other faces, not knowing that it was reflected from his own,—how could he stand up and draw the great words of Isaiah upon himself, and say aloud, 'This is the hour,'—'Lo! it is I.'? A consciousness less divinely calm must have grown confused under the crossing rays of so many sympathies. But with him the temptation was now passed: he had emerged from the desert that lay between the old life and the new.

The very Spirit of God had driven him thither to hear what could be said against itself: pale with fasting, alone by night with his Satan and his God, he had learned the worst; had not only flung the self away, but loosed the detaining hand of custom, and freely gone into the divine captivity. And now, he was no longer his own: his humanity was the organ of a higher Will: no flitting of the Spirit, off and on,—it rested with him now; no stormy skies that often blotted out the stars, but a pure and tranquil look into the infinite. And so, he could bear those native scenes again, for they lay in another light: the hills of Nazareth were transfigured before him: from all things round the dull and weary aspect had fled, that makes them press with the weight of usage; and he stood amid the well-known groups, as some immortal friend might return and look in among us here, with unabated love, but with saintly insight into meanings hid from us.

Lifted then into the full power of the Spirit, with the forces of evil already shrinking before him, whither, as least uncongenial, does he take his heavenly point of view?—To the village synagogue, on the stated day of rest: nothing newer, nothing higher; but just the place and time which had been sacred to the fathers. The first thing which he did, under freshest inspiration, was to resume the dear old ways, to fall in with the well-known season, to unroll the same venerable page; only to find a new meaning in words that had long carried their rhythm to his heart. What? had he not risen above *that?* could the dull preachings and the drawling prayers say anything *to him?* What charm could he longer feel in these childish Sabbath usages,—the decent dress, the restful hours, the flowing together of families and walking to the house of God in company? Did not he, above all, live in a constant air of divine communion, and mingle with the eternity where all is consecrate alike? Do what he might, go where he would,—walking early on the beach, sitting by the well at noon, or kneeling by night upon the mountain grass, jostled by the city multitudes or borne upon the sea alone,—was he not always with the Father,—himself a better sanctuary than he could ever find? What could a nature at that height have to do with any sacred enclosure of space or time? Yet, "at Nazareth, where he had been brought up, he went, *as his custom was,* into the synagogue on the Sabbath day."

We are sustained then by the sympathy of the highest inspiration, when we make it our "custom" too, to illuminate in our calendar some holy day, and to raise near every cluster of our dwellings a house where "prayer is wont to be made." Heed not the fastidious critic who tells you that the world has outgrown the church,—that the living voice of trust and aspiration shall soon have no response from sorrowing and struggling men. Depend upon it, *his* is the humour of the hour; and *you* who keep to the old reverent ways are taking sides with the perpetuity of our humanity. Fear not that you have here to do with any perishable work. Crowd the pavement of the church with the aged and the young: make it the favourite store-house of earnest vows and living sacrifice: train its echoes to sweet and holy hymns, that shall blend soul with soul, and carry all to God; and, thus sanctified, let it stand by night and day a silent witness to the world of invisible and heavenly things.

Against the Christian habit of *seasonal and local* worship the truth is often urged, that God is a Spirit, eternal and omniscient, abiding neither in "this mountain" nor in that "Jerusalem," and bearing equal relation to every mind and every moment. This truth is drawn aside into two opposite abuses. On the one hand, the *mystic* would mould himself into accordance with the divine constancy, by spreading the margin of his prayer till it covers the whole of life; and would let out the imprisoned glory of his highest mood to transfigure all the years. For him it is too small a thing to be "in the spirit on the Lord's day": any little Patmos-isle of vision is too limited for him: he must be always at the holiest he can ever be: he must sink his whole footing and himself away in the infinite flood whose perfection has no tides. To pass into a sacred equanimity and float evenly along, neither wrapt in chariot of fire, nor blinded with clouds of dust; to carry about in the heart a heaven that shall steep the commonest work in stainless colours; to let labour and rest, youth and age, with all intermittent things, stand for the body and be nothing to the soul, and inwardly live as if no shadows lengthened and no heavens rolled;—is the secret aim of one who loses himself in the spirituality and immensity of God. And this very same truth which urges him to worship always, *i.e. as much* at one time as at another, is, on the other hand, the plea with the *secular temper* for specially worshipping *never*, *i.e. as little* at one time as at another. How often do you fall in with one who feels himself above the superstition of real prayer; who is conscious of no personal relations beyond this world; to whom the whole expression and organism of religion is but a discipline for social duty,—a discipline necessary for the feeble, decorous for the good, but empty for the wise; who is rather its patron than its disciple, and maintains churches for the world as he keeps a nursery for his children, with as little idea of spending his own adult and earnest life there; and who looks on times and places of devotion, on the voice of contrition and aspiration, on the swelling hymn, on the impassioned words of psalmist and prophet, and the memorials of a Saviour's sacrifice, as an overwrought provision for sustaining the daily moralities of life. Serving God's will in the constant course of a faithful, manly, kindly career, he is out of his element elsewhere; has no burden to lay down, no height to seize: always equal to himself, he wants no reminder, appropriates no confession, and receives every ideal demand upon him as flowing water receives falling sparks. And so, he looks down on all special worship as a weakness to which he cannot descend; and, if ever social connexion or hereditary ties commit him to the interests of a Christian church, he upholds it for others rather than himself; or else encourages it as a platform of party self-assertion, and is proud of its dedication to his own opinions, instead of humbly offering in it the best that he has, and all that he is, to the real and living God.

Now what answer can we give to these two men, both apparently resting on a great and sublime truth,—the eternal constancy of God?—the one adapting himself to it by congenial persistency of devotion,—the other by ethical steadiness of will. Shall we ask from each of them some little allowance for human infirmity, which cannot hold on by a rule so patient? Shall we say to the Mystic, 'You must let us down at times from that untenable height of yours: why bid us

"Wind ourselves too high
For mortal man beneath the sky"?

we are on earth and God in heaven; and while we are here, our feet must sometimes stroll the easy grass, and the natural darkness hide diviner visions from us'? And shall we say to the other, 'You must not expect every one to be as even-minded as yourself,—as well able to dispense with the freshening of conscience and the fervours of faith: the atmosphere of the common human nature is of unstable balance, and so long as it has its belt of tropical heats, you must let its sweeping winds have way'? In answering thus, you plead on both hands for a concession to acknowledged weakness; and you treat just the opposite things as weakness in the two cases, making humble excuse, first, for ever touching the earth, and then, for ever springing towards heaven; and, in both instances, apologising for alternations of mood as something humiliating but inevitable, needing the tender mercy of Reason and out of harmony with the reality of God. These feeble self-contradictions I venture to leave behind, and to advance at once to a firmer position. In the *Occasionalism* of piety, I see not its shame, but its distinctive glory; and would lay stress on the *intermittency* of the devout affections, as the sign, not of poverty or weakness, but specifically of their grandeur in themselves, and their accurate accordance with what is highest in God's realities.

For, whether you stay at home, and look in upon the composition of our own nature; or go out into the universe and Providence of God, you will find this law:—that, of his agencies and manifestations, it is the lowest that are least mutable, and most remain the same from first to last; whilst the highest have ever a tidal ebb and flow,—moving in waves of time, and surprising hidden inlets of space with their flood.

In our bodily constitution itself this law already

begins to leave its trace. Two systems of parts and offices co-exist, we are told, in the human frame; one comprising the group of organs and functions which we have in common with the vegetable world, and by which, like the plants, we breathe, and take and use our nourishment, and throb with the sap of strength, and grow; the other including the additional endowments of an animated organism, the instruments by which we move, and perceive, and feel. By the *organic* life wo vegetate; by the *animal* life we suffer and we act. And in accordance with their respective ranks, the former and lower never ceases or remits from birth to death;—the beating heart, the heaving breast, and all the silent chemistries, persevering by night and day, whether half seen beneath the bloom of infancy, or shut up beneath the lines of age; while the latter and higher subsists by intermission,—springs into action, falls back into sleep; and even with the young child's eye, so bold and loving to the light, the lids droop and enforce a shade; and the quick limbs collapse and are flung upon the bed of nature till the spent tide returns.

Rise a step higher in our nature, and the intermittent pulsation of the finer energies becomes more marked. Mind is more fitful than strength, less under steady control of the will, faster and further in its ebb, in proportion as it is fuller and grander in its flood. The day-labourer with his limbs can bear longer hours than the man of letters with his pen; and can produce more even work. And precisely as the faculties which he tasks are above the level of intellectual routine, is the thinker dependent on moods which he cannot command or prolong :—to learn, to criticize, to judge, to arrange, being usually in his power ; but to combine, to discover, to create, being the free gift of happy moments not his own. Is he a compiler and fabricator of mental products ? his process, like any other manufacture, may go on, wherever the machinery of industry is set in motion. Is he poet or inventor ? then he seems to be the organ of another will, and to be now lifted into clear achievement, now sunk into deep humiliation. At times, a murky atmosphere appears to close in upon his soul and damp down its very flame to smoke ; and all his faithfulness and patience are unavailing to perforate the gloom, and end only in the dripping of the sad rain. At another time he seems to be planted high in a pure and lustrous air ; to look on nothing that does not shine with a self-light : the quick streaming thoughts flow upon him like a morning wind ; every darkening cloud swims off to the far horizon and melts into bars of indigo and gold : turn his interpreting eye where he will, he mingles with the meanings of things ; and his feet are on the mountains, and his heart with God.

And who will venture to say that the highest insight of the spirit is even half as constant as the highest action of the mind ? Ask the saintliest men and women of this world, whether their holy watch was continuous, and their faith and love as reliable as their thought; and they will tell you how long, even when they went up to be with the Saviour on the mount, have been the slumbers of unconsciousness, compared with the priceless instants when they were awake and beheld his glory. In every earnest life, there are weary flats to tread, with the heavens out of sight,—no sun, no moon,—and not a tint of light upon the path below; when the only guidance is the faith of brighter hours, and the secret Hand we are too numb and dark to feel. But to the meek and faithful it is not always so. Now and then, something touches the dull dream of sense and custom, and the desolation vanishes away: the spirit leaves its witness with us: the divine realities come up from the past and straightway enter the present: the ear into which we poured our prayer is not deaf; the infinite eye to which we turned is not blind, but looks in with answering mercy on us. The mystery of life and the grievousness of death are gone: we know now the little from the great, the transient from the eternal: we can possess our souls in patience; and neither the waving palms and scattered flowers of triumph can elate us, nor the weight of any cross appear too hard to bear. Tell me not that these undulations of the soul are the mere instability of enthusiasm and infirmity. Are they not found characteristically in the greatest and deepest men,—Augustine, Tauler,

Luther? Nay, did not the Son of God himself, the very type of our humanity, experience them more than all? Did he not quit the daily path, now for a Transfiguration, and now for a Gethsemane? did not his voice burst into the exclamation, 'I beheld Satan as lightning fall from heaven,' yet also confess, 'Now is my soul troubled'? And had he not his hours on the mountain all night? and what, think you, passed beneath those stars? Ah no! those intermittent movements are the sign of divine gifts, not of human weakness. God has so arranged the chronometry of our spirits that there shall be thousands of silent moments between the striking hours.

Nor is it in personal experience alone that we read this law. When we pass out of ourselves, and look abroad over the Providence of God in nature and in history, the same truth appears again. How it may be with God in his own essence, I dare not presume to think. He is the high and holy One who inhabiteth eternity; and if you will say of him those awful and mysterious things that flow from the conception of Infinitude,—that in him there is no succession, no transition, no emotion,—that he never comes and goes, is neither here nor there,—that he is the stationary Now, abiding still, with nothing past and nothing future; —I hold my peace, and breathe no word against you. But this I know, and in this I rather rest: whatever he may be in himself, his *manifestations to us* do not lie still before us in the sleep of a frozen sea: they break out of this motionless eternity: they sweep in mighty tides of nature and of history, with flux and reflux: they are alive with shifting streaks of light and gloom; and have the changing voice of many waters. And the clearer and more spiritual they are, the more marked is this fluctuating character; and they affect us, not as the dead of noon or the dead of night, but as the quick-flushing morning or the tender pulses of the northern lights.

God, you say, is eternal and immutable. If by this you mean that there never was a time, and nowhere is a place, empty of his agency, it is most true. But if you mean that his agency is everywhere and always equal,—that it cannot be encountered more or less,—that it is the same in the life of an angel and in the gravitation of a stone,—that there is for us no nearer to him and no further from him,—you give expression, I believe, to the largest falsehood that can be framed.

Where is it that we find the trace and illustration of the constancy of God? To what realm does your thought fly, when you would conceive his unchangeable Infinitude? You pass out into the field of *Space*, and carry with you the amplest measure of imaginable *Time*: you take leave of this historic earth, as of a village life, and move among the kosmic cycles on whose dial the little index of humanity can scarce play the part of second's hand: you step from star to star, and go to meet half-way the rays that have been travelling to you for a million years. And as you observe how orderly, how punctual, how balanced, how silent of its beginning, how unhinting of an end, that night-scene is, you adore indeed Him "that bringeth out this host by number"; but you return with a cold shudder from so fixed a face of God, and take refuge again in the green valleys of a more changing and ephemeral world. The great physical elements and laws which, from their inexorable regularity and gigantic sweep, stand before our thought as emblems of the Divine unchangeableness, are the largest, but also the lowest of God's manifestations. Speaking of his majesty, they are dumb respecting his *character;* or, at best, if they declare his faithfulness, they pronounce it stern as Fate, and drive into recoil the advances of affection.

But let us not fear. That immensity takes us the very furthest from him that we can go. The worlds he has made *out of nothing;* but man *out of himself:* the one, accordingly, he has put under necessity; the other he draws with cords of love. In the one, his word is pledged and bound; with the other, his Spirit still lives free. Nature is only his fabric, and is not like him; Man is his child, and is susceptible of his image. The human characteristics must for ever stand with us as, out of all that we can think, the very likest to him; and these are not a perpetual and unrelenting mechanism; but the thinking Reason, the aspiring Conscience, the elective Will, the gentle and self-sacrificing Affection. And when these speak to our hearts as his witnesses, we have our eye upon a more intermittent as well as a higher glory, than can be found in the great physical laws: for, as the Spirit bloweth where it listeth, the life of men and angels has at once a freer and diviner movement than the travels of a sunbeam or the revolution of a star. Nor is it in *all* men, or in the *whole* of human history, that it is given us to trace the impress of his Mind. However true it is that there is no private heart to which he is quite strange, yet it is not in all alike that the sanctities of his agency visibly appear. We see and own him in proportion to the nobleness and beauty of the lives which he inspires; and it is only now and then, at the great crises of society, that the common level of the human self and the finite understanding is transcended, and sages, prophets, saints rise above their nature and become the organs of a Spirit not their own. I presume not to say *how* it is God takes up his abode with us; *where*, across the melting colours the precise line should be drawn that divides the human from the divine. But wherever he so dwells with the soul as to impart his own character, and lift before our eye the beauty of holiness, it is his supreme expression, as it is his rarest. Accordingly it is this which he selects for the supernatural revelation of himself which stands unique,

—" the Word made flesh,"—the divine life humanised, and the human glorified,—the blending of both in communion and reconciliation. In that sacrifice culminate the intermittent visitations of God: it was not tidal only: it is once for all; and as it was supreme, it was solitary too. As all the special goodness, grace, and truth of historic men give pauses of blessed rest, and are not the week-day, but the sabbath of the world; so is the divine perfectness of Christ the sabbath of sabbaths, the solemn jubilee of our humanity.

Be assured then that in your ancient usages of seasonal and local worship, in seeking here to meet at intervals the high tides of God's spirit, you are in harmony with his sublimest Providence,—with a law of variation transcending any physical uniformity over which it sweeps. Reverence the holy custom, shelter from heedless slight the living impulse, that week by week calls you hither to remember, to aspire, to pray. Bring only the pure, lowly, childlike heart, tender to everything except the sins you must confess,—full of hope for the world and trust in God; spread out an eager and a gentle spirit for the dropping of fruitful seeds from Holy Writ and saintly hymn; freshen the fading vow of self-sacrificing love; and your worship here will not only resemble *his* who, in fulness of the Spirit, " went, as his custom was, into the synagogue on the sabbath day," but prepare for a higher communion, where " your life is hid with him in God."

II.

Seek first the Kingdom of God.

I.

MATT. vi. 33.

"Seek ye first the kingdom of God and his righteousness; and all these things shall be added unto you."

THOUGH the mountain slope may still be found on which these words were uttered, the figure of Jesus, as he sat on a basaltic block and taught, is seen by us only across the chasm in which eighteen centuries are sunk: the diminished picture rises in the distance, like a sunny knoll swelling out of a sea of darkness; and the voice reaches us, like the intonations, rather seen than heard, of a vision or a dream. Had we been on the other side of the separating gulf, and mingled with the peasant audience, and pressed the actual grass which is now but a verdure of our thought; had we felt the upland breath of that autumn evening, on which the great Teacher's fervent accents rose or died away; had we seen the lengthening shadows flung from that height upon the lake below, bisecting its blue waters, and creeping towards the white sails, the shelving beach, the lighted rocks, of the remoter shore; had we marked the eye of Jesus invited by the note of birds wheeling overhead, and caught his instant words, "Behold the fowls of the air;" or, as he pointed to the pastures brilliant with their golden amaryllis, heard his praise of the lilies that toil not; we should have owned that the heaven above was less deep in beauty than the divine soul before us: ashamed of our mean cares under the Providence he interpreted, we should have filled our evening with truth and trust inspired from him: we should have felt that we had been with one who stood alone among the sons of God; and who rose above all earthly spirits, as the snowy peak of Lebanon, now crimson with the sunken sun, towered above the dark world below. Who can wonder, if many a loving Mary, many an ardent Peter, many a true-souled John, took the vow from that hour, to "seek first the kingdom of God," and believe that "all other things would be added unto them"?

We receive these words, however, amid a scene quite different; and it is well if their truth and beauty, felt as they look up at us from the page of Scripture, do not cease to *live* as realities in our conscience, and become ideal and historical with the time that gave them birth. Does this ranking of human aims,—first spiritual good, then temporal necessities,—describe the actual order of our prevalent pursuits, or even the arrangement of our habitual convictions? Carry the precept in your memory, as you walk the city, musing on the *contents* of that hum of voices. Take it to the dock side, as you listen to the roll of traffic, and think of the history of all its wealth. Recall it in the mill, as you reflect to what end it is that all the giant mechanism heaves and whirls incessantly. If all this, it may well occur to you, is just for the things that *are "added unto" men* with scarce a thought of theirs, how transcendently strenuous must be their primary pursuit, to which this is but a trustful leisure! Assuming this scene, with all its bewildering intensity, as a sample of their indifference, what must be the measure of their holy zeal! Alas! you well know that those burning aspirations in reserve do not exist; that the stir around about you belongs, not to the secondary, but to the chief business, of men;—to the ends that *rule*, not to those that *serve*, in human life; and that far from being here amid its cooler temperature, you stand in the very focus of its most fervid heats. Nay, you will perhaps think, that it not only *is* so, but really *ought* to be so; that, after all, man's first great struggle must be to maintain his footing upon this world; that the means of life cannot but take precedence of the rules of living; that the Christian law of trust, though quite in place in the Sermon on the Mount, is positively *too romantic* for the warehouse and the street. Men must be allowed to make sure of physical support; and then will be time enough to look after their spiritual nature: let them "seek first" what they are to eat and drink; and, this once secured, the kingdom of God may be "added unto" it.

This style of sentiment is not likely to appear less reasonable, when you turn to those who, from horror at its irreligion, have fled from the world which it governs, and resolved to live out a sincere Christianity, in abdication of all the pursuits of human appetite and affection. Far up in Alpine heights, or in cloistered silence in the heart of cities, you may find fraternities and sisterhoods, renouncing everything except the kingdom of God, aspiring to it by the path of a holy austerity, and submitting cheerfully to a self-crucifixion of every affection below the standard of an angelic sanctity. But this attempt at entire dedication to Heaven produces a form of character which is far from satisfying our conception of a Christian symmetry of soul. Between fear of the abyss and aspiration to the skies, the blessed earth, our appointed place that lies in the midst, is too lightly touched, or even contemptuously disowned: the quest of God is too like a heartless flight from man; and it would be strange if the law of Christ,—the friend of publicans and sinners,—were suited only to the exceptional case of the saintly recluse, and incapable of being acted out by us face to face, amid the actual throng and press of life, without flight from our temptations, or suicide of our nature. Christianity no doubt would be a blessed thing, if it merely snatched a noble few by diviner attractions from a world heavy with incurable corruption, and drew them into its sanctuary with the awful invitation, "Ephraim is joined with idols, let him alone." But there is no true reflection of its great Author's spirit, till the Church and the World are not two, but one,—the inner and the outer courts of the same earnest worship; till the evil that is abroad is not despaired of but confronted and assailed, and disciples have the heart to say, "This earth is by no means Satan's, but wholly God's; come, let us chase away these demons of darkness, and win it back for him;" till religion, instead of shrinking within the altar rails, and lighting there a lonely lamp of incense, can turn its radiant face upon the people, penetrate their open life with its flash, and shatter and spoil the false idols of their hearts, and in all things reconcile and fuse together the human and the holy.

But how can this be, you will say? what means does Christianity afford of blending the secular and spiritual extremes of character, and, by union of these opposites, completing the healthful circuit of our moral power? Hitherto it seems to have kept them wider apart than ever; and while the minds at either end appear to have some force of Reason, it is in the one case Reason degraded into too gross a Sense, in the other raised to too ethereal a Sanctity.

There is no juster complaint against human exaggeration than this. And, strange as it may seem, the error of the two parties, however contrasted in result, is one and the same. They both feel, what the language of Jesus emphatically states, that there is some sort of opposition between the living for worldly and living for spiritual good. But they altogether mistake *the nature of this opposition.* They fancy it to consist in this; that the two orders of pursuit have quite different *spheres of work;* that what the secular man does, the religious man must avoid; that the quest of temporal advantages is one kind of business, tasking our industry with an appropriate set of occupations; the quest of heavenly sanctity another kind of business, prescribing occupations almost perfectly distinct. Accordingly there are employments which this pernicious moral superstition has branded with an equivocal mark of irreligion; and other employments which are supposed to constitute the substance of the true Christian obedience. The provision and government of house and home, the daily meal, the social hour of recreation or of mirth; the transaction of private business, or the control of public affairs; the enlargement of knowledge, the practice of art, the pursuit of truth;—in short, all the characteristic engagements of the citizen, the merchant, the politician, the student, are conceived to lie upon the secular side of human life, and to constitute our temptations to evil rather than our opportunities for good. On the other hand, works of charity to the needy, and visits of conversion to the guilty; the exercises of private devotion and of public prayer; the contemplation of saintly examples, and the accumulation of scriptural impressions and unearthly thoughts; direct and broad conversation about things invisible, and comparisons of inward experience, are supposed to constitute the religious staple of life, from which every distraction is a humiliating concession to the low and shameful necessities of a fallen nature. Hence, the popular conception of Heaven wholly excludes all idea of *activity and thought*, and admits nothing but a perpetuity of positive worship. Hence too, when a man of this narrow religion becomes entangled in affairs of the world, he carries into them no clear calm feeling of sacred obligation, to guide him in the path of noble uprightness; but rather a conscience half flurried to find himself there at all, amid things too profane to come within his province of duties: his faith can make nothing of such sinful materials, except resolve to escape from them as fast as it can; and need I say, that one who, with this feeling, gets, with no small stake at issue, into an unmanageable Devil's world, is very apt to let Satan have his own way, in despair of battling with him on his own ground? And hence, finally, he who with such belief, is determined never to capitulate, has no resource but the hermit's; to quit the scene of human energy and abandon the cares for subsistence, and going about some diviner work, expect the ravens to come and feed him, while he sits still. This he calls a trust in Providence; though it is manifestly a contempt of the established course of Providence, and a trust only in that which would directly violate it. He calls it a quest of the kingdom of God; though it is a flight from the realm of allotted duty, and a renounced allegiance of natural obligations. He calls it an emancipation from all thought of the morrow; yet it is plainly the surest way of filling the mind with real anxiety about "the meat that perisheth," and of engaging the whole religious affections, as in a gamester's play, in the precarious question of its failure or supply.

In fact, the godless lover of gain, and the gainless lover of God are fanatics both, taking hold of the opposite ends of the same falsehood. And the truth which suffices to rebuke them both, is this; *that the kingdom of God is not a business, set up in rivalry with worldly business;* but *a divine law regulating, and a divine temper pervading, the pursuits of worldly business.* It does not change the materials, but the form and spirit, of our life. It leaves our outward occupations essentially what they were, and opens to us still the domestic hearth, the public council, the field, the city, and the ocean, as the sphere of all our work: but it makes us conscious of the different orders of desire and affection that may guide us through all these; the brutal appetencies, the shrewd selfishness, the instinctive kindliness, the sense of justice, the love of goodness, the aspiration after the perfectness of God, with which the very same employments may be debased or consecrated. The feeling of divine duty is not a new faculty of action added to our mind, having a distinct set of objects indifferent to us before: all the impulsive forces that send us on to our theatre and take us to our work are instinctive gifts of nature, neither more nor fewer in the sinner or saint. But when devout Conscience finds entrance among them, it sets them in the relative order of their ranks; forbids the scramble of eager and unsettled claims; commands lazy appetite, already seated at the feast, to get up and gird itself and serve; sends impudent ambition to take the lowest place; and says to truthful love driven to the door, "Friend, come up higher." It reveals to us the comparative worth and authority of the several sources of action within us: it is simply, indeed, as the word denotes, the *consciousness* of this; and is therefore not properly a separate principle of the soul, but the inherent knowledge of their own place in the scale of excellence which attends the exercise of all our springs of action. It is not *a power*, but *a perception*, and performs a function *judicial*, not executive. No man, accordingly, can with any precision be said to *act from conscience:* he acts from some primitive instinct or acquired affection: but two of these may at the same instant be candidates for the possession of his Will; and when he puts aside the one which he knows to be the meaner, and obeys the other because he feels it to be the nobler, we signify the fact by the loose phrase, he acts from conscience. It is plain here that if there were no natural springs of volition, Conscience, left alone, would be wholly unproductive: it would be in possession of a sinecure, and its occupation would be gone. And what we thus say of Conscience, we say of the kingdom of God; for I know of no religion, natural or revealed, which is not a development of this divine element in our souls; an opening before it, by the apparition of some new greatness, of a higher and yet a higher than even its highest was before; a total passing away of worship into infinitude; and a sense of the sleepless watch of the Holiest around the path of life.

From this view of our nature it follows that *spiritual good* is not a *new object* given us by our religion, but only the *regulated and proportioned pursuit of natural good*, in entire deference to the relative excellence of its several kinds. Original instinct is altogether blind except to its own particular object, which it pursues as if it were the universe: hunger seizes upon food, anger strikes an obstacle, pity flies to suffering, with unreflecting impulse, seeing nothing else, and making no more estimate of its own end than the migratory bird of the seasons whose changes it obeys. Each instinct is sufficient for its own end, and for nothing more; lights our way and impels our activity, to its appropriate good, wholly regardless of the existence of any other; nothing can be added to it, nothing can be taken from it, without impairing its perfection, and turning it from an element of health into a seat of disease. Man, moreover, not only *has* instincts, but *knows* them, and is able so to compare them as to perceive which is higher, which lower: he not only *knows* them, but *rules* them, not letting each take its chance of becoming uppermost, but exercising preference among them, according to the divine right and rank of each. As this perception of relative worth among the springs of conduct is what we mean by *Conscience*, so the consequent *power* of practical choice among them is what we mean by *Will*. And *spiritual good* is nothing but the perfect consonance between these two: it exists where the moral vision is clear and wide, the moral volition quick and strong, and what the one discerns, the other executes. The proper and sole-appointed function of the Will is, not to form a partnership with any instinct, and add itself on as a fresh energy to its pursuit; not to rise up in rivalry to instinct, and by counterpoise subtract something from its force; but, letting the *quantities* of our nature alone, to guide us by its *qualities*; to make a true choice among the natural principles, when two or more are knocking at the gate of entrance to our life.

In what then consists the opposition between the pursuit of natural and the pursuit of spiritual good?—the desire of physical supplies, and the aspiration after the kingdom of God? It lies in this:—He who seeks after "what he shall eat and what he shall drink" is one whose *chief conscious aim* is *to get such things:* He who seeks first "the kingdom of God" is one whose chief conscious aim is *not to get them unworthily.* The one throws his whole reflective and directing powers into the work of instinct, madly enhancing, yet intellectually guiding, its intensity; infuriating the chase, yet giving it precision; and turning the innocent tendency of the creature, into the clever passion of the demon. The other applies his thoughtfulness to the *control* of his instincts, and the establishment among them of the true divine subordination of the lower to the higher. He never quits the helm to feed the fire; to steer the good ship, and not to double the tension of the steam, is the allotted office of his skill. He knows where his real danger lies; not in having appetites so weak as to need provocatives, but in not duly feeling the humble place they occupy; in sinking down among them out of sight of the higher principles of action; in absolutely forgetting, in the delirium of pursuit, the noble possibilities stretched along his upper range of powers; and, deceived by mere mental light, lapsing into moral darkness the most profound; with eye, like Lucifer's for ages fallen from Heaven, so accustomed to lurid fires and crimsoned steams that the white and virgin beams of the morning star, and all the cool silence of the skies, are unimaginable quite. In thus confining himself to the *regulation* of his natural aims, and the studious guardianship of the divine rights, so apt to be forgotten, of their highest ranks, he exercises a genuine *trust in Providence*, the very trust which Jesus enjoins. The worldly man is not content with the prompting of natural appetite: it is not strong enough for him to rely on its doing enough for him; and he must add to it all the deliberative energies of his Will. The fanatic hates and fears his appetites: so long as they exist at all, they are too strong for his repose and will do too much for him; and for their annihilation he hurls against them all the force of Resolution. The Christian *trusts* his natural appetites to find him all needful physical good: believing them neither an *over* provision nor an *under* provision, he lets their amount alone, and directs all his conscious aims to a higher point, the maintenance of the nobler affections in their loftier place. Were all these higher powers of his nature wholly lifted off and put away, he would cease to be a man, and would be simply dropped, where the creatures below him now stand, upon the ground of unconscious animal instinct: and would he not, though deprived of insight into himself, be safe as they? Would he not, like them, be supported still, without knowledge and without a care?

And if his instincts would suffice him then, and procure him what he wants with unreflecting simplicity, being incapable of solicitude, they may well dispense with thought and study now, and *refuse* the burden of anxiety. He may confide in the inevitable activity of these primitive springs of his nature, by which Heaven, "knowing that," in common with other creatures, we "have need of" physical good, has provided for its adequate supply. God feeds us, *precisely as* he feeds the fowls of the air, not by the suppression of instinct, but by its natural and unconscious skill;—a skill so sure, so perfect, if we will only believe it, as to set us at liberty for higher solicitudes and a more consecrated watch. And so the rule of our divine Teacher comes out perfect and unimpeachable. The more unconscious (*i.e.* without thought) our pursuit of physical good, the better for the ends of life: the more distinct and *conscious our pursuit of moral and spiritual good, the* nearer are we to the kingdom of God. The whole energy of our Will may be bent on the maintenance of a divine order, proportion, and harmony, among the principles of action. This may be our sole earnest concern; the engagement of heart, in favour of which we may resign all thought for the morrow,—for the morrow of time, or even, I would add, the morrow of eternity.

III.

Seek first the Kingdom of God.

II.

Matt. vi. 33.

"Seek ye first the kingdom of God and his righteousness; and all these things shall be added unto you."

In those teachings of Christ which appear to the worshipper of "sober sense" most strongly tinged with enthusiasm, a higher Reason perpetually discovers a singular exactitude of truth, which spoils them for the purposes of the fanatic, and dispenses with all apology for their "poetical licence." The passage, whose general lesson I have taken for my text, is not unfrequently extolled, in the first instance, for its beauty, and then frittered away as mere hyperbole. To minds sincere and pure, nothing can be more offensive than this kind of praise; as if there could be the beauty it applauds, except for the truth which it denies; as if sentiments could be fair to look at which it would be ridiculous to live by. It makes a true heart sorrowful, or even indignant, to hear the light way in which rules of life and forms of character are sometimes discussed as objects of taste, without the least apprehension of them as matters of obligation. Yet by all that we morally admire, we are practically bound. Human duties are not a mere picture gallery, in which we may loiter with our critic's glass; or a histrionic stage whose representations may delight us, while we sit still; but great and solemn realities, presented on a scene where every spectator practices, beneath the eye of heaven, the divine art which he beholds; where to discern an excellence is to receive a trust; and ideal admirations are the source of actual necessities. Whoever feels that there is an irresistible attraction in Christ's doctrine of repose on Providence, ought to distrust and disbelieve himself, when tempted to explain it into metaphor: he is bound to regard such propensity as the dictate of his lower mind contradicting the knowledge of the higher; and to search, with more open eye, for the divine wisdom that escapes him now. Beauty can no more exist in the moral world without *truth*, than without *light* in the natural.

In Christ's divine parable of trust, a contrast is drawn between that which men must seek for themselves, and that which they must leave God to provide. The one great end of all their active powers, is moral and spiritual good; while for temporal provision there is to be a surrender of themselves into the Divine hand. This doctrine, which is a truly characteristic principle of his religion, is treated, I fear, as a piece of pious extravagance; and is dismissed with the reflection that really it is out of the question for men, hungry, thirsty, domestic, social, not planted in any pastoral Eden, but dwelling in crowded cities, to think of living like the lilies. And so it would be, if by this were meant, any idle standing still, to subsist on air or whatever else the heavens might send. But see how far is any such poor thought from the mind of Christ. Does he mean that nothing should be done for subsistence? Only look at the example he offers of that implicit reliance which he enjoins on the Divine provision. He bids us "behold the fowls of the air"; and says, that "*God feedeth them.*" Do they, then, stay at home, and do nothing, expecting crumbs of manna to drop from rich tables in the skies? Are they found, empty of all appetency, regardless of the changing year, and hanging ever upon miracle? Why, their whole existence is a continued quest after that physical good which is *their* true and only end; and to pilfer the garden and the field, to skim and sip the stream, to dress their plumage with finer gloss, and sing the song of glad repletion, is their work from morn to night. What eager industry flutters in the spring around the skirts of the plantation, gathering the bits and brakes scattered for them by the winter's storm! What busy preparation, at autumn's first chill wind, wheels and musters overhead, for the long flight over Southern seas, the swift cheering on the slow, and the young wing supporting the old! What studious watch, under the semblance of flashing sport, does the home-loving swallow keep! And is not this truly called, a feeding of the creatures by their Maker? Is it not *his* hand that is opened, when they are filled with good? Yes; only, "that which he giveth them, *they gather:*" he supplies their wants, not without activity of theirs, but by means of it; not by casual miracle, but by constant law; by putting his skill *within* them, as well as spreading his affluence *without.*

But how then, you will say, can their life be quoted, as rebuking ours? If their dependence upon God consists in providing for themselves, what else do we? And why should the same thing be reproached as worldliness in us which is admired as pure trust in them?

The answer is plain; it is *not* the same thing that is thought fair in the creature, and base in us. It is only in the mere *outward act* of self-provision that they are alike; and, so far, they are not at all condemned. But this one act may correspond, in the two cases, to states of the *internal nature* wholly different: the springs of activity, where alone any moral quality resides, may have no resemblance; and the more, in this respect, man can restore himself to the condition of the "fowls of the air," the more does he fulfil the ends of his responsible existence.

The animals are impelled by an unreflecting instinct to pursue the good appropriate to their nature. By a relation, wholly incomprehensible to us, between the feeling of want in them and the existence of supply in the world, these two things, like the poles of an electric system, find each other out and meet. The appetite of the creature is not merely a passive sensation of uneasiness, but a positive guidance to activity; of which we can only say this one thing, that it is a blind tendency, not an intelligent foresight,—an abandonment to propensity, not an exercise of Will. And thus, while the insect and the bird continually *provide* for the morrow, they take *no thought* for the morrow: wholly surrendered to the infallible direction implanted in their nature, they are landed in good after good, and accomplish end after end, of which assuredly they had no preconception. Hence it is that their happy maintenance is held to be *divine;* for though the agility which achieves it is theirs, the skill and forethought, absent from them, remain with God. Mind and volition there must be to produce works of order and beauty and enjoyment surpassing our highest strength and art; and failing as they manifestly do in the creatures below us, we refer them to the Creator above us. To live then the simple life of lower natures, is to be fed by the hand of God; and by its unconscious surrender to involuntary, though internal, guidance, becomes the negative type of perfect trust.

Now man has within him the whole apparatus of instincts belonging to inferior beings; just as perfect for their proper ends; just as mysterious in their detection of the means; so that if he were endowed with nothing more than this system of animal direction, his subsistence, his habitation, and all the external conditions of his life, would be secure. Like the brutes that are joint tenants with him of this earth, he might pass his years in blind exemption from anxiety, enclosed within the moments as they come. He would have no mental, no moral, existence; but, zoologically considered, he would be complete. *Unconsciousness*, then, is *the natural and perfect state* of these fundamental faculties, and always belongs to them in the purest types of their activity; and in so far as they lose this attribute, they are injured by entering the presence of other powers liable to a different law. In man, however, this ceases to be possible. He is a responsible being, entrusted with the power of *self-direction*, and gifted with its pre-requisite, *self-knowledge;* and as there is no portion of his instinctive activity exempted from the dominion of his Will, there is no impulse that may not be made the object of his reflection, no pleasure which he may not turn into a deliberate end, no affection which he may not criticize. His whole being may become transparent to his own eye; and from the propension of the brute to the aspiration of the saint, he may lie analysed at his own feet. This power of introspection is the indispensable preliminary to the Conscience;—which is only the intuitive *knowledge we have with ourselves* of the relative excellence of our several principles of action. Thus, the three endowments of *Self-Knowledge, Self-Estimation, Self-Direction*, separate us by a vast interval from the creatures around us that only within the narrowest limits can be regarded as *reflecting*, or *moral*, or *voluntary*.

Observe now the effect of this *self-light* upon the different forces of our nature by which we are impelled. To a being thus let into his own secrets, the unconscious, innocent, life of the mere creature becomes impossible. He was hungry before, he can be dainty now; and the sway of the unknown stomach may be succeeded by that of the tasty palate. The wild animals can be guilty of no excess: their instincts stop at their proper boundary, and spontaneously keep their proportioned place. But what natural law effects for them, it is left for moral law to effect in us; and though precisely the same limits which instinct *would* assign to the appetites are the true and right ones, and the life according to nature coincides in its external form with the life according to Conscience, yet the rule which is involuntary in other beings, we have to enforce upon ourselves. We must forbid passion to break its bounds: we must set a stern police over desires to which self-knowledge has whispered dreams of disaffection and taught a thousand rebel arts. We must wield all the powers of the Will *repressively* against the lower impulses that solicit us, and *actively* in behalf of the higher. And we must do this till the insurgent propensities, made restless by their first self-consciousness, are driven back within their lines, and reduced to content with their primitive domain. Thus, the Moral order of the mind effects the restoration of these inferior appetites to their instinctive place; and the law of Duty in the pursuit of physical good is but a voluntary re-adoption of the law of nature; and the will of God within us is but the image rendered back, from the clear reflective soul, of the method of God without us. Here then is one meaning of high import evolved from the rule of Christ;—that the pursuit of physical good in a moral being is to have no larger range than in an instinctive being; that the superadded power of the Will is to be engaged not in extending, but in preserving the measures of this range; and so leaving the higher affections an unobstructed scope through the whole supplemental range of peculiarly human activity. And alas! it is needless to say, how little place the spirit of such a rule has in our actual affairs. Who can doubt, that the increase, not the divinely regulated pursuit, of physical good, is the leading object with the majority of men? that they are not content with the force of desire that nature has made strong enough in all; but throw into it all the higher faculties of the man, and hire into its service reason, affection, imagination? that the Will, instead of watching and restraining the aim, goes wholly over to it, works strenuously in its service, and even stifles the expostulations that intrude from the better mind? Whoever lives under the guidance of such a leading aim, and is more concerned about what he gets, than what he is, comes directly under the Christian condemnation, and is a servant of Mammon, and an alien from God.

But there is another aspect of Christ's lesson from the fowls of the air. The Moral law as to physical good is a return to the natural law, not only in respect to the *extent* of the pursuit, but even in respect to its *unconsciousness*. How, you will say, can this be, if we are so let behind the scenes of our own nature? How can a man daily determine his sleeping and waking, choose his meals, superintend his business, and yet not know what he is about? Assuredly, he cannot; and yet, throughout these processes there are curious snatches of unconsciousness, where once there was a laborious and intending will. The punctual walk, distracting when it was new, and wearisome when he was ill, for the most part leaves his attention free. The manual skill, or even the mental reckoning, acquired by painful effort, he throws off with the facility of speech. The temperate or abstemious diet, adopted not without a humbling strife, he finds a thing of course. In a thousand ways mechanical activity is creeping into his being, and releasing the living powers of the Will for new tasks of nobler enterprise. In short, *Habit* in man supplies the place of *Instinct* in animals, and enables him to *end* with the unconsciousness with which they *begin*. It releases him once more from the anxieties of self-care, and leaves behind him a protected realm, whence he may push forward to new conquests. It cannot elevate him to a state of holiness, for that implies fresh affection and pure choice breathing in the soul of action; but it can put him back into a state of innocence, and shelter a portion of his being within the security of nature, while he passes on the wing into the higher regions of the spirit. This necessity for urging ever onward, and applying the force of resolution to points of attainment still in advance, must always prevent the course of a responsible soul from being one of ease and restfulness: in a certain sense,—a sense however not depressing but inspiring,—it must be a strife, a glorious battle, protracted through eternity. We can never be free to stand still, and only *rule*, or receive manumission from our divine *service*: the mark of heaven is upon us, and we must for ever work, though in higher and higher fields. This is the true "*bond of perfectness*," from which it is the sign of a really servile and unloving nature to desire escape. I do not say then that *habit* will ever perform the task of obedience for us; but it will *shift* it to an upper and nobler stage; it will make peace where there is conflict now; and restore the reign of simple unconsciousness throughout the inferior principles of our nature. He who by strength of purpose has restrained his appetites and their dependent pursuits within the range of nature, and then by habit compelled them to act with mechanical unreluctance within these bounds, is virtually reinstated in the healthiness of Instinct. In respect to the parts of their being which they have in common with him, the fowls of the air are not more free than he. Only that his disengagement from the meaner anxieties of the Will is an earned deliverance, not a natural incapacity: his content with his allotted limits is a devout and open-eyed acquiescence, not a blind necessity: his self-surrender, for all things physically needful, to the guidance of God infused into his involuntary nature, is not an animal thoughtlessness, but a positive exercise of affectionate and holy Trust.

Here then is the exact interpretation of the Saviour's rule. Seek ye your physical good unconsciously, by strictness of habit restorative of the innocence of Instinct. Seek ye spiritual good, *i.e.* a divine order and temper in all pursuits,—with full consciousness, and an earnest tension of the living Will. In this doctrine there is no enthusiasm, no extravagance; but a union of beauty, truth, and goodness, that touches not our conviction only, but our deepest love and worship.

How then stands our practice by the side of this

divine rule? Does it reflect this estimate of the two sorts of good that solicit us? In conducting the great enterprise of life, have we established such a true order and holy strictness in our habits as to make the heavenly Art and Skill of the process, and not its worldly stake, our grand concern? Nay; do we even direct our aims, confessedly perhaps in confusion for ourselves, with a better regulation for our children? Do we not say to ourselves, "They must live," and take this as the guiding motto of their education, and plead it as an excuse for a thousand questionable things, that should make a Christian blush? Do we not most studiously train, most carefully elaborate in them, those desires which are sure of being the strongest, and place the rashest and most negligent confidence in those higher aspirations which, if they struggle into being at all, are likely to be all too faint? Do we not pamper the fiend of ambition in their hearts, and insult and starve the angel of devout humiliation? What care is taken to clip betimes the high excursive wing of the soul, beating already an air that worldly parents cannot breathe, and tame it to the miserable cage of wealth and display; destined, poor prisoner, to dash itself now and then against its bars, but to gain no liberty save the awful release of death! What can be more startling to a true mind than the crowded carefulness of secular instruction, contrasted with the negligent emptiness of religious education? Nay, is it not a fact that, for the sake of station and fashion, parents procure for their children a direct and systematic teaching in acknowledged fiction on the highest subjects; and, while they would stand aghast at a false quantity in Latin or a mistake in geography, care nothing if the whole system of the moral universe be misconceived; while they would be ashamed that Aristides should be confounded with Aristotle, or Marathon mistaken for Mantinea, are indifferent to the most gigantic errors as to the whole character and government of God? And when the young depart from the preconceived model of the parents' wish, what class of aberrations awaken the most manifest disappointment, and receive the severest rebuke? Is it the prudent profligacy, the sharp cunning, the well-disguised envy, the slippery yet presentable integrity, which imply the utter wreck of Conscience, and are the fatal symptoms of spiritual ruin? Or is it the conscientious eccentricity, the high defiance of conventionalism and convenience in the service of some generous heroism,—the resolve to live a true and earnest life,—which, wherever they appear, rebuke the littleness of men, and give a place among the nobility of God? These symptoms tell too true a tale of the frequent inversion of the Christian aim, and betray, in the sincerest and tenderest relation of life, an anxiety first for the physical good, with only a willingness that then the Kingdom of God, if so it chance, should be added unto it. "*They must live,*" do you say, in excuse for perverting the minds of your children? A true-souled parent, who knows the real contents and significance of life will say, "Rather than sustain themselves here on shameful and unworthy terms, Let them die!"

IV.

The Witness of God with our Spirit.

ROMANS viii. 16.

"The Spirit itself beareth witness with our spirit, that we are the children of God."

IT was a favourite idea with Plato, that in order to discover the true doctrine of personal morality, we should begin by studying the Commonwealth rather than the Individual. The single soul, he thought, was too small and subtle a thing to reveal its nature and the laws that bind it, to a vision dull as ours; but in a great community we have a magnified image of the same human nature, with all its relations made colossal to the eye, and its swift passions reduced to a stately and measurable march. In this conception there is at least thus much of truth involved; that large social phenomena often show what is passing through the private heart; that tendencies silently operating on you and me, unmarked by others, unsuspected even by ourselves, may have conspicuous expression in the literature, the taste, the morals of the age; that lights of self-knowledge may therefore flash upon us from the open spaces of the world, and the broad pavement of our time serve to us as the secret confessional. Thus we may find, I fear, a magnifying medium of self-inspection in a certain mode of speech about Religion which is every year becoming more familiar, and separating us further from the simple fervour of an earnest and prophetic age. I refer to the disposition to look at faith instead of living in it; to own it as a noble fact in human nature, without becoming personally committed to it; to feel interest in its representations, but evade contact with its realities. There is no more favourite object of criticism than its different forms: the origin of each peculiar worship, the meaning of its symbols, the character of its doctrines, are a topic no longer special to the divine, but familiar even to the newspaper. Yet the great objects of trust seem none the nearer for all this: they lie off at second-hand; and men discuss with the lips each other's creeds, instead of going into silence with their own God. The pure and simple faith of the elder time has passed away; nor is it any sufficient compensation for the loss, that unbelief has grown gentle and respectful. For, in truth, the loss of enthusiasm in the one case and the improvement of temper in the other are both parts of the same phenomenon: they are the meeting, or at least the approximation of the two extremes upon the common ground of a secret scepticism, empty of all power, positive or negative. Waiving the awful and fundamental question,—the only one that touches any living soul,—whether the voice of prophets and of prayer be *true*, men agree that at any rate religion is an indestructible affection of the human mind; that whether we regard it as a dream, a philosophy, or a revelation, it remains a *fact;* that it is an influence of such transcendent importance as to reward study and demand regulation and control. We find it accordingly not approached as a divine verity, but dealt with as a human product; dressed up and administered as a medicine for the maladies of character and society; judged of by its fitness to the wants of a nation or a class. The distastefulness of one extreme is studiously balanced by reaction into another; stagnant falsehoods are permitted to remain from indulgence to the sickly minds long used to breathe their exhalations; and to purer streams of thought no welcome is given, lest fevered mortals should feel too great a freshness, as of morning air. Churches are built, not as holy shrines to God, but as platforms of sectional opinion: doctrines and sentiments are estimated, not by the sincere rule of our private heart,—not by their intrinsic worth and sanctity—but by their supposed effect on the prejudices of others and the current usages of thought. All this betrays a disheartening unreality of faith. Such theological connoisseurship would sink abashed before the living look of God; plunged in the pure and sanctifying tides of his infinite Being, all fear and art would be baptized away. There clings to us some untrustful feeling, something that keeps us mere lookers-on, and hinders the surrender of our minds to the divine captivity that makes their freedom.

Were I to try to give expression to the sort of doubt which saps our moral strength, I should do it in the language of a theory which pervades the atmosphere of modern thought, and may well affect us, though we know it not. "Religion," we perhaps think, "is a beautiful creation of the human soul, the embodiment of her highest aspiration and intensest hope, her acknowledgment of Law, her sigh of guilt, her gaze of love, her solace for death, her picture of eternal perfectness. It is at least her sublimest effort, and an affecting testimony to the sweet and solemn depth of her nature. But whether, as she wanders through its scenery, she wakes and sees, or only dreams, is more than we can surely tell. Perhaps she has made her creed by giving names to the shapes of thought within her, and then turning them out to dwell as visions in the external space and light. As fear calls up the ghost it dreads to see, and grief projects upon the air an image of the dead, so perhaps may human faith only paint its heaven and invent its God." This is the misgiving which weakens the present age for great enterprises, and fills it with a certain tolerant sadness, patient of human trusts, but uninspired by them. No man of veracious mind can be content until it is dissipated. He cannot let it remain doubtful whether his religion is a mere phantom-world, floating across the wall of thought; or accept compliments upon its majesty and grace, as if it were a free creation of his soul. Talk to him as if its reality was only *relative to him*, and was unknown to the firm eternal universe, and your very gentleness insults and hurts him. "I speak," he will reply, "that I do know, and testify that which I have seen; and if you receive not my witness as true, spare me your praise that it is beautiful. The divine objects I announce *are there*, and the light by which I see them has no glory but as it flows from their reality; were it self-kindled, it would be but a darkness turned into fire." If others cannot perceive the Holy Spirit that looks on us through the veil of life and nature,—if in low moods of thought I lose the blessed Presence myself, and begin to ask whether it was a vision,—why should I trust the blind heart instead of the seeing, and believe the Night rather than the Day? Is it more likely that the pure soul, from its own sunbeams, should weave imaginary sanctities, than that the impure, by its turbid clouds, should hide the real ones? No; it is when inward confusion prevails in the conscience,—when care consumes the temper and duty is heavy to the will,—when the blood is hot, and the heart is cold,—then it is that doubt becomes our tempter, and says daily unto us, 'Where is your God?' When the fogs of earth lie thick around us, it puts the telescope into our hands, and says, 'Now show us your stars!' We may retort the charge of brilliant dreaming, and say that our miserable doubts are but the black shadow of our own spiritual disorder thrown upon the universe and turning it into the negative of God.

This controversy between faith and unbelief, between the better inspirations and the meaner suggestions of our nature, is not confined to the sphere of direct religion. There is no pure admiration, no deep reverence, which has not to vindicate itself against a similar imputation. What floods of unspeakable beauty may pour upon the artist's view from a natural scene of moorland or sea-beach, in which the literal observer, using his best eyesight, would find nothing to reward a look! What hints of wondering thought, what prayers of appealing love, may gleam through a clear eye, or quiver on a living face, where a common spectator sees nothing but the colour and the form! Which then has the truer appreciation of what is there? He who has only the ocular perception prides himself on seeing the plain reality, just as it is; and smiles at his imaginative neighbour who flings upon it a glory that dwells only in his dreams. He to whom the eye is but the spirit's instrument feels sure there is no falsehood in his vision, and sharply answers, 'Thou dull mortal, thy lens and retina are good; but there is something opaque which the optician cannot reach; may God give thee light!' So is it with every element and influence of life. There are some men before whom if you place some strain of deepest poetry, they will discern in it only the shape of the thought, the flow of the verse, and the fall of the rhyme; while to others it will bring tones of unearthly music for the hymns of their secret heart, and the very page, as it lies spread upon the knee, will meet them with a holy look. Nay, even in the scientific study of the outward creation, there is room for the same difference between man and man. One, with the penetration of a vigilant intellect, will watch nature sharply, as if it were an enemy, or coldly, as if it were a dead mechanism, and note its movements and methodise its facts: another, with a certain pressure of love and reverence, will not sit outside, but enter with a secret sympathy into the interior, and so catch the style of the creative hand as to surmise its laws ere yet he proves them. There is nothing which you may not try to understand in these two ways,—by observation from without, and by affection taking its abode within: by the first you learn only what it is *not*; by the second you appreciate what it *is*. How rarely do you meet any particular man, among all who fill the streets, to whom you find it a congenial thing to apply the Christian doctrine of immortality! The name on the shop or office-door seems not to stand on your register of heavenly things: the common features, the retail talk, the trivial cares, the mind filled up with the town news, appear so foreign to the atmosphere of God as to dash the glory of your religion; and when you go to his funeral, you think of the worthy tradesman who has lost his home, not of the saintly spirit that has attained it. But with his wife and his children it is otherwise. To them he is a light in the very heaven which he obscures to you, and mingles a dear and venerable reality with a scene that was but shadowy before; he is the nearest object to their thought of God; his image mingles with their prayers; and in the picture of diviner worlds, nothing seems more clear and natural than he. Yet they have chafed against his faults more painfully than you; and have had that near familiarity which, except to the deepest hearts, is rarely free from its moments of dispute and discontent. But you have looked at him with the scanning eye of criticism; they, with the penetration of affection: you have noticed his manifestations; they have had insight into himself; have known his temptations; witnessed his faithfulness; felt his tenderness; overheard his sighs for a nobler life. And it is wonderful how often, when the artificial glass of judgment is thrown aside, and you trust to the transparent air of a natural love, the vulgarities of a soul appear to melt away, and you are disenchanted of your fastidious scorn.

Which then, in all these cases, is the true view,—the

literal, or the *devout*? The depth and beauty which enthusiasm everywhere beholds,—are they *really there*, that we should try to rise into the vision? or are they a *romance*, that we should seek to wipe them off? Does the mind put them into nature, or take them out? Are we to honour their revealer as a prophet of divine endowment?—or their disenchanter, as the model of human wisdom? For my own part, without in the least denying that it is possible for an idealising fervour to see too much, I believe we are in more danger from the dulness which sees too little. In relation to the highest truth, mere sense and intellect, looking through the frosty air of a wintry heart, may be but instruments of delusion. If indeed we stood before the face of a dead universe; if nature were but an organization of atoms, pregnant with blind forces and teeming with unintended births; if the planets as they move did but dance the minuet of Fate; if the morning light were but a chemical glare, quite empty of the play of thought, and the waters and the winds had no meaning in their song; if duty, hope, and sorrow were the paroxysms of a puppet, a mere thrill upon the nerves; then, with our living mind to present before the scene, we should be above its meaningless materialism; there would be nothing to understand, nothing to reach, that is beyond the perceptions of the eye and the register of the cold intelligence. But if, while we are on one side of nature, the Infinite God is on the other; if, interposed between the divine Spirit and the human, it may become the veil to separate them, or the communion to unite; if the plain of the restless sea and the curves of the quiet stars are the tracings of his living thought; if the scenery before us and the experience within us are the symbols of his speaking Mind; if conscience be his voice, and trial his appeal for deeper trust, and every gleam of aspiration the kindling of his touch:—O, then, how can we expect to know either nature or life but by the hermeneutics of a godlike spirit,—the converse of sympathy between his will and ours? It is a work of *interpretation,* in which success will be chiefly won, not by the eye quick to apprehend the external characters of things, but by souls familiar with what holiest purpose and sublimest thought are likely to mean. A pure, faithful, devout and tender mind, borne down by no weight of stifled nobleness, and lifted above selfish fear and care, has the best key to the mysteries of humanity, and an insight into the counsels of the Infinite, clearer than acuteness and philosophy can give.

The scepticism which men affect towards their higher inspirations is often not an honest doubt, but a guilty negligence; and is always a sign of narrow mind and defective wisdom. Who ever found that the heavy mood in which he could admire nothing, be touched by nothing, sanctify nothing, permanently proved the true one? Who, when once he has escaped it, does not know this leaden look and solid air upon the surface of life to be the brooding cloud of his own heart? and how often do the more luminous perceptions of other souls reveal to us, in nature, in art, in character, a beauty we had not discerned before, but which is no sooner shown than it startles us by its reality out of all denial! Left to ourselves to peer about from the dull prison of our grosser mind,—unaided by the mighty spirits of our race, who emancipate us by their greatness and snatch us by their genius into the free light,—how little should we see of the sanctity and glory of this world! What a dim and subterranean life we should live! Yet the instant we are taken aloft we find that the darkness was the dream and the splendour is come true! If you will believe only in the perceptions of sense and distrust the intimations of the spirit, it is a question how low you will descend for your test of certainty. Will you depend upon your own faculties in proportion as they are simply animal, and deny them in proportion as they are divine? —confide in your eyesight and give the lie to the conscience and affections? The herds that low amid the Alpine echoes have, no less than you, the outline of the everlasting hills, and the verdure of the pine-cleared slope, painted on their vision, and the chant of the distant torrent swelling and fainting on their ear: is their perception truer,—are they nearer to reality, because they cannot, with you, meet the sublime gaze of nature and see through to the eternity of God?

The grandeur and the glory that you behold, are they not *there?* the divine expressiveness, the speaking appeal to your silent worship, the mingling of something secret with your spirit, as if unseen thought were flowing from the mountains and the sky, to meet the answering radiation of your soul,—are these, which are the human privilege, a phantom of unreality,—a delusion which the fortunate brutes escape? It is impossible! Call it imagination, call it wonder, call it love, whatever it be that shows us the deeper significance of the world and humanity and makes the difference between the surface-light of sagacity, and the interpenetrating glow of worship, we owe to it whatever highest truth, whatever trustiest guidance we have. Wherever there is anything beautiful to read, anything holy, anything tender and profound, this alone avails and commands the key of true interpretation. The hard and literal mind mistakes everything in proportion as its import is of priceless worth; misses, beyond all others, the drift of human language, still more the silent expression of look and action, and gropes without apprehension through the blessed hieroglyphics of life and nature. Does not the poet, does not the prophet, ask for a reader with enthusiasm enough to appreciate him, and complain that by others he is *not understood?* If the greatest *human* works and utterances demand for their apprehension a soul kindled with intense affections, can we doubt what is the qualification, and what the disqualification, for reading the *Divine?* May not their Author,—Soul of our souls, who breathes the eternal poem of the universe, and attunes our minds to hear it, who provides at once the hymn of the morning stars that sing together and the chords of the spirit that tremble to their strain, ask as clear a response from us as we demand from one another?

When, therefore, in higher moments brought by the sorrows of life, the tension of duty, or the silence of thought, you catch some faint tones of a voice diviner than your own, know that you are not alone, and *who* it is that is with you. Stay not in the cold monologue of solitary meditation, but fling yourself into the communion of prayer. Fold not the personal shadows round you; lie open to the gleam that pierces them; confide in it as the brightest of realities,—a path of heavenly light streaking the troubled waters of your being, and leading your eye to the orb that sends it. Learn to distrust the suggestions of lower and more earthly hours, and scatter the fears of the slothful, unawakened heart. If we treat the very "light that is in us as darkness, how great is that darkness!" Be it ours to doubt the glooms, and not the glory of our souls; to lie low beneath the blinding cloud, and simply cry, "Lord, that I may receive my sight!" and rise up to prophesy, only when the heavens are opened, and the divinest scope of things is clear; to court, and not to shun, the bursts of holy suspicion that break through the crust of habit and the films of care, and accept them as a glance from the eye of the Infinite,—the "witness of his spirit with our spirit, that we are the children of God."

V.

The Better Part.

LUKE x. 41.

"Martha, Martha! thou art careful and troubled about many things: but one thing is needful; and Mary hath chosen that good part, which shall not be taken away from her."

THE sketch of the sisters of Bethany presented in the Gospel, possesses more than a biographical interest. Discriminated as they are from each other with the utmost clearness, and representing, not simply individual peculiarities, but two natural orders of human character, they acquire all the force and significance of allegory. The figures would be striking and graceful, as mere domestic pictures, giving us insight into a family interior touched with colours ancient but unfaded, and filling us with melancholy to think of how old a pedigree are the cares and aspirations of the present hour. But the great household of the world has ever been divided very much as the cottage of Lazarus; occupied and directed by sister spirits, whereof Martha and Mary are the genuine types; deriving thence both its rivalries and its harmonies; and seeking in different but balanced ways to fulfil the mission of eternal Providence. And there too, Christ has sat divinely in the midst, watching the toil, teaching the wisdom, quieting the strife; appealed to by the competing spirits, and giving many an unexpected adjudication. The agency and affinities of his religion, in the private mind and on the theatre of the world, are not obscurely seen in the incidents of that village home; and the personal features, so small and distinct in themselves, expand, under the glass of a true interpretation, into lineaments of universal history.

What observer of human affairs can fail to recognise everywhere the class represented by the bustling, officious, indefatigable Martha, worn with her toil, yet ever making more, greedy of all the work, yet complaining of others' rest? There are men and there are nations that seem ordained to be the *fags* of the world; whose honest pride is to keep its larder stored and its wardrobe full; who exist only to sweep its passages and clean its windows; and find their most complacent dignity in spreading its table with the whitest cloth, and preserving its accounts in the safest order. They do not deliberately think these administrative cares to be the great objects for which man is set upon the stage of being: they are always on the way to some higher end: only they never reach it; for when they are just within a step of it, and the neatest preparation has been made for beginning to live, some new dust is discovered that must first be cleared away, and some finish, positively the last, constantly remains to be interposed. Fuming under self-imposed tasks, they think themselves the hardly entreated servants of all: deploring the slavery of life, they would be at a loss to use its freedom. Does any one suppose that if Martha had been more than taken at her word, she would really have sat at Jesus' feet, with surrendered and kindling mind? and that she would not rather have started up on the remembrance of some loose screw in the economical machine, which must be set fast ere her attention could be at liberty? And is it not plain that the half of mankind whom she represents, while lamenting that their years are spent in drudgery, and leave them no time for wonder, thought, and love, are at home only among the means of life, and, these once ready, would be perplexed to live. And so it is, that they are always preparing for a time that never comes: one trifle more of management, and then they will sit down to wisdom; and as they run out on this final errand without their hat, death overtakes them like a thunder-shower, and drives them to the shelter that forbids return.

Rarer and more scattered is the class formed in the likeness of the quiet, thoughtful Mary, less anxious to be the entertainers, than the disciples, of heavenly wisdom. Still such a class, being ordained of Providence for the harmony of the world, exists; and even in this busy, trading, struggling, England, the least genial to it, perhaps, of any climate in history, is by no means extinct. Here and there you may meet with those, who recall you at once from the accessories to the essence of our existence; who, instead of spelling its little syllables, interpret for you its great meaning; who do its work, not from a menial point *within* it, but from a lordly position beyond it, and rather *pass through* the present than are imprisoned *in* it. Other men appear to constitute life by small and gradual additions; jotting down act after act, as their will may happen to expend it; and only gaining a glimpse of the sum total, as the vast account is swelling towards its completion: and so they gather but an empiric wisdom that looks back on the beginning from the end, and miss the reflective insight that discerns the end from the beginning. But *these*, on the contrary, seem to comprehend the whole of life before experiencing its parts; to descend from its vast scope into its separate details; and to diffuse one indivisible character through the successive acts which measure, but do not make it. No doubt there is a good in that "knowledge how to live," which sagacity derives from mere length of days, and which gives a wholesome ripeness to the counsels of age. Such gathered experience is an indispensable antidote to the impulses of inexperienced self-will: it adds a fresh witness to truth and goodness, and strengthens the collective conscience of humanity. But, for personal guidance, it comes too late: the voyage is over, ere the chart is drawn; and after a thousand dangers of the deep, the skill to steer is won, at the moment when the anchor is about to drop in the still waters. Inductive knowledge is the glory of a progressive *race*, that can spare centuries without stint, provided science does but organize itself at last; but it is a poor reliance for the transient individual who cannot afford to wait for his moral wisdom till he dies. And so, to save our time and shorten the excuses of folly, God gives us, in the highest things, an intuitive knowledge and prophetic light: we are not left to the thread of memory ever in our hand, whereby to measure our past courses; but from the earnest eye, looking for the path before it, a radiance shines that shows the true way by night or noon. To clear and brighten this native light of conscience,—or rather to preserve its original purity,—is for every man the good part which shall not be taken from him.

The preference which Jesus manifested for the character of Mary, has, I believe, been often esteemed more poetical than just. It has been accused as a romantic judgment, giving countenance to the mischievous belief that the qualities best adapted for this world are uncongenial with the spirit of the other.

The passage has been read, not without a secret pity for the good Martha; and many a worthy housewife has thought within herself, "It seems rather hard that this is what we get for all our pains." From the outside it looks so easy to sit still and gaze up on the face of heavenly goodness,—so pleasant to take in the lessons of holy truth, that those who see the attitude from amid the toil and heat of the common day, regard it only as a mental luxury, a coolness from the tree of life upon the grass of thought; more fit to be envied of men, than applauded by the Son of God. And yet there is the deepest truth discoverable in this verdict of Christ; and the whole history of individual character, and of collective society, leads us to the same result. Those to whom *life is a succession of particular businesses,* however intelligent, energetic, and conscientious, must rank in the scale of human excellence below those to whom *life is rather the flow of one spirit.*

In the former there is always to be noticed a certain want of *proportion* in the parts and methods of their career. It has not the unity of a pervading aim, the ground-colouring of a latent affection. It is not the spontaneous expression of a given mind, but the activity provoked by a given lot; so that its highest energy is that of adaptation rather than creation. Every one understands, or at least *feels,* the difference there is, in matters of Art, between a work of ingenuity and a work of genius. It is a characteristic of all the "useful arts," those to which we dedicate the chisel, the furnace, and the mill, that they direct themselves to the formation of some definite mechanical product. The distinct preconception of an outward object which he is to complete, guides the processes of the artisan; and all his skill consists in the intentional application of means to his proposed end, and the gradual appearance of the result by due accretion of materials. He can tell you how he did it all; can enumerate the ingredients in a receipt; lay down the methods by scale and compass; and enable you to do the same thing again. It is the characteristic of "the fine arts," those which avail themselves of language, form, and colour, that they do not see at the beginning the outward result in which they end; that it comes out from their feeling, instead of standing before them as their guide; that it is reached,—as men say, *blindly*,—not *i.e.* by the artificial lamp of the understanding, carried in the hand and consciously turned this way and that to show the way, but by self-light from the sense of beauty hidden in the heart. The symmetrical unity of the work arises, not from contrivance, but from harmony in the mind which it expresses. Hence the incommunicable and purely subjective character of all high art. Its great masters can give you no list of its materials, no account of its procedure: they cannot teach you to do the same; and if you will serve an apprenticeship to them, it must be by veneration for their works, not by imitation of their ways. Rules may help you to manufacture, but cannot inspire you to create. Now there is a difference analogous to this in the moral administration of human life. Duty has its artisan, who labours by prescription to the will; and its artist, who shapes forth the love within his heart. The one lives after the manner of the journeyman, executing each separate order as it may happen to come in; the other, in the spirit of the poet, fashioning his own designs, and expressing through them all, one truth, one prayer, one hope. In the former case, everything is contemplated in detail: every particular task is an independent care and end, seen apart from the relations on which its worth depends, and for a time, remaining all in all. Hence arises a slavery of the mind to means and conventions; a worship of proprieties instead of obligations; an inability to follow the shifting boundaries of rule and habit, and an adherence to custom dry and dead. A conscientious will, without the light and glow of high affections, is almost inevitably the prey of superstition, and lies under the nightmare of fear. With what childish care may you often observe it tending and watering the artificial flowers of rootless usage, unconscious that they hold no seed and can ripen no fruit; while the true eye for nature can tell at any distance the blossoms of the meadow and the wood, from those of the ball-room and the stage. No degree of sagacity can protect the chafing will from false and disproportioned estimates. Its possessor carries with him a constant magnifying glass, which by exaggerating all trivial things, and leaving the grandest to spread far beyond his field of vision, equalises the little and the great. He sees no relation of parts. Each task in turn takes up the whole of him at once, and causes a wearing expenditure of effort on every successive point, without bringing the fruits of power in the end. A perpetual exaggeration of small things will never make a great one; and those who take a series of limited views, for want of the ascendant faith and love which blend them into one vast prospect, leave on you, after all, the impression that our existence is made up of petty matters,—that our world is a colony of busy insects making a mighty buzz about a very little being. They show the earnestness of all the parts of life; but not of the whole; and by their failure to present it in any noble aspect, or shed on it any tint that is divine, are apt to provoke others into cynicism and frivolity, rather than awe them with the sense of obligation. But a soul kindling with devout aspiration cannot mistake instrumental details for ultimate ends. The act of the hour belongs to the business of the day; the business of the day has its place in the scheme of years; the scheme of years is but the element of an eternal work; and all is the expression of a constant spirit, conversing with God in the present, and in quest of his higher mind in the future. To such a one, life is not a mere voyage by the log and line,—an experimental cruise over waters unexplored; but a course computed by the everlasting stars over an ocean unvisited indeed, but not unknown; with its relation to the heavens discerned, and sunny inlets and blessed islands ever in the thoughts.

The difference between a life pieced together from even the stoutest remnants, and a life woven, though with fragile woof and fading colours, from the continuous warp of a pure heart, is conspicuous especially in the *temper* with which the ills and wrongs of the human lot are borne. The mind intent on outward tasks and dedicated to mere day-labour cannot endure thwarting: its work failing or destroyed, it is left without resource; its only end is gone; the very world it had chosen for its abode has burst as a bubble; and it is precipitated into empty space, as a disconsolate ghost. If the disappointment is caused by the misconduct of others, the indignation of such a one has no natural check; sits amid the ruin in despair; bursts the bounds of reason; and recovers only with reflective shame. Shut up as he is in object after object as if there were nothing else, the habitual vehemence of his nature is easily explained. He lives a thousand lives instead of one. He is always gaining or losing his all: playing for the earthly stake and not for the heavenly skill, he looks with eager gaze at the slightest stroke, and is all eye for every move. He feels with respect to every untoward event as if it were an *injury;* and can scarcely refrain from being *angry* with his afflictions. From this unhappy thraldom, whoever "has chosen the better part" is delivered without effort. Regarding his whole life as the instrument of higher ends, he can lose this or that of its contents without its function being gone. Engaged not on what it *has*, but on what it *is*, he keeps the great object of his earnest spirit under every change. While it remains to be lived, its essence and its worth abide, and decay and disappointment touch its accidents alone. And so the vicissitudes which irritate and confuse inferior minds, leave him, though in sorrow, yet with undisturbed stability; and while others allow themselves to be provoked by afflictions as if they were injuries, he can receive injuries almost as if they were but afflictions; having ever in reserve the sense of a Divine Will, that limits the conditions of wrong, and checks it far short of hopeless ruin. This tranquillity of view imparts also a loftiness to life, which redeems even its poorest passages from the appearance of anything mean. Nothing menial, nothing contemptible remains in the inevitable relations of men, when once regarded as constituents of a Divine order. The lot which God provides, the trouble which he pities, the soul that he loves and visits cannot be beneath our patience and reverence: the scale of life within which he can hide his light, is no object of our anger or our scorn. Where self is dissolved in the all-sanctifying

Presence, no guiltless experience can bring humiliation. The emancipated nature rises into repose; and attains the sweet and quiet mind which never sways from its own centre; whose openness to love does not disturb its fidelity to duty; which passes through extremes of circumstance with a serene and touching constancy; and is so attuned that, whether caressed by summer winds, or quivering before rending storms, it can give forth only harmony. To such a one, the littleness of the parts of life loses power to deprive the whole of greatness; inversely, the greatness of the whole gives every part a large significance, and secures even the least from disregard as not worth the carefulness of a devout aspiring conscience. The gentle spirit of piety holds in it no contempt; cannot feel itself above anything that bears the sacred name of duty; is thankful enough if it be only equal to it. No! it is quite another temper,—the false imagination of romance, not the true heart of religion,—that despises the small component elements of life, and fancies that in such foolish scorn there is some wise liberty. A certain freedom, no doubt, the two may be said to have in common. They can both fling themselves loose from usage, and strike into paths eccentric with the movements of the world. But when romance dashes out of the established ways, it is to please itself; when religion, it is to serve others: the one in self-display, the other in self-forgetfulness: the one in defiant joy, the other in modest reluctance: the one in triumph over inferior men, the other in surrender to the higher will of God. And here we touch the inmost difference between them; that with the one, it is the claim of liberty from what is below; with the other, the need of submission to what is above. And so, while the face of the one looks superciliously down, that of the other turns reverently up, and lets the feet be directed, not by eager and foreseeing choice, but by the felt hand of an Unseen Guide, whose counsels are known only moment by moment. And thus a sacred calm falls upon the soul, forever hearing the whispered words, "Fear not, for I am with thee."

VI.

Perfection Divine and Human.

MATT. v. 48.

"Be ye therefore perfect, even as your Father which is in heaven is perfect."

FROM no lips but those of the great Mediator between the divine and the human in our world could this precept fall without failing of its beauty and suffering reproach for its extravagance. Had any teacher less near to God, less dear to man, given utterance to it, it would have been taken to imply either a presumptuous estimate of earthly possibilities, or a low conception of heavenly sanctity. How often is the Christian preacher,—nay, even the Stoic moralist,—accused of demanding too much from human nature, of urging the wing of aspiration beyond its appointed height, when he merely asks for some faint lineaments of the Divine image on the soul, and rebukes the petty thoughts and low ambitions which completely shut it out! When he looks among them for only some reflected trace of the infinite purity, some pious nobleness to mark them as the Children of the Highest, how readily is he charged with losing himself in the regions of romance! Yet here the Teacher of teachers, the great interpreter of Conscience, tranquilly demands, not merely the consciousness of God, but the living likeness of him; not only the resemblance of an involuntary feature and a transient hour, but a similitude intentional, constant and complete: "Be ye *perfect*, as your Father in Heaven is perfect." And from him we accept the injunction, as giving not only the ideal of our life, but the actual of his. Himself the middle point of reconciling harmony, where the attributes of humanity are touched with the glory of a divine perfection, he renders it credible to us that, all minds being of one race, the Supreme Holiness may repeat itself in all: he destroys the hopeless distance at which an unapproaching worship stands; and brings into conscious sympathy and resemblance the goodness of the finite and the infinite.

Self-evidently, it is not in the scale, but only in the kind, of character, that our nature can be brought to the similitude of God's. Cut off, as we are, from all sensible approach to him in dimension, we can bear his image only in the spirit of our souls. It is just in this, however, that the perfection of a moral agent must consist. He might have great magnitude and long duration and intense force, yet be no more than a monster and an anti-god, a gigantic depositary of passion and disorder. Space and Time and Power are mere physical elements, quite neutral in the estimate of character, and conceivable alike of Devil and of Deity. It is in the kind of sentiment ruling within the mind, the balance of its graces and the proportion of its love, that all its perfectness consists: and these are colours that may be no less faultlessly blended within the miniature frame of a mortal nature than on an amplitude boundless as the sky. To change our physical relation to God, of absolute dependence and incommensurable littleness, is no more possible than for the wave to become the ocean: but just as the same laws that sway the masses of the sea also trace the ripple and shape the spray, so may the very same divine principles, the same preferences, the same constancy which belong to the spiritual life of God, reappear in the tiny currents of our will and even the very play and sparkle of our affections. It is but the affectation of humility, or the dislike of noble claims, that can make us shrink from our affinity with the Father and Inspirer of all souls.

There is a special feature in the Divine perfection on which Christ in his exhortation emphatically dwells. God warms with his sunshine the evil and the good, and refreshes with his rain the just and the unjust. No impulse of anger, no persuasion of complacency, diverts him from his steady ways, or alters the fundamental ground-work of beneficence, on which all his administration rests. There is a common mercy, an inalienable love, which he never permits to become contingent, and from which nothing ever falls away. It abides with the sinful as with the saintly, and returns the same mild look to guilty defiance as to trustful prayer. Looking on Nature as the theatre and on her methods as the activity of God, we cannot fail to be struck with his serene perseverance through the storms of human affairs, and the heavings of human passion. Once having established a physical law, he persists in doing thus and no otherwise without weariness from lapse of time or deviation from change of place. Go where you will, live where you may, you are in the presence of his silent veracity, his unswerving consistency. The rules which he has laid down for this terrestrial sphere, which dispose of its matter, distribute its growths, and determine its movements,—which we read off from the ocean, and the mountains and the air,—are followed no less in the furthest fields of telescopic vision; and processes observed in the newest continents and never traced till yesterday explain the geologic vestiges of incalculable time. Science cannot find a Law, provincial or provisional: intending to interpret one spot, she alights upon a truth for all: struck with a momentary phenomenon, she seizes the key of a periodic combination. She cannot detect the orbit of the moon, without discovering the plan of all the solar worlds; or catch and expound the sunbeam in a crystal without telling a truth of Orion and Pleiades. Ere yet there was any *moral life* upon this world, a material order had been established, and was slowly building up and garnishing the future dwelling-place of man: the rippled sand, the gravelled beach, the sedgy marsh, the treasured and the melting snow, have left their record of seasons and successions like our own. And through all the subsequent moral vicissitudes of human history, this steady order has continued, as if those vicissitudes had not entered on the scene. There are indeed legends which tell of a visible sympathy of the elements with the affairs of man,—of Nature angry with his crimes: but no such convulsion at her heart has left a trace upon her punctual record and her calm face. Over Arctic wastes or teeming cities the Sun is equally lavish of his flood, and glances alike from the sword of an Attila and the crucifix of a Xavier: the full moon indifferently flings her purity into the windows of revelry and guilt, and paints the Saviour's image on the chancel-floor where lonely sorrow and devotion kneels.

What Science calls the uniformity of nature, Faith accepts as the fidelity of God. They are but the settled ways of his sole causation, the program of his everlasting work, the dial-plate which the index of human expectation is to traverse age by age. When we speak of their unerring regularity, we do but attest his truth, which keeps the time-piece steady for us, and warns us how the shadows lie. He that framed these rules might have made others in their stead, and at any moment change them by a thought. But once he has announced them, an eternal Word has gone forth, and shall not be made void. It is a promise made alike to just and unjust, and must be punctually kept with both. Without a reliable Universe and a trust-worthy God, no moral character could grow. A fickle world admits only of a lawless race: no obedience could be required from those who are planted among shifting conditions, to whom foresight is denied, and whose wisdom is as likely to go astray as their folly. As well might you attempt to build upon the restless sea, or to steer by shooting stars, or keep time by the leaves dancing in the wind, as shape a mind or train a character amid a scene whose courses were unsteady and where action was a lottery. All human habits are formed by a mutual understanding between man and nature. Who could be temperate, if the food that simply nourishes today were to intoxicate to-morrow? Who would put away sloth to be in his fields betimes, but in faith that the sun would not forget to rise? Who build his observatory, were not the heavens still the same that Kepler and Galileo scanned? Thus the constancy of creation is the direct expression of the good faith of God; of his regard not only for our security, but for the culture of our reason and the insight of our conscience. He disciplines us thus to his own love of beauty and order. His eternal patience takes away our excuses of surprise, and rebukes our pleas of disobedience. The wild sophistry of temptation is put to shame by the serene light of his natural countenance and the steady swing of the pendulum that counts his ways. He secures us against all *passionate* sway: no *impulse* rushes into space with irruption of blessing or of curse: no *devilish element* bursts the bars of his prohibition, and maddens us by dashing with discords the music of the spheres. He keeps the everlasting watch himself and, if there be chaos any where, takes care it shall not be here. That he may be true to us, he foregoes a portion of his infinite freedom, and binds himself to methods whose cycle we can measure and whose exactitude we may trust. The natural Universe is God's eternal act of Self-restraint: and if he is willing to descend into finite system and trace the fields of his presence with the orbits of accurate custom, is it too much for us to answer him with a life of faithful regulation; to repress within us the sources of confusion; to mark the flow of time with intersections of punctual duty; and so pursue our way that neither the just nor the unjust may be able to distrust us? To enter spontaneously into the bonds of inflexible veracity, and habits of holy order, is the first element in that perfection which brings us into the similitude of God.

If however there were nothing diviner than the punctuality of Nature, God after all would *not* be perfect.

Precisely *because* his sun shines and his rain descends, *alike* on the evil and the good, do we feel that, if this were all and represented his whole thought, his forbearance would be a cold indifference, and his mercy more terrible than vengeance. He would be indeed above the realm of passion, but still below the heights of pure affection; and while we should be safe from the flash of impulse, we should have the promise of no dear love. We can revere and worship the universal goodness which spreads a common ground for the thankful and the thankless; but only if it be a real *long-suffering*,—a *self-repression* put upon a higher sentiment,—the temporary *silence* of a holy Mind, that for truth's and pity's sake treats for awhile as the same those that are felt to be infinitely different. Could we think that the just and unjust in being dealt with alike by the courses of the universe, were not discriminated in the deep reality of God, there would be no beauty, no tenderness in the comprehensive sky and the impartial showers: the restrained flashes of retribution would touch us no more than the stony lightnings hanging from the fist of some sculptured Jove; and the neutral smile upon the face of nature would be ghastly as the mildness on the features of the dead. We admire the evolutions of a tranquil and persistent order, the precision, the symmetry, the smooth chronometry of unwearied Law; but only as the expression of what is higher behind; only if the mechanism is put forth by what is not mechanical; only if its inexorable necessity be the product and determinate act of an Infinite Will. As the usage of a Mind whose activity is free, the accuracy of the heaven and the earth is marvellous; as the balance of forces with which matter is bound, it is not marvellous at all. As a voluntary sameness amid the profusion of possibilities, as the calm look of living Holiness on a drama so often passionate with guilt and sorrow, it subdues us with adoration and consoles us with the deepest trust; but as the involuntary dynamics of a rotatory necessity, it would grind us to despair. Often indeed, with our best faith, there is something hard to bear in the fixity of nature around the dangers and the agonies of men. Over the village stricken with the plague, why does the sun rise with such a dreadful glory, and the morning breeze sweep with so mocking a freshness in its breath? When the ship strikes and rends asunder with a shriek, why does the water swing about as if it held nothing better than itself, and the surge fling and beat the mother and her child, as if they were a senseless log? When a tyrant's army sleeps encamped upon the field, ready in the morning to crush a nation's life, why do the patient stars look so divinely down, and glide over the wicked watch-fires as if they were a lamp of sacrifice? Were this unconcerned steadfastness *all* that our faith presented to us, there would be no perfectness in God: Providence would be no more than Fate;

Duty, an accommodation to necessity: Science, the negation of worship. Were this *all*, then would man, in imitating God, lose the highest attributes of his soul; would dry up into a mere unbending organism of habit,—a machine punctual, precise, and polished; never slackening to think, never pausing to weep, never quickened with joy; beating off his steady stroke of work and disappointing no one's computation, till death cuts off the steam. A faithful and reliable man is a priceless and wholesome blessing in this world: but this cold exactitude is *not* faithfulness. Springing from no life of conscience, and graced by no varieties of love, it is neither a sacrifice to God, nor a heart-offering to man, but only that absence of disturbance which arises from an unimpassioned and plodding nature. The human *piecework* that is got through by those who are content *to do much and be nothing* is doubtless great. But its good is only negative: the moment it ceases to be the expression and outcoming of a living soul, its very copiousness is dearth and its success is failure. When the regularities of habit and the perseverance of will become simply automatic, they lose their claim to moral admiration: however they may pace with heavier grist the mill of wealth, they have ever less to offer at the shrine of worship: the windows are darkened through which gleams of divine and solemn light once entered and enriched the soul: the voice loses its mellow tones, and is no longer flexible enough to sing a song of hope to the heavy hearts of sorrowing men. No withered unconcern, no dead exactitude, is fitted for a life like ours,—a life full of free elements, related not merely to the punctualities of material nature, but to the heaving passions of living men;—a life strewed with various sorrows and full of struggling nobleness, where no open ear is ever far from the curse, the sigh, the prayer;—a life of outward heats and inward thirst, that no sleeping mill-pond can keep clear and fresh, but only the running waters of the pure soul descending from the upland wilds. Neither in the human nor in the Divine existence does the most faultless uniformity in itself constitute perfection.

But there is something far other than this in God. He is not only the Author of Nature; he is also our "Father *in Heaven*." Above and around all his action in the physical creation there lies a diviner and a tenderer realm, an infinite circumambient space of his mind, that does not act on matter but is only present with spirits, and whose transcendent nature we can only express by saying that here he is "*in Heaven*"; —not on the earth, not in the planets, not with the sun, though the place and orbits of them all are in the natural sky; but out of the whole astronomic realm, in a *præternatural* sphere, more beautiful and glorious than any where bounden law and rigorous necessity prevail. However vast and majestic the uniformities of nature, they are nevertheless finite: science counts them, one by one; and completed science would count them all. God however is not finite: he lives out beyond the legislation he has made; and his thought, which defines the rules of matter does not trans-migrate into them and cease else-how to be; but merely flings out the law as an emanating act, and himself abides behind as thinking power,—an eternal Spirit with a boundless inner life still unexpressed. In this silent ocean of his being,—this transcending spiritual sphere of his life, dwells the remaining element of the perfection which we seek. It is an all-embracing Love, an inexhaustible holiness, an eternal pity, an immeasurable freedom of affection, whence all the regularities of his will spring forth, and which leaves enough behind to visit the private wants of every soul, to linger with tenderness near every sorrow, to be present with rescue in every temptation. This it is that is the real ground of our trust and love: God is not merely the power of nature, but the Father of spirits: his resources are not spent and used up in the legislation of the physical universe, but are large enough to overflow freely and copiously into the spirits that are in the likeness of himself. Hence, without violated rule, without breach of pledge, he can individualize his regards, enter with his gentle help into every mind, and while keeping faith with the universe, knock at the gate of every lonely heart. Stupendous as may be the network of determinate law, with threads fastened on every world and continuous through all kosmic ages, there is room enough in the interstices for the free play of the Spirit that passeth where it listeth,—for the movements of an everlasting moral life amid the natural,—and all the swift pulses of Divine affection. It is precisely in the union of these two,—a customary order he will not loose,—a free Spirit he will not bind,—that he is perfect in himself and open to near communion as well as distant trust.

And if it is with *this* perfection that *we* are to be perfect, how clear becomes the type of our highest good! and how truly it speaks to our purest aspirations! An imperturbable Order penetrated with an ever-fresh and pliant Love,—is not that the very balance we need, to bring the conscience to repose? First, like God, to reclaim the wild spaces of our life, to reduce its chaos of possibilities, to divide it into times and seasons, and tell each punctual duty when to rise; to organise a scheme of faithful habits, against which impulse shall dash in vain, and within whose barriers the waters shall lie safe and still; to be accurately reliable and true, to begin no cycle we do not maintain, and of all the lights we hang aloft to see that "not one faileth";—is to vindicate our affinity with the creative method of his mind. But then there is a higher kindred with him, the kindred of the spirit, yet to claim. Through all the inexorabilities of habit the living breath of every gracious affection must flow at its own sweet will: around the rocky fixtures of resolve, the tides of a great heart must freely dash and sweep. If once we allow the method and mechanism of our being to stiffen on us and shut us in; if in the rigour of our duty we have no love to spare; if, within our rules of justice, pity cannot stir; if toiling day by day in our field of patient work, we forget what it is to mingle with the beauty of the world, to wonder at the mystery of life, or sink into the meaning of death and sorrow;—we become what the universe would be without a God, a fatalised organism, in servile bondage to its own lowest forces, transcended and wielded by no Diviner Soul. From this uttermost blight no trustful disciple shall seek deliverance in vain. Let him but keep close to the fountains of living inspiration, and the spring will not run dry. Let him go even to the task-work of action in the spirit, not of egotistic mastery, but of reverent obedience, and it will bring no withering to his heart. Let him keep his thought and faith in sympathy with both sides of this great world, which manifests the life of God,—its everlasting ways,—its ever living spirit; and he shall renew his strength like the eagle's; he shall blend the ground-note of constant duty with the sweet and running melody of an ever-varying love; and by the harmony of opposites, become at length "perfect as the Father in Heaven is perfect."

VII.

The Moral Quality of Faith.

2 TIMOTHY i. 5.

"(When) I call to remembrance the unfeigned faith that is in thee; which dwelt first in thy grandmother Lois, and thy mother Eunice; and I am persuaded in thee also."

IT is not often that the old Reformer, preparing to quit the scene of his labours, bequeaths to his young successor such parting counsels as those of Paul to Timothy. The usual product of experience, especially of an experience gained in attempting a great moral revolution, is a certain caution and lowering of hope: and when, looking back upon the past, the spent enthusiast measures the smallness of his achievements by the splendour of his early projects, he is tempted to regret the magnitude of his aims, and to advise for the future a zeal too temperate to live through the frosts of circumstance. Towards the end of life, the precepts which most naturally flow from our lips express themselves in *negatives:* we warn the fresh aspirant *not* to expect too much; *not* to confide too implicitly in men; *not* to be too certain of the truths he loves; *not* to wage a fruitless battle with the obstinacy of human affairs, or waste his strength in seeking to force the bounds of possibility. The disposition to judge every enterprise by its event, and believe in no wisdom that is not endorsed by success, is apt to grow upon us with years, till we sympathise with nothing for which we cannot take out a policy of assurance. It was otherwise with Paul. He had many friends of his own standing, connected with precious memories of the past: at Antioch, his earliest patron Barnabas, his partner in many a trust; at Corinth, his associates Aquila and Priscilla, with whom he had so long lived and worked; at Ephesus, the faithful Onesiphorus who, wealthy merchant as he was, was not ashamed of the apostle's chain, but when at Rome visited and refreshed his captivity. But none was so dear to him as Timothy, the youngest of them all: not one, he says, did he find likeminded with him.* In him there was nothing to check and chill the great apostle's unexhausted heart; whose rich tones found full response in the young man's fervour and disinterestedness, and whose yet elastic hopes gained a new spring in the presence of a kindred enthusiasm. The friendship between these two men, so unequal in years and so different in powers, is one of the most suggestive episodes in the early history of

* Philipp. ii. 20.

the gospel. It was apparently the one mellowing affection that toned down the impassioned vigour of Paul; that bound him tenderly to life, and, when he would spring to grasp the heavenly crown, recalled him with a sigh; that mingled a constant human image with his prayers and brought them trembling on his voice; that, homeless as he was, made him feel amid his wanderings the sadness of absence and of loneliness. The travelled ambassador of Christ, who snatched Christianity from the hands of a local faction and turned it to a universal faith,—whose powerful word shook all the gods from Cyprus to Gibraltar,—who turned the tide of history and thought, giving us the organization of Christendom for the legions of Rome, and for Zeno and Epicurus, Augustine, Eckhart and Luther, he, with his indomitable soul, was conquered by a Lycaonian youth, and now in Rome sat, with his chained hands upon his knee, musing, as he says, with joy, on the tears and embrace of their last parting. And then he writes to say he cannot do without him. All have deserted him but one; at his hearing in the palace he had to meet his accusers almost alone; and now he waits his sentence, and ere the imperial sword can fall upon his neck, he must see Timothy again. What is the tone of the letter, written at a crisis like that,—the letter which resigns the expectation so long cherished, of living till Messiah comes? Does he indite a threnody of disappointment? Does he caution

Timothy against sacrificing himself to impetuous hopes, and tell him that zeal is well enough, but that after all we must take men as we find them? On the contrary, his words fan every noble fire in the young man's heart: like the voice of the retired victor, looking on and feeling the blood glow at sight of the race again, they spur the dear Athlete to fresher effort, and bid him mark the goal. The spirit of *fear!*—'tis no gift of God's;—only the spirit of love and power! let the good soldier of Jesus press on in hope, heedless of any shame and hardship that may befall a faithful man; stir up the gift that is in him; be instant in season and out of season; keep a patience never spent by failure; and in the last extremity remember in whom he has believed. Glorious Apostle! Would that every leader's voice could burst, as he falls, into such a trumpet-sound, thrilling the young hearts that pant in the good fight, and must never despair of victory!

The secret of this deep affection between the aged apostle and the young disciple is to be found in a quality common to them both,—which made Timothy wise beyond the measure of his youth and Paul fresh against the tendencies of age;—that energy of *faith* which, from its wondrous conquests over our lower nature, is by many regarded as *supernatural*. By *faith* I do not mean their common belief in Christ and devotion to his cause: I do not refer to any agreement of their intellect in relation to the propositions of a creed; but to a certain quality of heart and character so rare to find in these days, that it is scarce possible to explain. He calls it an "unfeigned" faith, and takes it as the mark of transparency and simplicity of soul. He treats it, not as an apostolic gift, but as flowing down in the maternal succession, from the gracious heart of Eunice and the blessing of the good grandmother Lois, ere yet there was any Christ to believe in. It was therefore an attribute that might pass across the line from nature into grace; that could descend in the track of hereditary religion, and link a faithful family to heaven. Nothing so marks the degradation of our modern Christianity as the notion that *faith* is only *opinion*,—that a man may have it or not without affecting his moral worth,—that it is the result of intellectual accident or opportunity, for which God will never call him to account. It is, on the contrary, beyond all comparison, the most complete and distinct exponent of a man's character; and if only we can get to know it, he is revealed to us more clearly, than if the whole catalogue of his actions were given us to read. Matters of historical theology, no doubt,—critical questions about the authorship of books and the authority of councils,—may be differently judged by inquirers of the same spiritual grade. But it is not so with the deep essence of religion; and the view which we may take of our moral relations, of the life here and hereafter, of the ruling laws of this universe, of the being and character of God,—is the direct product of the radical affections of our nature, and will be false or true simply as these affections are mean or noble. Our devout beliefs are not built as we suppose, upon the dry strand of reason, but ride upon the flood of our affections; safe and joyous, bounding over its waves, when its surface only plays with the sweet breeze of heaven; but engulfed, when it rages in the storm of passion, or fixed in stiff death, when its flow is stopped by the winter of an Arctic intellect. We do not simply learn from experience what we are to think; but we carry into experience feelings and preconceptions by which we read and interpret experience. Faith is the natural hypothesis of a pure and good heart, whence it looks on the face of nature and of life, and deciphers and welcomes their diviner lineaments. Want of faith is the hypothesis of a low and unaspiring heart, which feels the presumption to be *against* whatever is high and glorious, and gives the benefit of every doubt to the side of the flat and mean. In some men there is surely a visible openness of impression to what is excellent and noble in character,—a readiness to believe in goodness,—a willingness to take for granted that all is right till proof arises of something wrong,—a manifest assurance that at the bottom of all things lie the foundations of eternal truth and holiness, so that whatever is faithfully and lovingly done has God and nature, and therefore hope and promise on its side.

This presumption in favour of all beauty and sanctity in human life, and in the universe, is *faith*. It has a *moral* character, because it implies a personal knowledge of the higher principles and affections of our nature as able to rule the lower: they have been listened to as oracles: they have vindicated themselves as realities: they have submitted to no fatal insult, but have kept upon their lawful throne. No man can believe in a rule over creation which is powerless over himself; or see in other souls a goodness traceless in his own.

We readily acknowledge this moral character of faith in our relations with one another. You come for the first time into intercourse with a stranger. There is a clear confiding light in his eye, and a free sit in his features, and a frank flow in his speech, which make you feel in a moment that you are not watched, but trusted; that you have no part to play, no cautions to adopt, no prejudices to evade, but simply to lie open as you are, and be believed. You are introduced to another man, more studiously gracious perhaps than the former: but the smile upon his face is not alive; his laugh has not the sincere ring of the vibrating soul; his eye seems to carry his attention beyond what you are saying to yourself; his words, with all their smooth flow, reveal his thoughts and nature as little as a protocol. If you admire anything, you feel that you amuse him like a fresh child; and if you are indignant at some wrong, you see that his response is a flash of the lips without any charge within the heart. You stand before the *unfaith* of the critic, not with the sympathy of the man; and you know what to expect, if you say a thing too foolish or too wise. Each of these men comes into your society with an hypothesis lurking in his heart,—the one of trust,—the other, of distrust: these are no conclusions from evidence, no deliberate opinions, but the mere predispositions of their own nature. Moreover, when the acquaintance has ripened and you have given them real grounds for positively judging you, the same indications on your part will produce a different effect upon them: be the signs of character what they may, they will prove different things to the two men; of whom one will be the first to believe the evil, the other to believe the good; the one finds food for the appetite of derision where the other makes occasion for love and approbation. We cannot say that there are *no* opinions formed by men of one another, in a true judicial spirit: but certainly the vast majority of such judgments are mere self-revelations showing the native affinities of soul which experience is used to justify and confirm. The avidity for detraction springs, I believe, as often from want of faith as from want of charity. There are some unhappy beings, whose life is a long wasting with the canker of jealousy; who have an exhaustless store of suspicions ever circulating among their friends; on whom innocent words fall with a sting and are returned to you with poisoned point; who toss ever upon the fevered bed of scorn, and fall only into troubled dreams, and find no Saviour to take them by the hand, and bid them rise to the light of love and rest. Had they "*faith* as a grain of mustard seed," they could say to this mountain of oppression on the breast, "Be thou removed, and be thou cast into the sea," and it would be done! But, with them, the presumption is always in favour of the dark and evil: *that* is the ground colour of the universe to them; all else is but a phenomenal play above the surface,—a fair and evanescent show that has no perennial root, and which the season's sunshine fades away. And so a brooding night is ever throwing up its black waves again to swallow the blessed islands that had begun to be verdant in the heart. No doubt, this temper constitutes in itself a violation of charity: indeed the three Christian graces of Faith, Hope, and Charity, perish in it hand in hand: but Faith, I believe, is often the first to die; and then the others say, "Let us also go and die with her." Indeed a vital sympathy binds these graces together in the soul; and where one is wounded or in bonds, the faintness or constraint will reach them all.

There is indeed a certain temper, often usurping the name of Charity, which springs, not from faith, but from the utter want of it;—an easy laxity, a good-natured indulgence towards the sinfulness of men, arising from mere dim-sightedness as to its reality; a smiling complacency to which character is indifferent, provided enjoyment and good fellowship are unimpeded; a sunshine of mere animal cheerfulness, dry and constant and tedious as the staring summer's noon, that has no tearful lights, no hiding-place of majesty and storm, no bursts of moistened glory tracing a penitential way from some green spot of earth to the veiled yet reopened purity of the sky. There are those who talk patronisingly of *forgiving* human sin, as if it were theirs to deal with as they liked,—as if it were a personal affront to *them*, about which they might exercise their magnanimity at will; as if there were no God of awful holiness, in whose presence and before whose law the guilty and the guiltless stand, and with whose pity or whose frown it is not ours to play. The spurious charity that is simply tolerant of moral deformity, because untouched by aspiration towards moral perfection, is an odious burlesque of the pure Christian grace. The true charity is not that which *thinks lightly* of evil, but that which is *slow to believe in it;* whose presumptions are ever those of a trustful and holy heart; and which, even when a brother's guilt is indisputably clear, thinks, amid its shock and grief, that he has fallen from his real nature, and cannot be at peace with himself,—that there must be a better soul behind, where God's long-suffering solicitation may find a hearing yet; and that any how, through whatever suffering and discipline, the right ways of heaven, the everlasting sanctities, must triumph in the end. And so it is, that without faith there can be no charity.

When we pass from the domain of human relations into that of the Divine, we shall inevitably carry our habitual temper into the survey, and our faith or unfaith will be still suffused with a moral colouring. I do not say that no other causes than the predisposition of our affections operate in determining religious belief, so that we can at all justly infer the character from the creed. Among men of equal excellence and similar cast of feeling there are doubtless purely intellectual varieties of conviction: and we should go fatally wrong in our estimate of others, did we form it by the narrow rule of agreement with ourselves. But in measuring the solidity of our own thoughts on Divine things we should be strangely self-ignorant, did we not allow for the mood in which they visit us and take their shape, and place more or less of confidence in them according as the moral atmosphere is large and lustrous within us, or contracted by mists of fear and dull with dejection of heart. And to suppose that the test which holds for ourselves has no application beyond would be to ignore the plainest phenomena of life: for what fact is more evident than that men's views of the unseen as of the seen world, are, for the most part, less expressive of their range of knowledge than of their tone of sentiment, and, even when affecting to be intellectual conclusions, betray the marks of moral assumptions. It is the mere pedantry of liberalism, to treat all the humours of religion and no-religion as so many differing philosophies, and to insist that our sympathies shall hold towards them a bearing of impartial indifference. Legal equality they must assuredly have; but, secure in this, they must remain exposed to the free play of love and aversion which flows around all the indications of human affection and will.

We are not spontaneously drawn to one who is always suspecting his friends, and who deems it so natural a thing for them to wrong and hurt him, that he imagines it on hints the most inadequate. When his mistrustful eye is lifted beyond the immediate circle and looks into the invisible world, do you expect its expression instantly to change and become sweet and childlike before God? It cannot be! the habit of unrestful vigilance, of courting the dark corners of possibility, of giving the benefit of every doubt to the worse alternative, will still assert itself, and expose him to misgivings of Providence, and an exigent demeanour towards heaven. The Cynic in society becomes the Pessimist in religion. The large embrace of sympathy which fails him as interpreter of human life, will no less be wanting when he reads the meaning of the universe. The harmony of the great whole escapes him in his hunt for little discords here and there. He is blind to the august balance of nature, in his preoccupation with some creaking show of defect.

He misses the comprehensive march of advancing purpose, because while he himself is in it, he has found some halting member that seems to lag behind. He picks holes in the universal order; he winds through its tracks as a detective; and makes scandals of all that is not to his mind. He trusts nothing that he cannot see; and he sees chiefly the exceptional, the dubious, the harsh. The glory of the midnight heavens affects him not, for thinking of a shattered planet or the uninhabitable moon. He makes more of the flood which sweeps the crop away, than of the perpetual river that feeds it year by year. For him the purple bloom upon the hills, peering through the young green woods, does but dress up a stony desert with deceitful beauty; and in the new birth of summer, he cannot yield himself to the exuberance of glad existence for wonder why insects tease and nettles sting. Nothing is so fair, nothing so imposing, as to beguile him into faith and hope: as the language of men is "for the concealment of thought," so the professions of nature are to be read in reverse; so that in every promise he sees its breach; in every inspiration, its collapse; in every life, its death. On the soft cheek and clear eye and springing limbs of the infant he gazes in the spirit of a pathologist, to ask himself which of them will soonest rot away; and the jubilant throng of playing schoolboys suggests to him the forecast of sad fates, from broken strength and sickened hearts, or faded innocence. In all this melancholy view there may still remain a tinge of humane regret, and the scepticism may hang compassionately round others without a tone of personal complaint. But in selfish minds the same temper takes a meaner turn, and resorts to the pettiest reasons for the most desolating thoughts: "If God were good why should I be born with a club-foot? if the world were justly governed, how could my merits be so long overlooked?"

It is not often that this moral defect of faith works itself out into such full-formed type. But the germ of it lurks in us all, and puts forth its tendency at least in transient moods, when the vision is dim and the heart is low. In flat and heavy hours, the tones of conscience are so muffled that, by not listening we can miss them, and can say of the Holy Spirit, "it is nought." Amid the tragedies of life, in the haste of sudden grief or the crises of appalling suspense, the quick and vehement waves of passion that sweep within us break angrily against the steadfast sternness of nature; we resent its silence, we deprecate its periodicity, we are in despair at its calmness, and say "it is the face of the blind:" we forget the long years quickened by the felt life and love of God, and the high moments kindled by his freshest inspiration; for it is strange and sad how small and brief a darkness may quench for us an everlasting Sun. The healthy mind has no deeper assurance, none closer to the very springs of its energy, than that it is entrusted with itself, able to rise with wing that strengthens in the flight, or to drop into unfathomable fall. But when the moral nerve relaxes and life is looked at more than lived, sickly subtleties invade us, and, fitting us into the universal mechanism, oppress us with the ancient nightmare of fate. Has the time come when some dear saintly soul vanishes from our side, and leaves us to our lonely path?—As we think of all his noble and lovely ways, the realised heights, the ever-growing depths of his nature, nothing seems more natural and sure than his migration into a sanctity of larger and immortal scope. But if, holding the vigils of death till we are faint and numb, we cease to listen to our love and let go the visions of our memory, and surrender our weakness to the waxen look and cold touch of those shrunk features; if in imagination we are dragged along the physiological history because easy to conceive, and baffled by the spiritual, because it has no pictures to help it; and if thus we permit ourselves to dwell on the unanswerable problems of so transcendent a hope; it wavers from too sharp a contrast with the present darkness, and fades from sight by very immensity of glory. In all these experiences, we blindly yield to material pressures, and sink always from the native faiths of our higher mind; we go over, not to more valid evidence, but only to meaner suspicions; and are like one who is ready, in unhappy mood, to forego a lifelong confidence in the first of friends and give heed against him to some paltry calumny. It is an offence, not less against the calmness of Reason than the constancy of love, to be thus haunted by the visions of an untrustful mind, and, like some poor sleep-walker, be led by ghosts of fear over marsh and moor till the home of rest is lost. Be it ours, in all things human and divine, to keep the good heart of faith; and as we accept the clearness of a brother's face and the simplicity of his word and the freedom of his affection, so to throw ourselves open to the expression of God's life and love, in the beauty of the world, in the law of conscience, in the ample range of thought and aspiration, and in the promises, already pressing to fulfilment, of saints and prophets. It is never a good sign, be it remembered, when doubts beset us founded on no better reason than that the thing in question is "too good to be true." The suggestion, we may then be sure, is not from our best and noblest mind; and should be dealt with, less as an honest plea, than as a low temptation, and swept away as an ungenial mist, by a breath of fresh affection, clearing the stars again. There can be no pure intellectual eye for heavenly truth, till this meaner order of moral suspicions is dismissed with the quick and resolute prayer "Lord, I believe, help thou mine unbelief!"

VIII.

Divine Justice and Pardon Reconciled.

1 John i. 8, 9.

"If we say that we have no sin, we deceive ourselves and the truth is not in us. If we confess our sins, he is faithful and just to forgive us our sins and to cleanse us from all unrighteousness."

There are two extreme tendencies in human sentiment respecting God, from which a devout and thoughtful heart shrinks with equal repugnance; a religion which begins with fear, and a religion that ends without it. On the one hand is the passionate faith of remorse, which throws the shade of its own despair upon the universe of God; lies prostrate in the dark cell of alienation; and declares that, if no mediator interpose, there is no hope or respite from the curse of inexorable Law. On the other is the creed of lenient good nature, which spreads the light of its mild indifference over all things; considers the sins of men as chiefly venial frailties; is pleased with its own tolerance; and trusts that Heaven will overlook what it must have foreseen and did not think worth while to prevent. The former places us under a rule so pure, that the faintest guilt appears before it as something infinite; and beneath a law so strict, that the word it speaks can never be recalled. The latter represents the Sovereign Judge as measuring sin rather by the standard of our weakness than of his own true perception,—as full of tender allowance for a tempted nature,—as holding out to our aim an ideal which he does not really expect us to reach,—and as leaving it to be understood, that if there be only some decent approach towards his standard, he would be glad of a pretext for avoiding painful severities. The former would deserve the praise of moral loftiness, were it not used as a mere prelude to a doctrine of atonement offensive to every sentiment of right. The latter might boast of vindicating the divine clemency, but for making free with it on somewhat easy and sinful terms. Indeed, by a singular inconsistency, the former overstrains the law of conscience in order to prove it impracticable and get rid of it: the latter too amiably relaxes it, in order to retain its force. The system which most depreciates morality starts with the sternest view of duty; and that which is most exclusively moral begins with frittering obligation away.

Think what it is to affirm, that amendment only is needful to forgiveness, and that from penitent sin the punishments of God are freely withdrawn. Does the guilt then go for nothing with him, and are his penalties an empty threat? May his law be violated, his oracle of conscience insulted, his expostulating spirit quenched, with impunity, provided only this does not run on to the end? Does he treat his children entirely according to their present temper, and make no difference for their previous unfaithfulness? Then it is quite false that he "rewards every man according to his works": he puts on the same footing the old offender and the young saint: he thinks nothing of the hugest amount of wickedness, once thrust into the past: his word, so solemnly given against it, is all recalled, and its warning was never more than a pious fraud, like the nursemaid's threat to give the refractory child to the black man. Everything veracious, everything august, everything holy vanishes from a government thus pretending to inflexible rules yet surrendering all to the pressure of the moment.

And yet, it seems equally difficult to maintain as to deny the strict veracity of the Divine warnings and promises. Is the presage of the guilty mind literally true, and does every sin find us exactly out, and pay us just our due? Is the word of Heaven, that is gone forth against the wilful, never made void, and precisely "as a man soweth so also must he reap"? Alas! then, what hope remains for us? for then is there "no place for repentance" though we "seek it carefully with tears." If the accounts of justice are strictly kept; if their balance is carried forward from page to page; if it is impossible for us ever to overpay, and certain that we are always falling short; what can prevent the reckoning from being ever worse, and our existence from being burdened and borne down by an everlasting debt? The past breathes despair upon the present, and sends its icy wind on every fresh and blossoming growth within the heart. Could we but throw off the weary nightmare beneath which we feebly gasp, could we spring up and start anew, the forces of the soul are not yet broken, but are young and hopeful still: only, while chained to this mortal weight, they lie as if crushed and dead. We cannot stir till we are pardoned; yet cannot be pardoned till we stir. Thus, if there be forgiveness with God, it cannot but loosen the tie between conduct and its consequences; or, if that tie be strict, there can be no forgiveness.

There is no more serious dilemma presented by human faith than this; nor any more productive of looseness and confusion in the soul. Minds not much in earnest about their moral and spiritual life may not feel it or may suppose it a mere nicety of theory; for it is not the character of such minds to demand any unity or consistency in their religion: they are content with a plain truth here, and a good rule there, a little that is pretty sure to be right, and a great deal that can hardly be wrong: but taking up each in turn as an external thing, and finding for none a vital root within the soul, they are unconscious of incoherencies and contradictions by which many a loving heart would be torn to pieces. These easy believers cheerfully worship the good-natured God, and deny all difficulties. But to whomsoever the human surface of things has opened and shown the divine; to whomsoever mere *wrong* has deepened into *sin* and *regret* into *remorse;* whoever has found the need of forgiveness to be a want more real and urgent than that of daily bread; whoever cannot be off and on with his Maker, as in the play of taste and mood, but must see himself an outcast or be reconciled; whoever, in short, *lives* instead of *dreams;* —he well knows, that this perplexity is speculative only to those whose religion is not practical; and that to the daily task of service, the hourly spirit of peace, nothing is more needful than a clear and uncontradicted light of divine forgiveness.

The truth is, it is a hard thing for our narrow mind to take in the infinite harmony of Divine perfection. Our conscience and our affections make incompatible demands on God. We require for our support that he be faithful; we look, for our comfort's sake, that he be tender too. Certainly, if we are to trust in his holiness, there must be a law sure and universal, that binds together guilt and punishment; a law without exception to its grasp, without swerving in its execution. It is to reveal this law that the misgivings of conscience shake us with their awful voice; that spectral shadows flit across the heart of guilty gaiety; that boldness before the sin sinks into abjectness after it; that, in proportion as we lose our moral count, and the skein of life, wound no longer smoothly off, is ravelled into a broken and tangled waste, we rush into vain distractions to quell the fever of our secret misery, and yet find no peace. To assure us of this law it is, that our only rest is found in true simplicity; that under the clouds of evil passion the mind is tossed and heaves in storm, but under the heaven of pure affections, lies calm as the summer sea; that, till the stubbornness of pride gives way, there is no quiet in the soul, no smoothness on the brow, but only furrows of ever-deepening care; that the stiff Will of self, so rigid to resist, proves feeble to achieve, and gets no power, save to fret itself and others, till it is melted by some noble inner love, and flows down into the moulds of a divine obedience. It is an ineradicable faith, that every tendency to disturbance and disorder follows the direction of human guilt; and that every approach to repose is on the path of human faithfulness. No shade of doubt is to be cast upon this faith; it is as much our primitive, instinctive guidance, as our expectation of the future from the past. As, for purposes of knowledge, it is appointed us to believe that the sun which has risen today will rise tomorrow; so, for the ends of duty, it is given us to feel that sin has a bitter fruit to ripen, and that having sown the wind, we shall reap the whirlwind. This is the corner-stone of our whole structure of confidence in the moral government of God. Without it every lost battle of justice would appear irretrievable, every truth, eclipsed for the moment, would seem as if quenched for ever; and the hope which has supported injured goodness in every age, which has taken away the edge of suffering and the terrors of death,—the assurance that God and time are on the side of right and will put its persecutors to shame, would be at once the highest sublimity, yet the vainest reliance of our world. If anywhere in this universe it were discovered that the law of cause and effect did not universally hold, that the conditions under which physical phenomena occurred were not steady, that the supposed connections of events were broken, and the signs of their coming which were noted on one day could not serve for another; this would be the death-blow to human science,—a proclamation that creation had run wild,—that nature, relapsing into chaos, was knowable no more. Not less true is it, that if, anywhere upon the track of time, one sin were found to have escaped its menaced punishment, if the rule were seen to waver and relent which joins suffering to the faithless will as its inseparable shadow, if ever He who "sets the poor with princes" were to set the wicked with his saints; this would be the death-blow to all moral faith,—a declaration that the foundations of life were crumbling beneath our feet,—a premonition of universal dissolution. As reason cannot move without presuming on the uniformity of nature; so must conscience rely on the unchangeableness of Law; and can worship only a God pledged never to treat those who have been guilty like those who have not.

And yet, if this be all, the truth is more terrible than we can bear, and God severer than we can love. Does he then judge always by the past, and shut the door conclusively on the moments as they go, so that the touch of the present, and the cry of its entreaties can reach them no more? Is there no meaning in the prayer "Blot out my transgressions, and remember not my sins"? no divine truth in that saying, "Her sins, which are many, are forgiven; for she loved much"? Did it make no difference to Peter, that a look recalled him, and he went out and wept bitterly? Whence then the "joy in heaven over the sinner that repenteth"? If compassion be impossible to God, it is strange that he has implanted any in us; for he has more reason to pity us, than we can have to pity one another;—we, gazing in the face of an equal and a brother; he, looking from his serene Almightiness down upon our nature, tempted, sorrowing, struggling, dying. No, it is as much a part of perfection to receive the penitent as to reprove the sin; unless the noblest impulse of the human soul seeks vainly for its image and prototype in him. Indeed it is matter of experience that contrition, with all its sadness, is not without its answer of relief. At first, no doubt, transgression drives us from before his face, and we wander in awful solitudes like Cain. But the banishment is too dreary to be borne. We are first stopped in our flight to sit down and think upon our shame; and then are drawn to steal back, and doubtfully seek the old neighbourhood again; and its dear looks smite us to the heart, till we lift up our voice and weep aloud, saying 'If perchance the Lord would look upon our tears'; and at length we hint our prayer no more, but catch his very eye, and say 'Lord put me to grief, but cast me not off: not from thine absence, but from thy hand, let me receive thy chastisement: let me be stricken, but bear with me here: thy darkest frown is better to my soul than the dry light upon the wilderness of exile.' And with this self-surrender there comes an unexpected peace, so sad and solemn that surely it is the response of God; and must be accepted as a token that, truly, "the contrite heart he does not despise." If therefore, on the one hand, he cannot treat penitent sin as if it were innocence, so neither, on the other, can he treat it like impenitence: and the present temper reflects back some light upon the past transgression.

But how, alas, you will still say, can these things *both* be? how can God at once swerve no hair's-breadth from his threatened punishment; and yet be ever ready to forgive? Rightly to understand this, we must mark the distinction between his interior nature and his external government, between what he is in himself and what he has written out and proclaimed in the legislation of this universe. Not all that dwells in his thought and lives in his heart has he put forth; and vast as is the field, and sublime the record, of creation; solemn as we find the path of life, and awful the insight of the conscience; these are but a part of his ways; and there is yet a hiding-place of his thunder that none can understand. Everything in him is infinite; and all the splendour of his revelation in the old earth and in the older sky, and on the heart of humanity, and even in the unique life of the Man of sorrows, are but a few front lines of light, streaking the surface of immensity. He says to us much; but he is silent more: his law is open and remains; his Spirit that made it abides behind, and is committed to nothing save by its own nature to all that is beautiful and perfect. Thus, his infinite disapprobation of sin has not all found utterance: part is expressed, and part reserved. The former is embodied in the moral law and stamped into our moral nature: it is written on the agitated brow of passion and gleams from the eyes of guilty men: it is heard in the sighs of the broken will, in the plaint of purifying sorrow and the sweet hymns of souls redeemed and peaceful. The latter is not embodied at all: it is a free existence: no lines define it, no bound encloses it: it is as the divine colour of all truth and majesty without its form, with hues ready to bathe all things but fixed on none. Now, exactly corresponding to this division between the legislated word and the secret thought of God, there is a distinction in the guilt of man: part comes out in action and part remains behind; the one fixing itself in ineffaceable characters in the realm of nature; the other diffusing a taint of degradation through the secret soul. Here too, the element which pushes itself into expression is *finite*: it is an overt and determinate offence, bringing nameable mischiefs, and inflicting visible and calculable wrongs: but the evil spirit which has shot out this curse is something infinite, and is conscious, if ever its vision becomes true, of a vileness that has no bounds, a sinfulness which no definition can enclose. Both lie exposed to God's holy disapprobation: the *act* however to his expressed displeasure and purpose of retribution: the deformed mind to his *reserved* abhorrence. With respect to the perpetrated volition he has irrevocably committed himself: his veracity is pledged to go on: his word has gone forth, which binds together guilt and pain, and it cannot return unto him void. Not one consequence which he has annexed to wrong-doing will fail to appear with relentless punctuality: no miracle will interpose to conduct away the lightning of retribution. Within that realm of law and nature, he is inexorable, and has put the freedom of pity quite away; and as the Atlantic storm turns not aside to avoid the ship where sanctity or genius are afloat, so neither does the tempest of justice falter and pause to spare the head uplifted in repentant prayer. But it is otherwise with respect to the soul and person of the sinner himself: the sentiments of God towards him are not bound: and if, while the deed of the past is an irrevocable transgression, the temper of the present is one of surrender and return, there is nothing to sustain the Divine aversion or hinder the outflow of infinite pity. Free as our soul is to come back and cry at the gate; so free is He to open and fold us gently to his heart again. Weak indeed from the waste of all our strength, lame with our many wounds, in peril from our dim sight, and pain from treasured agonies, we must still be; and God can only say 'My poor child, I cannot help thee here: this burden must thou carry to its end.' But still the penitent lives no outcast life: the light of reconciliation is upon him: he suffers and is very faint, and often his heavy cross weighs him to the earth: but he can bear the scourge of nature, now that he is withered by no scorching look of God. Wrestling with the Almighty no longer, he can move on upon his journey with a cheerful heart, though ever after halting on his staff. And so ceases the contradiction between the exactitude of Justice and the tenderness of Pity; and we may say with understanding heart "If we confess our sin, he is faithful and just to forgive us our sins, and to cleanse us from all unrighteousness."

IX.

God Revealed unto Babes.

LUKE x. 21.

"In that hour Jesus rejoiced in spirit and said, I thank thee, O Father, Lord of heaven and earth, that thou hast hid these things from the wise and prudent, and hast revealed them unto babes; even so, Father; for so it seemed good in thy sight."

THAT the sage should miss what the infant can see seems at first but little possible, and still less a subject of thankfulness. It would appear to discourage the highest attributes of our nature, to throw contempt on the patience of thought, and cruelly to visit the prayer for light with the deeper darkness. Can it be that the more pains we take to know, the less will the truth be found; that the rich and practised mind is at a disadvantage compared with the inexperienced and empty? And if so, why exult in the frustration of the noblest of human aims, and the confiscation of the prize to those who have no aim at all? Many a zealot, baffled by the acumen or indifference of more polished minds, has found in these words consolation for his own ignorance and the rudeness of his followers; as also in the similar words of Paul, "Ye see your calling, brethren, how that not many wise men after the flesh, not many mighty, not many noble, are called; but God hath chosen the foolish things of the world to confound the wise, and the weak things of the world to confound the things that are mighty; and the base things of the world, and the things that are despised hath God chosen, yea, and things that are not, to bring to nought things that are; that no flesh should glory in his presence." Tertullian, for example, dwells with a savage satisfaction on the supposed exclusion from the kingdom of God of whatever we hold fair and great in the old heathen world and richest for the adornment of all time; and exults in peopling it with hordes of triumphant barbarians like himself. Is *this* the spirit of Christ's thanksgiving? Are we required, out of sympathy with it, to believe Socrates an outcast and clap our hands as he vanishes from hope? to stifle our reverence for Æschylus and Plato,—for the Scipios and Antonines,—and declare God's preference for mendicant monks and illiterate missionaries? Must we condemn, as secular and carnal, our own natural admiration for the gifts of wisdom,—the disciplined powers, the large and supple thought, the balanced feeling, the accurate expression, of a well-cultured nature,—and force ourselves into harmony of taste with the raw religion of unmellowed sectaries,—their loud voice, their rude speech, their narrow zeal, their tumultuous inspirations? Far from it. It is not intellect from which God hides himself, but selfishness and pride; which may belong alike to taught and untaught, and darken the soul of sophist or of clown. The words of Christ no doubt imply that knowledge of other things may co-exist with blindness as to that which is divine; and the apprehension of divine truth with ignorance of other things. And how it is, that the two kinds of discernment are separable, without being incompatible, will be evident if we unfold a little their difference of nature.

There is light both in the "babe" and in the "wise": but in the former it is wholly spontaneous; in the latter it is chiefly derivative. In its infancy, the soul simply apprehends what is given it to perceive; lies confidingly on the bosom of nature and lets the morning beams come into the full and wondering eyes; does not read off by skilful signs the absent and the future, but mingles with the present and takes it in; starts no doubts, is entangled in no reflections, but lives straight out of the unquestioned instincts of the hour. Later on, this impulsive freshness is all changed. Second-hand information is added to the first: the order of events and the classification of objects are registered: much that is invisible is ascertained by analogy, and that is yet to come predicted by laws of succession; and by well organized combinations of thought new deductions arise, new possibilities disclose themselves, new courses of imagination are open, that withdraw us ever further from the primitive sources, and make us forget, in the fertile plains and park-landscapes of our migration, the lonely uplands of our birth. We have reached so much by circuitous paths and mediate contrivance, that the early starting-point and assumed base of all our mental reckoning has been lost: we no longer know the simple from the complex, the artificial from the natural in thought: we use the tissue which we have woven to dispute the fibre of which it is made; and follow down the streams of reasoning, exploring as we go, in hope of truths that all the while lie far up at the fountain head. It is this *loss of the habit of natural trust,* this tendency to anxious quest of something distant instead of pure repose on what is *here,* that, according to Christ's prayer, hides God from the "wise and prudent." And, conversely, it is the surrender to spontaneous light and love, the simple passing out upon it into life, without doubt of its guidance or scrutiny of its claims, that reveals him unto "babes."

How profoundly true this is,—that in divine things the little child may know what the great philosopher may miss,—will appear if you only think what God is, and whether he is likely to be discovered on any explorer's track or by any artifice of calculation. Two things science enables us to do, from which all its triumphs spring. It shows us how to put the parts and products of nature *into true classes;* and it qualifies us to *foresee* phenomena else unsuspected. But God is neither a being to be classified, nor a phenomenon to be foreseen. Such procedures of the mind are quite inapplicable, except to the finite and the transient; and he who goes forth upon them may find whatever *begins to be*, but not that which for ever *is;* may rightly dispose of *this* and *that*, but never meet the All in All. As well might you attempt to put space under your microscope, or weigh gravitation in your scales. If you believe that God exists, and understand your words when you call him "infinite" and "eternal," you cannot expect to find him as *one object among many*, but as a *Spirit in all*, the living reality of all appearance; the firmament of thought that holds the stars; the omnipresent deep that throws up the tides of history and the ripplings of private care; the sole power of the universe without; the archetype of the free soul within; and the secret source of the meaning that dwells in everything. Were he at all away, we might step forth to seek him; did he ever slumber, we might watch for the date of his waking times. But living for ever in us and around us, he does not enable us to compare his presence with his absence: if we miss him, it is from his perpetuity and nearness; if we meet him, it is not by feeling after him abroad, but by dropping inwards and returning home. The differences by which he is revealed are in us and not in him; in our faculty of recognition, by no means in his constancy of action. His light is alive in the very hearts that neglect or deny him; and in those that most own him is latent a thousand times for once that it flashes on their conscious eye. But there are moments when the beauty of the universe looks in at us with a meaning quite divine; or the crises of history shake us as the visible drama of Providence; or the eye of appealing misery burns into the place of pity in our souls and we know it to be *his* sympathy as well as *ours*; or a new insight of duty opens a path which he alone could show. In these instances, we strain no ingenuity to discover him; it is he who comes to us and finds us; his presence rises of itself, and the revelation is spontaneous. Our sole concern is to accept it, to revere it, to follow it, to live by it.

Thus the true attitude of the devout mind always involves a certain quietism and self-relinquishment. Instead of pressing curiously forward, it sinks in meditation back, rests upon the moment as divine, and feels the very pavement beneath its feet as holy. It has neither any distance to go, nor any time to wait, in order to close in with the Spirit of God; only to own and trust him now and here,—to pass into his hand with simple faith, a disarmed and unreluctant captive to his will. To look at the Christian conflict from without, you might suppose that it was achieved by lashing the soul to intense volition, by an ever-hasting never-resting agility, by breathless eagerness to mount the height. An energy so great seems to strain all the powers of Resolve: a victory so arduous over ease and passion has in it a royal air of mastery: an aspiration so lofty appears to set the eye on what is distant and toil for it with determined vow. Yet, if you will look within, you will find quite another mood of mind from this; not rigid purpose, but pliant affection; not kingly command, but docile submission; not even any passion for far-off excellence, but a willing heart for the duty that is near. The spirit of highest heroism before men stands as a little child before the face of God. When the Christian lady, endowed with whatever is choicest in the gifts of nature and the enrichments of life, exchanges the cultivated home for the noisome hospital, pledges the highest accomplishments to the lowliest charities, carries gentle graces and clear faculty into the presence and service of wounded and fevered exiles, and lives only to see and do what few men, in their strength and hardihood, would dare approach: we ask ourselves with reverent wonder, how a resolution so magnanimous could declare itself at all, and how sacrifice so costly can bear the constant drain. Perhaps the struggle we imagine never has been there. Perhaps the difficulty, the reluctance, the stern mustering of conquering force, are all a dream. Perhaps there has only been a simple *yielding up of self* to the asking look of God, a dropping of all resistance, an acquiescence in the moulding touch and pressure of the divine will. The originality and greatness of such minds arise not from præternatural effort, but from unreserved surrender: they do not determine whither they will go, but only say, 'Yes,' whithersoever they are led: they do not fret to find the way or complain because they cannot trace it far, but, hand in hand with an everlasting Guide, set a foot of firm content on the next ground that he may show. Hence the quietude and evenness of all their ways,—a certain gentle and solitary air that seems too mild to give out so much power,—a half-mystic reserve whence strangely issues a rare organizing and administrative faculty. For it is the great marvel of the Christian character, that the completest *self-sacrifice* gives the completest *self-possession;* that only the captive soul, which has flung her rights away, has all her powers free; and that simply *to serve* under the instant orders of the living God, is the highest qualification for command. This is the meaning of that great saying of Cromwell's, "*One never mounts so high as when one knows not whither one is going*": a saying which "the wise and prudent" scorned as a confession of blindness, but which reveals to simpler minds the deepest truth.

There are, in fact, two types of human greatness,—the Pagan and the Christian,—the moral and the religious,—the secular and the divine. The former has its root and essence in *trying hard;* the latter, in *trusting gently:* the one depends on *voluntary energy;* the other on *relinquishment of personal will* to cast every burden upon God. The one chooses its own ends, elaborates the means, attempts to see several moves before it, and secures the unity of its course and character by plan and vigilance; the other, possessed by a God-given end, becomes its organ and its implement, and simply lets it use, from day to day, the entire powers of the soul. On a nearer view, there is here, after all, not so much an abnegation of will, as a return to its primitive simplicity. The child, impelled towards some object of his wish,—*e.g.* to run after a ball, to imitate a phrase, to make a drawing of a horse, is wholly preoccupied with his conception, and never measures his resources against it, or thinks of the chain of movements that must lead from the idea to the accomplishment. He lets the end find its own means; and flings himself upon the unconscious tentatives that carry him to his goal without telling him his way. In such instinctive execution of his remote aim there is ever the grace and freedom of an inspiration. But when, in order to frame it into an expertness, you draw back his thought and fix it upon the process, and make him count and register the steps, the flow of power will fail him; the feet will totter, the voice will hesitate, the finger stiffen; and the spontaneous faculty, lost by your analysis of Nature, has to be doubtfully regained by combinations of Art. Similarly, in the higher intuitions, it is the unconditional surrender to an authoritative end, with implicit trust in its command of means, that arms them with a force serene and irresistible. Free from every care, entangled in no web of calculation, the thoughts gain an unanxious elasticity, and the life derives unity from the singleness of spontaneous feeling that pervades it all. Both these heroisms may be high and noble: both may be untainted by mean passions and unworthy aims: both have left their trace of glory on human history. But the strenuous self-reliance must yield the palm to the quietude of self-sacrifice and the victory of faith. However intense the stimulus which ambition or even conscience may give to the intellect and will, it is not to be compared with the might assumed by the faculties of their own accord, when released from fear and care, and flung into the Almighty hand to be wielded at his will. There is no instrument so tremendous in this world as a human soul thus committed to what is diviner than itself: it is as the two-edged sword of the Spirit with the scabbard thrown away; and wherever difficulties are to be cleft, and fiends of evil to be cut down, there it will be found, flashing on the Providential field. Be it the saintly woman, or be it the God-fearing Puritan, "None mount so high as those who know not whither they go."

It is not then so difficult to understand how the most wonderful Christian activity proceeds from the quietest and most passive surrender. Equally true is it, that the more you studiously attend to divine and infinite things, instead of letting them attend to you, the less are you likely to learn of them. Why pry about to find the universal Light? why wander through the dark to meet the Night? The Light is here and bathes you all the while: the Night is around, and hides you in its embrace. Drink-in the beauty of the hour: lie open to its deepest hints and holiest meaning: be still, and ask for purity of heart; and the blank will fill, the cloud will glow, with One who is often found of them that seek him not. Those who in this matter prate most about "progress" are just the people to make the smallest way; and none seem to win less knowledge of sacred things than those who make a watchword of "truth" and a parade of "free inquiry." This posture and direction of the mind is false except for finite and evanescent things, and must be dropped to begin the life of faith. The Infinite is not hid in a corner; or locked among the treasures of the Vatican; or lingering among the antiquities of the first century; or waiting behind some future and undevised experiment,—that we have any key to turn, any bar to remove, any choicest instruments to invent ere he becomes accessible. Were it so, were he at the end of some hard problem, the mere prize of logical skill, what hope would there be for the multitude of toiling men? We sometimes hear it said, by well-read people; "If we, with all our advantages of mental training, find it so difficult to banish doubt and realise the holy truths which we profess; if we are often obliged to have recourse to subtle reasonings and close reflection in order to clear up a perplexity and shake off a misgiving, how can we expect from the untaught poor anything but inapprehension and unbelief?" Were religious faith the creation of dialectic or the fruit of erudition, this despondency would be just. But its source and place are far different. It is rather the first root of life than the last blossom of thought; and is secured upon the native love and unsophisticated conscience which may lie torpid through some wintry seasons of civilization, but can never die within the soil of our humanity. To commune with God, there is need of no subtle thought, no foreign tongue, no newest philosophy: "the pure in heart shall see" him; and Fox and Bunyan can more truly make him known, than "Masters of Sentences" and "Angelic Doctors." It is not till we fall from the platform of our natural trusts, that the wheels and pulleys of argument are plied to lift us back again; and the artifices of reason would never be needed but to meet and balance the artifices of doubt. The dark spirits which the restless intellect evokes, a brighter intellect alone is able to disperse: but when it has cast them out, it has but chastened its own work, and reinstated us in natural health. Religion is born ere thought begins: it is re-born, when thought is consummated and enters into its glory. But meanwhile, as the familiar measures and methods of intelligence are given for the finite order of things, it is no wonder that they embarrass the apprehension of the Infinite, and increase the difficulty rather than the facility of faith. And so long as this lower mind takes no counsel with the higher and spiritual nature, and does not widen the horizon of its view, it will be blind to what the other sees; and our mental advance will be marked by the alternation of an ever-creeping shadow on divine things scattered by an ever-answering light. In order to emerge from this struggle of action and reaction, we need, not increase of acuteness, so much as return to simplicity. The supreme prerogative of cultivated Reason will then be to reopen the native pieties of early love and trust; and the truly wise will see around them, in richer hues and sublimer proportions, the heaven that lay around the child. While the curious intellect tries this and tries that, with an ever-shifting call of "Lo! here," and "Lo! there," to the tender conscience and the unspoiled mind the kingdom of God has already come.

X.

The Messengers of Change.

PSALM lv. 19.

"Because they have no changes, therefore they fear not God."

To one who tries everything by the standard of enjoyment, there arises a curious contradiction between the inner nature and the outer lot of men. We are thrown upon an existence where nothing is permanent, nothing asleep. We bring into it a soul that sighs for repose, that struggles with the restless tide, and ever hopes to drift into the still waters, and lie within the shelter of the hills. Our life is planted on the surface of a whirling sphere. Our prayer is to find its tranquil centre and revolve no more. Not that we are passive all the while, and borne along by powers wholly foreign to ourselves. Strange to say, we are sharers in the very stir and turmoil of which we complain. We create the race which we say outstrips us and leaves us faint. We fling our voice into the hum of human history; yet stop our ears, lest it should drive us mad. It is not the mere lapsing seasons of the heavens and the earth, not the passage of our physical life alone, by which our remonstrance is called forth: but, not less, the vicissitudes of society, the shifting attitudes of thought and feeling, the evanescence of habits, institutions, and beliefs; processes, of which our own agency is the producing cause, and in pleading against which we are plaintiffs against our own will. Thus, we are at variance with ourselves, as much as with our God; and are like wayward children, breaking their toys and then weeping at the wreck which their own passion has made. The yearning for rest is no doubt deeper and stronger with the old than with the young, with the conservative than with the reforming spirit. But it exists in all. The very desire for progress is for the sake of some fixed goal: the most burning aspiration hopes to sit and look forth at last from the cool and freshening height. The intensest action sustains itself on the thought that it may soon subside: it loves not the burden it is impelled to bear, but trusts ere long to lay it down. When the poet or the moralist touches on the transiency of all earthly things, and the perpetual succession of fresh relations, it is always with some sadness in the strain: as if he went forth to take a tender farewell of the old, rather than to swell the triumph of the new. And even the philosophy which has brought itself to think that the universe is but an eddy of eternal change, an ocean composed, all through its depths, of crossing currents of phenomena, has usually taught the doctrine either with a sorrow in the voice, or in the metal tone of heartless arrogance. The decree of vicissitude manifestly presses heavily upon the soul: and whether it be the outward condition of established comfort that crumbles beneath the feet; or the beliefs of earlier days that change like the morning clouds before the kindling light; or the affections that have given a quiet sanctity to life, and are now called to drop their objects one by one at the word of Death; the cry of the heart is still the same, "O that it were with me now, as it was in the times never to return!"

This regretful glance at the fading colours of the past, this longing to find rest from the ceaseless flow of change, has two different meanings and tendencies: one false and evil; the other true and good. Its impulse is false, when it leads us to the mere negative resource of ease and exemption, instead of the positive repose in God; when we only cry to be let alone, that our sleep be not disturbed too soon; when we simply shrink from the touch of new duties and new sorrows; when we are angry at the noble passion that urges us to toil and danger, and repent of the love that brings us grief. Its impulse is true, when it makes us, in our quest of peace, go out beyond vicissitude, instead of weaving a nest within it; when it refers us to a centre of stability, a spirit of Almighty constancy, a presence of pure and infinite affection, amid and behind the fluctuations of created things; when, instead of returning to our ark at the first spray of the cold flood, we do but rise upon the wing to look through the upper air, and then take our resolute track to the fixed and illumined hills. The soul is faithless which, when it is stung by severities and bowed by afflictions, tries to choke its sympathies and bring a frost upon its mellow seasons. It is not by reducing life to less, but by expanding it to more; not by muffling its stern tones, but by ringing its sweetness clearly out, that a serene harmony can be obtained. When duty is severe, we must be more reverently dutiful; if love brings sorrow, we must love more and better; when thought chills us with doubt and fear, we must think again with fuller soul and deeper trust.

The changeful lot which our lower instinct deprecates is, in truth, the very discipline by which God would draw us to himself. Repugnant to our animal and sentient nature, it kindles the diviner element to life. There is none but God himself that can abide for ever holy, for ever perfect, for ever wakeful, without any experience of alternation. As for us, if we have no changes, we fear him not. Our faculties of intellect and feeling, our sense of beauty and of right, the opening out of character and affection, are made dependent on the stimulus of incessant change. The passiveness of the infant's existence is overcome by a thousand soliciting impressions; the light that fascinates the eye; the touch that puts a spring into the limbs; the ever-varying challenge of the mother's looks, forcing the tender cheek into a smile. The great apparatus of external nature, which would teach us nothing if it and we were fixed, glides with transitory images before the sight, and, ere we can sleep before one scene, presents us with another. This is indeed the very condition of all apprehension and intelligence. Dipped ever in the same scene, plunged in one colour, filled with one monotone, no perception would be startled into birth: the glance of attention sleeps, till the moment of transition; it leaps forth at the edges of light and darkness, of sound and silence, and in crossing the line first learns the realm on either side. So long as life is young, a perpetual stream of wonder pours on the mind and bathes it with exhaustless admirations: even were no lines of unexpected order, no new regions of knowledge opened, the rapid ripening of the faculties themselves would alter the apparent lights on every scene, and dissolve the outlines of each prior experience. And in this training of constant change there is a marvellous tendency to drive us upon faith in the Unchangeable. Finite things can be discerned only against the background of the Infinite. The visible body that glides before the eye is as an island in the Space that has no bounding shore. The passing event that marks the moment is but a point of contact where the curve of our being meets the tangent of Eternity. No appearance emerges and arrests our thought, without raising questions of Causation, and speaking to us as from a hidden Mind that meditates in beauty and speaks in law. To the pure and unspoiled heart, all phenomena that present no deformity, and all experience clear of sin, open a way for the consciousness of God: gleams of him will frequently break through; and a certain tacit sense of his reality and nearness will linger around even common hours and daily tasks. Where the first lessons of life, the first stirrings of the soul, are hindered by no hardening and ungenial culture, its features of earthly gladsomeness will have a certain modest setting of heavenly reverence.

But the cycle of young experience soon completes itself. At each return its repetitions become more and more familiar. Change itself becomes customary, and visits the mind with monotony rather than variety. The spring seems to burst with a fainter verdure, and the winter hearth to burn with a less vivid glow. The morning-breeze of young enthusiasm, so fragrant of the night, so fresh from heaven, grows drowsy with the steady heat, and sinks to rest: and the mental and moral life which had been nursed in vicissitude threatens to perish under the opiate of usage. Not that Providence abandons us in our maturity, or omits to ply us with awakening appeals. No sooner has life ceased to be a *constant* flow of novelty, than it enters on a series of grand crises, which intersect its even course: its current orbit has become as a beaten track: but there are nodes it cannot pass without a spark and thrill. When life-long ties are contracted, and the green path is entered at one end at whose other the death-shadow waits in ambush; when first the home of marriage is set in order; when the child is born; when the parent dies; when the friend deserts, or the business fails, or the sickness prostrates; the Angel of Change looks in again through her veil of light, or her curtain of shadows, and reminds us of Him who abideth in the midst for ever. All these are epochs of natural devotion; and only the most insensible heart can pass them with the neutral heedlessness of instinct, and without any enriching hue of awe-ful thought. The incidents of the great mortal drama are so prepared as never to permit the interest to flag; and even in its quietest development, where the plot seems most evenly to act itself out, we cannot be long without some scene whose pathos touches us, or whose misery appals. These times, moreover, are irregularly scattered on our way, that they may the better surprise our insensibility, and that we may not kill them by anticipation ere they come. They are not like the steadily recurring hours that announce the stated duty and find us mechanically prepared. With whatever wonder we watch the dial-plate of life, we cannot find them there. The deeper crises are marked in invisible characters there, legible only to the Omniscient eye; and as the index traverses, we know not what birth, what death, what sudden hope, what blighted joy, lies just upon its touch. When these hours strike, neither matin nor vesper has such a holy sound: it is God himself that tolls us in to prayer, and calls us to listen to his great Sermon on the Mount; and whether we are in the field or on the sea, we must throw down the common implements of our work, and go and stand before his face. As one crisis after another is brought upon our lot, it gives us the means of moral admeasurement and deeper self-knowledge: it reads off the reckoning of our spirits, and tells us whether we more deeply live, or more begin to die. Each newest sorrow revives the thought of those before, and spreads out the past in tender colours before the eye: the pictures of other years, the scenes once pressed by our more elastic feet, the dear forms that were with us there, and held us by the hand, stand out in the clear and silent light: and their very looks may tell us whether any grosser film has gathered on our soul; whether we can meet their calm and holy face; whether, as we are further from them in one direction, we are nearer to them in another; and whether the same atmosphere of God seems to enfold us both and make us one with them and him. The emergencies that reveal things to our sight are a discipline which, however grievous, we can ill spare; and, to those that give them worthy welcome, they leave a trust nobler than security, and a wisdom better than any joy. The men who most escape them, who most completely realise the false elysium of an easy life; whose heritage saves them the rough battle with difficulty, to win an honourable footing in the world; whose health is never shaken by disease, and whose home is invaded by no anxiety; are rarely those who most penetrate to the moral significance of life, and are alive with the quickest affection and the promptest alacrity of conscience. Too often a sluggish cloud gathers on their mind and hides from them the finest expression, the divinest look, upon the features of nature and humanity. All things fall tamely to their lot as matters of course: the prizes for which others spend all their manly strength, the decent and ornamental comfort, the provision for the sinking parent, the education for the rising child, the store of books, the fund for charity, the time for kindly deeds, the place of influence in society; all are theirs without a thought, and, grown flat with usage, have none of the rich flavour of hope and toil. Great is the danger that, because they have no changes, they may cease to fear or love. It is only by strong and noble effort to shake off the slothful weeds as they creep over the surface of such a life, and keep the margin clear by the running waters of pure affection, that they can retain the native clearness of the soul, and continue to reflect the gaze of Heaven. What the natural history of the heart, the quickening necessity, the subduing sorrow, accomplish for others, is left in their case to the strenuous vow of their own will. It is one of the great compensations which balance, more equally than men suppose, the good and ill of human existence, that where there is more affliction there is often more affection too: if the burden is heavier to be borne, the soul is more elastic to bear it; and by many a sorrowing creature, flushed with the inspiration of love, duties are thrown profusely and spontaneously off, which the painful struggles of unawakened ease could scarcely lift.

So completely is it the Providential plan to secure to us the discipline of change, that, when we fall asleep on the crust of usage, a fire is immediately kindled beneath us, and we sleep on a volcano. Our very inertia operates as an instrument to prepare for us new crises that shall force us to spring to our feet once more. Whatever be our appointed work, the first moment of its neglect is the first moment of its decay; and where we cease to grow our corn, the poison plants will cover all the ground. God has made nothing in this world *to keep*—nothing, at least, that has a beauty, and that bears a fruit; death only and negation, deformity and barrenness, will flourish when let alone. The individual mind, abandoned to negligence, watched by no eye of conscience, bathed in no presence of God, exercised in no athletics of duty, loosens all its healthy structure, and sinks into moral decline; little, perhaps, suspecting its own degeneracy, till surprised into some awful degradation, and wakening into shame. No institution, no state, no church, will go on of itself and hold its footing in the nature of things, while its guardians and trustees are dozing on their watch. There is ever a little speck of disease, a canker of evil and falsehood, secreted in the substance of terrestrial things, which is sure to spread, if you omit to wipe the dust from their surface, and wash them with the waters of purification. If you persist awhile in your unfaithfulness, you will be startled at length by the spasm of a sudden agony; and it will be well, if by repentant efforts at renewal and the use of painful remedies, a disastrous dissolution is staved off. In nations, as in persons, too great a calm, too mild an indifference, too peaceful an apathy, is ever a dark and boding sign, the lull that comes before the storm, the dead silence ere the thunder breaks. If we stir the atmosphere and fling it upwards from no soil burning with noble passions; if every zone of our world reduces itself to temperate and timid heats; if no circulating breath of pure enthusiasm passes from land to land, bearing on it the cry of sympathy with the down-trodden, and of defiance to the oppressor; God will clear the air for us from above, and fling across our fields and cities the whirlwind of revolution. Thus it is that "He who abideth for ever will afflict us," if, "because we have no changes," we cease to stand in awe of him. There is no peace but in waking to all his seasons, and moving freely with the windings of his Will; quick to seize each fresh surprise of duty; alert before day-break to strike our tent of ease; patient to endure the crown of thorns which must press upon the brow of every son of God.

If, then, the very law of life is a law of change; if every blossom of beauty has its root in fallen leaves; if love, and thought, and hope would faint beneath too constant light, and need for their freshening the dark-ness and the dews; if it is in losing the transient that we gain the Eternal; then let us shrink no more from sorrow, and sigh no more for rest; but have a genial welcome for vicissitude, and make quiet friends with loss and Death. Through storm and calm, fresh be our courage, and quick our eye, for the various service that may await us. Nay, when God himself turns us not hither and thither, when he sends us no changes for us to receive and consecrate, be it ours to create them for ourselves, by flinging ourselves into generous enterprises and worthy sacrifice; by the stirrings of sleepless aspiration, and all the spontaneous vicissitudes of holy and progressive souls; keeping always the moral spaces round us pure and fresh by the constant thought of truth and the frequent deed of love. And then, when, for us too, death closes the great series of mortal changes, the past will lie behind us green and sweet as Eden, and the future before us in the light of eternal peace. Tranquil and fearless we shall resign ourselves to God, to conduct us through that ancient and invisible way, which has been sanctified by the feet of all the faithful, and illumined by the passage of the Man of griefs.

XI.

Secret Trust.

JOHN iv. 32.

"I have meat to eat that ye know not of."

THE sense of dependence, it has been declared, constitutes the essence of religion. At all events, it is an essential condition. A nature perfectly self-possessed and self-sufficing, in equilibrium with the world without, and at rest from the balance of its powers within, would be so rounded off and complete in itself as to float through existence unconscious of the attractions, untroubled by the resistances, which determine its path. It is when we feel the jar of actual adjustments, that the sphere of the possible bursts open to us; when we are borne out on the wing of affections which find nowhere to alight, but only floods below and clouds above, that we set our heart on the rock beneath the waters and the light beyond the gloom. And there are such provisions for this experience in the whole constitution of our life, that not even the most robust and limited of men can escape the sense of instability. There are times when we cannot but feel the world too strong for us;—the world *without;* when its strain of duty loads us with too heavy a weight; or the stroke of its laws shatters our reliances and leaves us wounded and alone; or the tyranny of its opinion baffles in us what is wisest and tortures what is best; or the brevity of its duration for us brings us at the same hour to the last verge of its opportunity and the full discovery of its scope. Nor are we less liable to be overmastered by the world *within;* when the will is struck down by the lightning of passion, or moves creaking with the friction of temper, or sinks in the collapse of depression; and whether we are taken up and borne along upon the storm, or checked by the secret threads that bind us to the ground, we seem to be disposed of against vain remonstrance of our own. Even if the winds were calm without, the floods would roll within; for in our unstable soul the very bottom heaves beneath; so that we are tossed between the elements and ride on a surface that never rests.

What provision then is there for conquering this uncertain sea? what means of holding an even way through the fluctuations of impulse and vicissitude? In the habits of human life, and the resources of human character, there are helps of various degree to this end. To steady us amid the dizzy sweep of change, it is good to be under a rule of *outward necessity*, which weights down our sudden caprices and goads our flagging resolves, and compels us to pace a round of achievement we should else deem it too monotonous to take. Be it only the drill of an army, the discipline of a frigate, the punctual bell and inexorable machinery of a mill, whatever mingles law and measure with the forces of the will, and constrains them to work in rhythm if they work at all, is a beneficent corrector of irresolution and vehemence, and builds up those habits of outward order, in which inward right most loves to dwell. It is still better to pass under the sway of a *fixed purpose* of our own, which shall be worthy of our conscience and adequately tax our powers; to make it the master of our industry, the counsellor of our doubts, the victor of our temptations. And whether it be to write a history, to solve a problem, or to remedy an abuse, whoever has clearly before him such an end in view, sails with his compass alight through the wildest night, and, bearing onward, is heedless of the pelting rain, and unbewildered by the gloom. From all who are intent upon great works, a Luther, a Cromwell, a Clarkson among reformers, a Gibbon, a Humboldt, a Grote among intellectual men, the distractions which weaken life naturally fall away; and even its griefs strike upon them with gentler touch; and over many a dead lift of obstruction which would bring less concentrated energies to pause they are carried by a quiet persistency. But neither the service of an involuntary necessity, nor the execution of a voluntary purpose, reaches the ultimate sources of unrest; and, in order to steady us from the centre outwards, it is best of all to be possessed by a *hidden faith*, which keeps its tints of beauty and its lines of truth behind the flying shadows, a secret image of what life *really is* before the verifying eye of God, a preoccupation with its rightful perfectness as seen in the supreme visions of the heart. Once let there be this felt difference between the seeming and the reality of things; let them carry an inward idea which is moulding them even while they mar it, and which will persevere and emerge through their transient deformities; let the phenomena pass in front of this divine light, while the mind sinks deep into it, and abides there with perfect trust; then, having the interpreting key to changes which baffle others, it dwells in an element of peace, and identifies itself, not with the discords of the world which are working themselves off, but with the harmonies that are striving to be. To look upon the scene of things as thus pervaded by the thought of a just and holy God, and charged to work it out, in unconscious servitude or conscious partnership, to live with heart and hope fixed upon the higher ends instead of imprisoned in the poor beginnings,—this is to have power perfected in weakness, and joy kindled amid tears: this, as we toss upon the deep and are covered with the night, is better than the fragile compass: it is the compass lifted to heaven, and turned into stars that are never clouded and never set.

"I have meat to eat that ye know not of." What words could more pathetically hint at the spiritual source of strength in that unique career,—that aliment of the holy, true and good which Plato says is the common well-spring for the thirst of all minds, divine and human. Thus to live out of the invisible and higher, and cling to it as the last reality, is Religion; and this it is which alone takes away the hardness of duty and gives a sweetness to affection, and mingles a sanctity with experience.

1. There is an invisible and transcendent element in *Duty*, which at once defines and inspires it; clears its form and turns it from a human reluctance into a divine joy. It is in vain that we look around and consult the outward world, and take up now with this example, now with that, in order to find what we ought to be and do. So long as Conscience tries to "live by sight and not by faith," and cannot stay at home with God, but must go forth into the desert or the city at every call of "Lo! here," and "Lo! there," it can only pass from thraldom to thraldom and find no true Deliverer. Neither models that appeal to the eye, nor maxims that speak to the ear, can ever, without abatement, send us to the divine light or tell us the

divine thought. Plant me where you will upon *that which is*, I must look across a chasm to *that which ought to be*. The kingdom of heaven remains within; and only broken gleams from it are reflected from the world without. Right and wrong are nowhere clearly set in the sunshine, or painted definitely out in the opposite characters of men; but are mixed up together, as if the combinations of fact took no notice of the distinctions of thought, and some weakness of nature fell short of the design of God. Where have you ever found, even in the selectest gallery of the good, one whom you could make your absolute rule of life? Do you fix, for instance, on the pure soul which sits behind that uplifted face, and, the more it retires within, shines the more through the transparent eye? He who looks at you with that sweet pathetic light and whose voice makes music in the heart, may never have known a passion that is ignoble or a vision that is unclean; but see! his home is in confusion, his appointments are unkept, his wife is overworked, and he heeds not that he has left her to serve alone; in dreaming how the world might be better he lets it drop into the worse. Do you turn then, in your disappointment, to one who shall be "safe from all illusions"; whose clear discernment and firm will keep him well adjusted to the world around him; and who suffers under no disproportion between the intellect which apprehends and the conscience which works out the practical problems of life? If you keep close to him, his calm and constant mind may hold you punctual to duty and secure against mistake. But, alas! if you are in doubt and wayward sorrow, you never dare confess to him; if you go astray into some folly, he will only upbraid you; if the wing of some high passion lifts you from his beaten track, and struggles to reach the blue and visionary distance, he will part from you with contemptuous adieu. Sick at heart with the cold repulse, do you take for your comrade and your guide that young apostle of righteousness, the enthusiast of self-denial, who flings himself as an organ of divine pity on the sins and grievances of the world, and shames them from a presence instinct with faith and hope and charity? It is well; while you are at his side, conscience can never sleep, and the will, touched by the love of God, can bend with a tender grace to the smallest things. But he will hurry you hither and thither, faster than your reason and more capriciously than your conscience can go: stable only in nobleness, he is carried, with the hectic flush of restless impulse from one compassion to another, and misses the quiet unity which alone can compress any achievement into the few human years. Not the beauty only, but the possibility of his life you find to be exceptional; and with loving sorrow you have to leave him on his path alone.

And if in even the higher characters of men no

adequate rule of life is to be found, still vainer is the trust in the current sentiments and recognised standard of society around. It is a miscellaneous multitude of the foolish and frivolous as well as of the wise and faithful, which votes into existence the moral opinion of a community; and its level can never rise above half-tide, except when some mighty wind of genius and goodness sets in from the deep, and for an hour builds it up to flood. From its very nature, social law asks no more than men of all sorts agree to demand of one another; and lets off with impunity the follies it is prudent to wink at, and the sins it is not convenient to forego; and if *this* is to be our measure of right,—to uphold us where we are,—low indeed must be our moral position, and precarious our standing even there. If you have only your little share in the public conscience, all that dignifies existence is at the mercy of the veering winds, and all that consecrates it retires behind the cloud: not the goodness only, but the beauty and true adornment of life, oscillate into senseless distortions; and you will deck yourself, under Cromwell, in the winding-sheet of Puritanism, and in the next age in the lascivious robes of the Restoration, and will helplessly deliver yourself in our time to those outrages on taste which bespeak vacuity or shamelessness of character. Unless you have some selecting principle within, the native affinity, the incorruptible reverence of a pure and modest nature, you have nothing to steady you under the swaying movements of custom; nothing to protect you from any favourite folly; nothing to hinder your captivity to the false admirations that for ever lie in wait for the idle and the faithless of mankind. It is by looking up beyond the actual, not by looking down into it, by seeking God within, not consulting men without, that you will truly measure the divine claims upon you, and find your duty clear and calm and sacred. Commune with him, the All-holy, and it will become a secret understanding between his spirit and your own,—a trust from him, answered by assent and love from you; an escape from the poor twilight of human mediocrity into the precincts of a lustre which can never fade. A soul that goes apart with this divine vision of goodness has that to feed on which others think not of.

2. There are also invisible capacities in *Human Nature*, a latent fund of diviner affection, without an eye on which we shall ill sustain the depth and freshness of our charity, and the very fountains of the heart must dry. Look only at the surface of life, either where the triflers loiter or the competing crowd pushes its eager way, and tramples the weak upon the ground; or enter just the first stratum of motive immediately below, where men dress up their seeming to one another, and invent decorous disguises for their selfishness; and you have the scene before you which turns the observer into the cynic and satirist. And carry *that* temper whither you will, you will never see more than this: all

that turns up will confirm it; for it elicits what is akin to itself; it creates its own evidence as it goes, and publishes it in the journals and the clubs; and drives whatever contradicts it to hide in the forest shades of the inmost spirit and be alone with God. If we have *no trust*, and frame our speech and tune our voice as having none, we shall often find it difficult to love even our friends as they *appear* to us: our very presence will harden them, and put them on their defence; and by many a carping word, or chafing of the spirit, they will do injustice to themselves. How often may you hear the querulous dialogue, the mutual complaint, the artificial fence of hurting speech, between those who, if they would but burst the barrier of their pride, would fall into each other's arms, and in dismissing the fiend, let the reconciling angel in! The pure and tender eye which is not arrested by the troubled and broken surface, but sends its glance behind and within, not only sees the actual love that lives there, but warms and wakes the possible love that was asleep and never stirred before. Our humanity, touched with a divine freedom, has larger and more liberal limits than its critics and its students dream: it is not base; it is not noble: it is a vast possibility of baseness or of nobleness; and nothing so kindles its high spiritual consciousness and transfigures it with light divine, as the appeal of trustful sympathy, and the expectant light of a brother's faith. Could we not treat the guilt and degradation which deform the world as something unnatural, a spoiling of the idea of God and the possibilities of man, could we not rely on some supporting response when we bear down upon them with expostulating call, it would be all over with our patience and our hope. But when we pass the poor deforming exterior, and enter the inner nature, and ever so faintly trace the sleeping lineaments of the divine image, pity despairs no more, and love recovers from its recoil.

3. There is, finally, an invisible meaning and Providence in *Life*, which alone, through the clashing voices and dizzying movements of the scene around, can steady the tremblings of nature, and bring a quietude to the heart. Were we sent upon this stage with blind spiritual eye, and committed to our sensibilities alone to grope about and judge by what the moments bring, all things would appear confused and fragmentary; and however divine the poem of the world, the scattered shreds would not reveal its thought or the broken strains its melody. From our own position, simply as we feel it, all security and peace often seem to pass away: the ground breaks beneath our feet, and, as in a dream where there is nothing solid to clutch at, we sink we know not whither. On the bed of pain, when thought and will swim feebly away and we are condensed into the poignant moments; when we long for the night, but, when it comes, the stars glide too slowly and the silence will not let us moan; and we watch for the

morning, but, when it dawns, the soft light mocks us with its sweetness and the birds with the blitheness of their song; in the vigils of anxiety, when some life which is our all trembles in the scale, and we extort a thousand contradictory oracles from the flush upon the features or the cloud upon the eye ;—under the sting of calumny, when things we most abhor are told of us, and averted faces and sarcastic words show that the lie has proved too strong and the love of friends too weak; —in the countless vicissitudes of broken fortune and shattered health and disappointed hopes; all must look like ruin, if we have no stay beyond the impression of the hour. And even though we should not be upon the rack of suffering ourselves, how often, if there were nothing behind the things we see, might the immediate aspect and courses of the world disturb us! When the minds of men seem to fall into confusion, deserted by the simple sanctities of their fathers but not yet emerging into any clearness of their own; when, for want of any firm foothold of right, authority quails and rude forces triumph; when audacity seizes upon states, yet is itself afflicted with the wavering of irremediable doubt; when churches, enfeebled within by puerile superstitions, stand amid a rising flood of atheistic denial; when the distinctions slip away between veracity and pretence, between trade and theft, between modesty and license; we might well despond, if we did not look beyond the present, and interpret it by the light of a diviner thought than animates its actors. But lifted to an adequate distance from it, and assigning to it its place in the Providence of humanity, we discern it but as a pulsation in the line of time, one of those moments of alternate tension and relaxation which are separately dark, but together make the very light by which we see. Thither, to that divine elevation above momentary things, let the soul resort in faith; and the sorrowful clouds that shut it in are surmounted, and the everlasting sunshine reached. In frailty and in trembling, we rest in an eternal calm. In loneliness, we have still an ever living communion. Deserted by the voices of affection, we are with Him who attuned their sweetness, and will console their loss. And dying, we do but pass to the very source and home of life.

XII.

The Sorrows of Messiah.

JOHN xii. 27.

"Now is my soul troubled; and what shall I say? Father, save me from this hour? but for this cause came I unto this hour. Father! glorify thy name."

IN Rome there are ancient catacombs which were used by the primitive Christians for interment of their dead. As depositories of the ashes of a lost generation, they are nought to us: the dust of believer or unbeliever, of the sinful or the saint, is drifted by the winds of time into the common wreck of our humanity. But a single mark made by a living hand is worth all the remains of death sealed and treasured with so much care; especially when traced in moments of truth and tenderness on the curtain drawn around the sleep of friends: and the outside of the urn and the sarcophagus may teach a more instructive lesson than can be learned from the emptiness within. Now throughout the decorative emblems and inscriptions in the early Christian cemeteries, it has been remarked, one uniform character may be observed,—their spirit of cheerfulness and hope. By some fresh breath, the gloom seems all swept out from the chamber of so many griefs; and a sweet and placid light to fill the place, other than the glare of earthly day, and like an enclosure of starlight from the skies. The images and pictures on the walls exclude all the horrors, and present only the sanctity, of death; assuring us that survivors kept over it a secure and quiet vigil, invested it with peaceful thoughts, and looked through it to a holy and passionless existence. There, the evergreen leaf protests, in sculptured silence, that the winter of the grave cannot touch the saintly soul: the blossoming branch speaks of vernal suns beyond the snows of this chill world: the good Shepherd shows, from his benign looks, that the mortal way, so terrible to nature, had become to those Christians as the meadow path, between the grassy slopes and beside the still waters. Yet were these mausoleums peopled by no favoured race. They were the last asylum of the persecuted; they opened the first shelter to the weary and despised: side by side with those who had fallen asleep on the pillow of domestic care, were many who had died the martyr's death, and mingled their last sigh, not with the sobs of affection, but with the fiendish shouts of the amphitheatre. When this is borne in mind, the impress of cheerfulness on the symbolic memorials of the place cannot fail to strike us as remarkable. That the victims pelted hither by the storms of a merciless world should be laid down upon the earth without a mark of anger or a burst of mourning, but only with the mild farewell of affection and of hope, attests the power of the new faith to still with its word the fiercest tempest of grief and passion.

This indication however is in perfect agreement with other signs of a fearless and glad enthusiasm pervading the early Church. Rome was startled by the appearance, in her effeminate cities, of a people whom it was impossible to terrify; on whom torture and death, consecrated by some invisible charm, lost their deterring power; who reminded her of her old republican hardihood, only that it was not so much manly as godlike; who amid the pestilence, or after the siege, came into the streets to cool the fevers of death, and soothe the rage of despair; who escorted the martyr to his end with envious gratulations, and greeted the earthquake itself with the hymn of redemption.

And even earlier than any organized Christendom, we find, in the apostolic writings themselves, abundant traces of the same spirit. What can be more free and buoyant, with all their variety, than the writings of Paul? Brilliant, broken, impetuous, as the mountain torrent freshly filled, never smooth and calm, but on the eve of some bold leap, never vehement but to fill some receptacle of clearest peace, they present everywhere the image of a vigorous joy. Beneath the form of their theosophic reasonings, and their hints of deep philosophy, there may be heard a secret lyric strain of glorious praise, bursting at times into open utterance and asking others to join in chorus. "Rejoice in the Lord always! and again, I say unto you, Rejoice!" His life was a battle; from which, in intervals of the good fight, his words arose as the song of victory.

The primitive followers of the faith then were all of one heart and mind; and that was a heart of free and natural joy. Yet they were disciples of one who is known to all ages as the *Man of sorrows;* of one serene indeed in spirit, and of a strength divine and clear; but with the tinge throughout of a sad earnestness,—sometimes flushing up into a transient glow of hope,—rarely deepening into the shade of a visible anguish; and yet throughout, from the wrestlings in the desert to his cry upon the cross, showing itself in miracles of pity and in nights of prayer; in the light of his love and the flash of his invective,—his delight in nature and in childhood, his abhorrence of Pharisees and hypocrites; in the deep beauty of his parables, and the melancholy wisdom of his prophecies; in the sedate unity of his life and the quiet majesty of his death. How indeed is he represented by the emblem in which Christendom has embodied its veneration? The crucifix is the accepted symbol of grief divinely borne.

Whence is this contrast between the disciple and the Master? Why, when we look beneath the garment of praise, do we find, at the heart of the religion, the spirit of sadness? The outward lot of Paul was not less severe than that of the Crucified himself; and he had certainly no hope, no trust, no comfort, which had not been imparted by the author of his faith. Could Jesus *give* a gladness it was not permitted him to share, and by the gentle hand of his religion wipe away all tears except his own? All theologies are much perplexed to afford any account of this. If he was an inspired man, why did not his inspiration lift him beyond the range of grief, and awaken in him the temper which it produced in others at secondhand? If, as others say, he was God veiled in the flesh, how could he have sorrow beyond even the measure of a man?

Nothing in truth can be more natural, if we did not persist in looking for the explanation in the wrong place. Assuming that, under one name or other, there was in Christ a blending of divine and human elements, we fancy that it was his participation in the human nature which bruised him with sorrow, and that his higher attributes, by their imperfect amount or occasional retreat, fell short of power to heal the wounds. Had this been so, then those who, with the disciples, stood upon a lower level of humanity, would have been sunk into a deeper darkness, instead of being lifted into a more cheerful light. No, it was the Divine spirit in Christ,—as it is in every noble heart,—that subdued him to that earnest sadness, which, under human impulse only, would have been soon forgot. However true it may be that "Man is born to trouble," he owes the distinction not to his inferior, but to his highest powers. Reason alone has the privilege of tears: Conscience trembles with remorse; creative Thought laments its poor performance; and the light of Love casts the long shadow of death. Lift off these crowning faculties, and you remove at once our griefs and glory, and let us down to the poor level of unfallen Adam. If labour and sorrow come of the lapse in Paradise, we have reason to bless the sinning mother of all flesh, that she held not her hand from the forbidden fruit, and exchanged the grass and flowers of Eden for the rock, the thistle, and the thorn. It is not as child of the earth, but as a Son of God, that man has his heritage of care. And in proportion as the Divine spirit is transcendent over the inferior nature, and through higher and higher brightness becomes a supernatural light of the world, must the shadow deepen too; till in Messiah we reach the limit of inspired sorrow; where the lot and outward scope of being is finite as in other men; but the soul, immeasurable and infinite.

Far from its being wonderful that the disciples should have a joy to which the Master was a stranger, it is the necessary consequence of their relative position. He who himself *is* a religion, must needs miss the chief solace of religion. Others believe in him;

but he has no mediator in the immensity that leads to the Most High. They gather, with reverent affection, round him, and feel a perfect rest; finding in him a representative image of all that is Divine, a mid-point of clear conception beyond which they cannot go: but he stands, with uncovered head, beneath the Infinite, and has no help to God but his own poor thoughts. They live, as we all do unconsciously, by communicated religion, the instinctive dependence of lower souls upon the higher, and the divine right of the greater to hold the less: but he has no higher, no greater, and, while ruling systems of minds, floats through space with no guiding attraction except to the awful Centre which is everywhere. No Messiah of heaven can find a disciple's rest at the feet of them who sit in Moses' seat. And yet no one can be his own Christ. It is this singular position, beyond all the beaten ways and city lamps of the habitable earth, on the confines of eternal night, and amid the breaking lights of a new world, that fills the prophet's soul, ever genial and tender beneath its sublime strength, with sorrow even unto death. He cannot love and have a home in a sphere which is not yet hung up in heaven, and which he spends himself in creating: and so, the meanest things have a shelter denied to him; and the saying comes to pass as it is written, "the foxes have holes, and the birds of the air have nests, but the Son of Man hath not where to lay his head."

Consider, for instance, the difference there is between obeying a Law, and following out a heart of Love. It is poorly represented by the difference between the piecework of industry and the creation of genius. The apostles were entrusted with a definite and prescribed task, requiring indeed alacrity of heart and fidelity of will and heroism of resolve, but still a task clear and fixed, and in which settled ways were possible, and skill and habit would avail them, and visible progress might be made. And this type of life, viz. of Duty within appointed limits, and desires coextensive in their range, is the happiest of all. It has the healthiness of labour in its progress, and the rewards of labour in its close. It is essentially the life of childhood, environed with an invisible protection, and with the freedom of an unreluctant obedience. Tell me only the burden I have to bear, and weigh it out before me day by day, and let it but be according to the measure of a man, and I can lift it up with joy. And so it was even with the various life of Paul. He had a thing to say, and then to take the consequences: his instructions never changed; and in peril and in prison, he was still an *ambassador* in bonds. When he had done at Antioch, he could go to Corinth: when he had affrighted Diana at Ephesus, he could take passage over the Ægean and defy Minerva on Mars hill: having made his defence in Jerusalem, by appeal to Cæsar he could see Rome also, introduce the Prince of Peace in the metropolis of a nation of soldiers, and plant the cross above the capitol. And as he went, he could count the synagogues he had converted, and the centres of Christian light he had left behind. He had moreover some forty years of toil, in which to see how the labour of his hands could prosper and grow; how the blessed seed could burst the sullen soil and show its green young life, now here, now there; till in the winter of his own age, the seasons of God seemed to bring a warmer sky, and crown his tillage with a reproductive blossom ere he dies. But the Master's mission was different from this. It was a work not to be reckoned by *quantity* at all, but by *quality* alone, so that one might almost doubt, from any measurable symptoms, whether it had a real existence. No long and versatile career was permitted to spread and multiply its power. He was gone before mid-life; and three years at most achieved the work which two thousand assuredly will not exhaust; and the poor villages of Galilee, and the precincts of Jerusalem bounded the steps of him, at whose name the front ranks of all mankind, for fifty generations, have bent the knee. And his sorrow, therefore, lay in this; that he did not know, and as a consequence of his inspiration could not know, what he did, except that it was his best, or whither he went, except that it was whereto God was sending him. No standard of usage or habit availed him to compute his way: false formulas can no more estimate a true soul, than equations can solve you the beauty of the morning light. He could not move for a single step in the beaten ways which were the high road of hypocrites and had their ending in destruction; yet he fell upon a time over which no other path was traced. So he had to dispense with the help of custom; to break through all dreamy traditional veneration for things abominable to his inner heart; to see for himself the true and divine path of light through the clouds which his age and place had thrown around him; content if he could only discern the next step clearly; and ready to follow the pointings of the finger of God, though it directed his foot upon the sea, or bade him walk sheer off into the darkness of the abyss. At every instant he had *to find* his work by the living spirit of love and truth and trust, without and against the dead momentum of habit and of law. It was a moral life without sleep; a watch in the great observatory of nature through a night that never yielded to the dawn, with eye ever strained on the eternal stars. Hence the sublime faintness of the inspired soul; kept awake by the resistless glory of the Creator; yet sinking with the pale exhaustion of the creature.

The prophet's heart, moreover, is rich in deep affections; open to all gentleness and beauty; quick to pity; eager to love; and in spite of its clear perceptions of spiritual things, not without a certain distrust and self-renunciation that make it long for the answering suffrage of other minds to say 'Amen' to all its prayers. Yet, from the necessity of the case, he lives in absolute loneliness: he stands where sympathy cannot reach: he leans his head on the bosom of no equal, and must put up with poor disciples' blind sorrow at his sighs. He is alone, except with God; and God alas! is silent always;—a thing that makes a great difference to a loving and dependent soul. "Answer me, O God!" is the cry not only of ancient seers, but of human nature in its grief and aspiration in every age. The tone of a living voice, coming across the misgivings of nature, and rendering response to the aspirations of the wrestling and solitary spirit, would raise it up in conscious and joyful power. But this is denied to the doubts and anguish of the saviours of the world. Their cries and tears are dissipated and lost in the immensity into which they are thrown; and there is "silence in heaven" unto this hour. This it is that makes the grandeur, yet the desolation, of a life of absolute faith; this, which brings to the Redeemer the deep trouble of the soul; without, however, tempting him to say "Father, save me from this hour!" but, seeing that "for this cause came he unto this hour," leaving him content to say "Father, glorify thy name!"

XIII.

The Bread of Life.

MATT. xiv. 19-21.

"And he commanded the multitude to sit down on the grass; and took the five loaves and the two fishes, and looking up to heaven he blessed and brake; and gave the loaves to his disciples, and the disciples to the multitude. And they did all eat, and were filled; and they took up of the fragments that remained twelve baskets full. And they that had eaten were about five thousand men, beside women and children."

JOHN vi. 49-51.

"Your fathers did eat manna in the wilderness and are dead: this is the bread which cometh down from heaven, that a man may eat thereof and not die; I am the living bread which came down from heaven."

THE Israelitish tradition of the manna in the wilderness left behind it a long bequest of imagery and doctrine. To the nation whose romantic history it enriched, this "angels' food" became the favourite emblem of the providing care of God; first, of the affluence of his natural supplies; then, of the fulness of his spiritual grace. To the Poet telling of His pity who hears the raven's cry,—to the Prophet promising His answer to the deeper hunger of the soul, no illustration so readily occurred, as the dry desert sparkling in the morning with his riches as with the dew, and the shower of plenty that fell as crumbs from the table of infinitude. The earliest records of our religion cannot otherwise express the influence which diffused itself from the presence and spirit of Jesus, than by at once comparing and contrasting him with the old Lawgiver and his miraculous supplies. Moses gave the fathers support adequate to the perishable life of nature: Christ cherished in their children the undying life of the soul:—Moses furnished them with an outward food, gathered on the ground and not less strange to him than to themselves: Christ offered them no foreign discovery, nothing but himself: he found the divine element within him, and in his own person *was* the bread of life. He also, though on the grassy hills of Galilee instead of among the sands and rocks of Horeb, was with a mighty multitude in a desert place; and there he fed them too, so that they need never want or thirst again; but withal gave them nothing but himself: when he was there, he was his own sacrament;—the most lifegiving element that ever came from heaven. This is the meaning which, according to the fourth Gospel, he himself has put upon his feeding the multitude; and in treating it as expressive of the essence of his religion and the mode of his influence, rather than as a bald wonder of the material kind, we do but obey his injunction to look not at the meat that perisheth, but at that which endureth unto everlasting life. The narrative is evidently emblematic, and finds its true and permanent significance in the idea which it embodies, and of which the occurrence it relates is but the vehicle. If you take the fact as historical, then it is the picture-writing of Providence, the allegory of God, by which he represents to us the ministrations of Christ to the eternal cravings of our secret nature. If otherwise, then it is the human product of the very same truth, the attempt to fix and sculpture in the substance of concrete incident the reality of his creative energy as the supporter and vivifyer of souls,—the flowing feeling, congealing itself, as consciousness grows cold, into the solidity of history; just as the mystic imagery of Jesus, as he breathed out his last words of affection, and brake the bread of parting and handed the wine of his remembrance, has been turned into physical dogma, and petrified into a eucharistic incarnation. In any case the fact exists only for the sake of the divine truth which holds it in a permanent abode.

The little basket, carried up among the hills, furnished beneath the hand of Christ an ample feast. And no less a marvel does God work with all the pure in heart who go up into the lonely place to meet him. Be they only not quite empty of truth and love; let them have but the poorest pilgrim's unleavened cake of sincerity and faith; and when they have spread their insufficiency before God, and broken it into its worthlessness for his blessing to enter, they shall return richer than they came and gather more than they had brought. The rules of quantity, the laws of weight and measure, do not hold beyond the outward world; they disappear wherever the Holy Spirit claims its own. The smallest spiritual store, taken into the most retired spot, has a self-multiplying power; and if only used with holy trust, will pass the dimensions of nature and betray the resources of the infinite. The great Creative Spirit is ever ready to touch the merest grain of manna in the heart, and make it numerous to shine on all the ground. He to whom space is the seed-plot of stars has in the human soul a tillage more lustrous in the sowing and more enduring in the fruits. When he flings a handful of moral endowments into the furrows of our nature, he never withholds the mellowing winds and dews; and the germs will not perish unless we deny them root. Within the smallest genuine grace he has wrapped up boundless possibilities; and whoever will but believe in it and apply it faithfully shall never fail of more. There is no one so miscreated or misplaced as to have within him no germs of good, from which a fruitful circle may be made to spread. Just as in the Pacific Ocean, if once a coral rock is built up to the level of the tide and feels the caresses of the wind, some little speck of life appears, and as the island rises, widens till it dips into the salt waves;

so in the most desolate mind, born furthest from the main-land of hope and power, there is never wanting some point of native green, that may creep, as it were, from stone to stone, till it fairly drive the barrenness away. If you will but find God's living gift within you, and simply trust it when it presses into growth, there is not a waste place of your nature that shall not become habitable, and even glorious with a wild beauty. Whatever you may doubt, *something* there is which you deem true ; however much is common and unclean, you have your gleams of what is surely holy ; wherever you are weak, there is some matter on which your secret eye is clear, and your foot is firm. *Here* then is the ground on which your moral life is to be raised. Whithersoever others may lead you, here is your native well-spring of faith and love ; whatsoever others may teach, this is the divine oracle to you. Sink deeply into this, and be at one with it, worship in it, live from it, ere you even try to know or undertake to do aught else. Till you get down to the foundations of your natural piety and touch sacred ground, you cannot raise the superstructure of either your knowledge or your action. Heed not what is dark, play not with what is perplexed, believe not your unbelief, till you have flung yourself into your real faith, and done the thing you most revere. He that will follow the will of God where it is clear shall find less than before that is obscure ; and no step on holy ground will ever bring you nearer to a soil barren and unblest. There is a wonderful power in simple pure veracity, that knows its own pretences and can tell its seeing from its dreams; that has an ear for the still voice of God, instead of drowning it in the hum of its own sophistries; and an eye to watch his lights and shades, instead of suffusing all things with its own colouring. From such guileless and open conscience he is never entirely hid; some dear and holy secret, minute it may be, but precious as a known star upon an unknown sea, he makes distinct and clear: and since his infinite nature, perfect as a sphere, surrounds us every way, it matters not from what bright point you begin to trace its glories: there are a thousand great circles of truth and goodness stretched across its immensity, any one of which will take you to fresh lights, yet bring you whence you came. If a man will but leave off deceiving himself, lay aside his intellectual and imaginative arts, and reduce himself to spiritual simplicity; he will find a path by light other than his own,—a light from which doubt and unreality flies away. Faithful to his first grace, he is enriched with a second: devoutly serving the authority of this, his gift is still enlarged: he becomes wiser and nobler and nearer to God, at every stage; till at last the very fragments and leavings of his faithfulness, the dropped words of his insight, the casual deeds of his affection, exceed the first entire amount. And he that begins with fasting himself leaves enough on the ground to fill the satchel of a dozen apostles.

The reduction however of the mind to spiritual simplicity, the return to a childlike transparency, is a change which, though it seems but the cessation of art, is often beyond the mere wishes and strivings of nature. Most men, when they have discovered their own unreality, and suspected their miserable delusions, continue in them all the same; and feel like one who undergoes shipwreck in a dream, and sees the firm land close by, yet can put forth neither hand nor foot to reach it. Strange that, of all possible tasks, simply *to be what we are* should prove, not the easiest, but infinitely the hardest! It is the saddest evidence, if not of a "fallen," yet of an abused and sin-beclouded nature, that to revert to our primitive faith, to come to ingenuous terms with our genuine love, and live out of the hearty kernel of our being, is at once the nearest and the rarest of attainments. Needing only quiet surrender and bringing only heavenly peace, it is evaded by incessant efforts and postponed for a corroding misery. But wherever this pure grace of simplicity exists, it has for men a secret and irresistible charm. They recognise in it the traces of God's immediate presence,—the conditions of his inspiration,—the light from him which they too have felt and lost. It is the holy prophet's grace, that keeps from before his eye every deforming veil, and leaves him face to face with divine things, and gives him communion with the Spirit of all truth. Quite different from philosophic reflection, which employs the mediation of reasoning and the instrument of analysis, and arrives at its conclusions by methods of which it can render logical account, that purity of heart which sees God discerns him by the immediate glance of sympathy. Standing in front of the great curtain of appearance, on which the shadows of his thought are thrown, it watches them as they traverse, and interprets them with the infallible apprehension of a congenial soul. *How* he reads off the meaning and expressiveness of things and meets in them the very heart of God, such a one is unable to explain: only, that meaning is plain and certain to him as sorrow in human tears and aspiration in the lifted eye. The divine Indwelling in the mind of man is ever, I believe, in some *unconscious* grace at first,—some reverence, some love, which *possesses* him; which is not the object of his thought, but the very colour of his thinking; which he did not form by the laws of his movement, but which constitutes his invisible axis of revolution. He does not know his own gift, but only the duty and the God to which it bears him. It makes him feel the falsehood of the world, without being aware of his own truth: it impels him to be alone, and to go up above the mists into the solitude of prayer: it places before him a universe of realities different from that which occupies ordinary men, and throws the great drama of existence, with all its intense interests, off from the transient stage of material semblance into the eternal theatre of invisible justice. He is detected by others to be a revelation ere he finds it himself; and when he retires among the hills for private communion, he draws all men unto him. They follow him by an impulse scarcely more conscious of its nature than his own; looking indeed with wonder on him, but unaware what it is in themselves that needs him and looks up to him for help and guidance. They know not the depth of their spiritual hunger: he knows not the riches of his divine supply; yet by the mystic attraction of mutual fitness they wend their way to the same spot, above the world and alone beneath the sky.

Once set however face to face, they cannot fail to find each other out, by the directing instinct of inward wealth and inward want. Meeting upon that height, with disturbing voices and deluding sights away, and only the simplicity of God between, they can hide the truth from one another and from themselves no more. Jesus had gone up from the populous valleys with no view to look on any eye but that of God, or breathe a word, except of prayer: he went, because there the hills shut out the lower world, and only space and silence reigned: he went, to avoid the false press of human admirations and satisfy the true aspiring of divine want; not to distribute, but himself to taste, the blessed bread of heavenly communion. But when the reverence of the people disappointed him, and they went out afoot from all the cities and preoccupied the mountain grass, he was moved with compassion, "because they were as sheep without a shepherd"; and he let his soul descend in its abundance on them, instead of laying it low in its need and sorrow before God. Wondering, it may be, what he has to give,—having retreated thither just because he had not enough for himself,—yet unable to withhold his supply, he tried how far his store would go, and threw among them the frugal morsels of heavenly truth he had collected from the infinite: "he began to teach them many things," and continued till the day itself was spent: commencing with the scant estimates of aspiration and humility, he found what would suffice for all. So it ever is with the influence of a holy mind. With the quickness of sympathy and pity, the prophet's soul so believes in others' eternal hunger as to take no scrupulous measure of his own supply. Were he asked, he would say, "it is not much, and hither I came that it might become more"; but called out to make the most of what he has, he finds a miracle of bounty; for not one among thousands goes empty away. In all the higher gifts of the spirit,—in the graces of a pure, devout, and loving nature, in a simple and holy faith that takes lonely walks with God,—there is this marvellous and blessed paradox:

they are the most absolutely inalienable, yet the most freely communicable of all treasures. Nothing is so strictly private, so characteristically personal, as the temper of a mind lifted above earthly delusions and filled with a divine and all-reconciling light. Its trust, its hope, its vision, live in it, it knows not how: it can tell them, but can show no path to them; can sing them out in hymns, but not demonstrate them in problems; knows them to be first-hand truth, cut off from second-hand approach. Yet so far is Religion from being, on this account, a purely individual thing, —a reserved account between each worshipper and God, that it cannot even live at all upon these terms: as well might you try to condense the lightning into a chamber-lamp to shine for you and your little tasks alone: it exists only by flashing from heaven to earth, from cloud to cloud, down on the sea, up from the western to the northern sky. Divine faith is the most diffusive and kindling of all things. Kept as a private store, it wastes away and perishes; it becomes so meagre that you can feed upon it no more: you yield to a worse temptation than befell your leader in the desert, and turn the bread of life into a stone. No one, I suppose, ever deeply believes, or even thoroughly disbelieves, alone and by himself. He cannot dispense with others' sympathy; he listens for what they say of these great things: he looks into their eyes: he wonders about their thoughts: he waits till they give a sign; and not till they hint his secret feeling, does he dare to think it right. If none ever confirmed the leaning of his affections, he would suspect it was only a distortion in himself; and would be ashamed to bow down and kneel, were there no bended head but his. No! faith is no individual property, to be shut up in the closet of personal silence; it is a thing of *Catholic consent;* the ultimate element in which our common human soul exists and which spans the interval between it and God; the spiritual atmosphere in which the vibrations flowing from the tones of truth and love are propagated from mind to mind, from region to region, from time into eternity. Faith is not less an intercommunion and mutual confession of souls with each other, than of all with the Father of spirits. The condition of its vivid existence is, the profound consciousness of common wants and common aspirings, and the presence of some clear and faithful heart inspired to express and interpret them. Where no such earnest want is felt, where it is suppressed by the ascendency of sense and the indulgence of ease, to the neglect of the higher demands of every noble nature, the possibilities of religion are crushed out. To minds in this state it seems as if there were nothing in it; and if Jesus had had with him only a company of well-fed and self-satisfied Pharisees, assuredly there would have been no miracle, but only a repudiated basket of scanty loaves and small fishes. Let any man only *be* satisfied, and God himself can find him no repast. But Christ relied on the natural hunger of honest hearts, and trusted to the yearning soul and multiplying grace to make what he had suffice. And lo! the answer to his prayer is the great continuous miracle of Christianity itself;—millions from every height of history testifying unto this day, that they in their time have been divinely fed!

XIV.

The Unknown Paths.

Is. xlii. 16.

"I will bring the blind by a way that they knew not: I will lead them in paths they have not known. I will make darkness light before them and crooked things straight."

THERE is undoubtedly a sense in which all faith is "*blind.*" Science steps only where she clearly sees; faith can dispense with seeing. Science boasts of her prevision; faith can advance into the dark. Science is proud of her power to lead the order of events; faith gives the hand and is thankful to be led. If the whole of life were distinct as a diagram before us and manageable as a machine; if we could command its issues and measure out its years; if, by our own skilled choice, we could determine our health, our genius, our family, our lot; if, further, each passing age of the world could lay out the next and foresee the future as it reads the past; we should have attained the Elysium of science and found the "Happy Islands" of civilized ambition.

But in the literature of such a spot would be no poetry, in its music no hymn, in its architecture no cloister, in its voices no prayer: amid the staring daylight, no altar lamp would be trimmed to keep the watch; and, in the hard elastic air, no ear would listen for the faint steps of any Divine visitant. The reality of God would be still there, as the stars hang over us no less at mid-day than by night; but our vision would not suspect him, his deep would be a dazzling blank; and for relief the eye would drop back and rest on the near fields where the plough is moving and on the striped sea, and the outline of the beach and hills. The scene of our own surveying, the work of our own tillage, would lie as an empire beneath us and detain us from any apprehension of a higher authority beyond.

It is ever the ambition of men to walk by sight: it is the method of God to lead them as the blind by a way that they know not. They naturally try to diminish the amount of *guess-work* in their life, and to make sure of the grounds of action in whatever they undertake. To take nothing on trust,—to fasten the thread of every enterprise on fixed laws of nature,—to venture into no field that is unexplored, to fill up no blank with images of thought, but turn away from the invisible because it is not visible:—constitute their maxims of highest prudence. Carry out this principle to its extreme consequences, let it become a universal rule of living; and it lands us in a mere secular materialism.

Why trouble ourselves, it suggests, with anything beyond this world? Who can tell us anything about it? Here we are, in a sphere of which we know something, abounding with remediable evils and unrealized possibilities of good; in the midst of men like ourselves, to whom we cannot fail to be a blessing or a curse. Let us hold to the work which we understand; make ourselves and our neighbours what is fitting and worthy *here*, and leave the hereafter to take care of itself. With model cottages, well-drained towns, universal instruction and cheap recreations, protected by just laws and free institutions, we shall make the most of the world we have; and do better than by sighing after one that we have not. Dealing with the alphabet, with the account-book, with the laws of health and the arts of skill, we know what we are about, and cannot fail to grow cleverer, richer, stronger, and to leave the earth more habitable than we found it. But when we propose to operate on a future, whose conditions are unseen, and to shape what is given us by that which is as yet withheld, what is this but to sacrifice the more real to the less, and to vest in our ignorance the casting vote against our knowledge? By appeal to considerations of this kind, men justify a total disregard of their diviner relations and encourage in themselves the purely secular taste which refuses to draw on faith for the sources either of wisdom or of charity.

Nor are they altogether wrong. Whoever wants to

N 2

find the *proper thing to do and how best to do it* must look about him and gather it from the visible scene in which his lot is cast; and if, instead, he fixes his eye beyond, and reckons his task backward from what he imagines there, he may think a penance more sacred than plain justice, and a sacrament higher than a charity. All the *matter* of our human work must no doubt be determined by the actual relations in which we stand today,—by our necessities, our opportunities, our powers. What a man can do best is the true task for him; what his neighbours and his age want most should prescribe the form of his self-sacrifice. Now is the time, and here is the world, committed to our trust; and any form of activity that looks another way in neglect of their pressing appeals, may well be suspected as an evasion or a romance. If, therefore, any one comes to us and, under pretext of sanctity, disparages the business of our working days; if, as *his* condition of anything divine, he wants from us something else than to drive the plough, to navigate the ship, to order the house, to teach the child, to help the weak;—if, in our labour to remove every canker from the life of men, he sees nothing to disprove our being aliens from God; then we may justly assert the claims of our common human world, and defy him to fetch anything diviner from the skies. No slight or scorn is to be endured towards the duties which God has made ready for our hand; nor is eternity to be railed off from time, as if *that* were the high altar and *this* the profane street.

But does it follow that, because our business is with the present, we go astray when we trust and meditate the future?—that, since we have to deal with the visible and finite, all affection is misplaced on the invisible and infinite?—that, unless we are surrendered, heart and soul, to the temporal claims of human life, we shall but wander from our true end? Not in the least. This is indeed the inference drawn by superficial men, who persuade themselves that dreams of religion are the great hindrance to the real amelioration of the world. But its utter falsehood is attested by the whole course of human and especially of Christian history; which rather proclaims, that, if you would improve this world, you must have the hearts of men set upon another; if you would give any grandeur to life, you must pale it beneath the splendour of an hereafter; if you would prevent the waste of industry, the contempt of moral economy, the indifference to the lesser humanities, you must train the soul to a worship that goes immeasurably beyond them. There is not a secular reform in the whole development of modern civilization which (if it is more than mechanical) has not drawn its inspiration from a religious principle. Infirmaries for the body have sprung out of pity to the soul; schools for the letter, that free way may be opened to the spirit; sanitary laws, that the diviner elements of human nature may not become incredible and hopeless from their foul environment. Who would ever lift a voice for the slave, that looked no further than his face? or build a reformatory for the culprit child, if he saw nothing but the slouching gait and thievish eye? Nay what impulse would even science itself have had, if sustained only by the material utilities? what inspiring zeal, but for that secret wonder which feels the universe to be sacred and is a virtual thirst for God?

I know it sounds like paradox to say that the more you magnify the present, the less you can make of it; and that, if you exalt man to be highest of all, you will reduce him to the meanest. Yet is it undeniably the thought of immortality that imparts dignity and depth to whatever in us is mortal: and were we not fitted for communion with God, there would be little to revolt us in the vacant mind, the unchastened habit, the servile lot. All the pathetic appeals and reverent usages of life, the patient love, the costly pity, lavished on sorrow and infirmity, all the graceful ceremonial of the affections at the birth, the marriage, and the funeral, assume that everywhere more *is* than *seems;* that whatever happens has holier meanings than we can tell; that the characters written on the screen are flung out by light behind. Take away the divine symbolism from our material existence, and let it stand only for what it can make good on its own account, and what is there to redeem it from selfishness and insignificance?

The home sinks into a house, the meal into a mess, the grave into a pit: honour and veracity are appreciated chiefly as instruments of trade; purity and temperance, as necessities of health; justice, as the condition of social equilibrium; mercy, as the price of a quiet time. Does this literal aspect really satisfy you? Does it give any adequate account of your natural feeling towards these several elements of life? If this were all, would they stir you with such passion of love, of awe, of admiration, as sometimes carries you off your feet? No; we are not made upon this pattern; and in our composition are colours mingled which are native to no earthly clay. In every good man there are affections, moral impulses, aspirations, far more intense and deep than would accord with any secular proportions; and he instantly becomes aware of this, if he falls into unsympathising society, where he is put upon his self-defence. As soon as he tries to justify an enthusiasm, however true, and casts about for visible and definite grounds on which to rest it, he is conscious of weakening it by the argument designed to give it strength; he feels that it has rights of its own beyond the reach of all his words; he is hurt that his advocacy, vainly struggling to speak for it, has but spoiled the charm with which it speaks for itself. Let any one endeavour, upon a mind of hard, clear surface, to infiltrate some moral conviction to which it has hitherto been impervious; and he will find how little he can open the living pores of conscience by showering down pleas of reason and interest that turn to dust ere they alight.

What then do we gather from such experience? That the purest inspirations of men have other grounds than our secular life presents, and would lose their justification, were there nothing else; that it is they, nevertheless, that have led, and must ever lead, every worthy enterprise by which the world is ennobled and adorned; that, therefore, did we cease to trust them, did we let the world rule them in place of their claiming to rule the world, the very springs of improvement would decay; the progress we admire would turn to retrogression; and the present life, for which we make the costly sacrifice,—the finite plot, reserved for such careful culture on condition of being screened from the infinite dews,—would become a waste of fallen foliage and rotting fruits.

In this respect, as in so many others, does God lead "the blind by a way that they know not." He realizes other ends than they contemplate; and the ends which they contemplate he achieves by other means than theirs. Ever since the gospel was first preached, of Christ the risen, his disciples have set their affections on things above, and held this world in relatively light esteem: yet the heaven they sought remains as it was, and the earth they despised is enriched and glorified. Were *we* to contrive a way of improving this life, we should set men to think of nothing else: yet God contradicts this ruinous device, and reaches the end by drawing men away from it, and pre-engaging them with a higher. It is the great principle and mystery of all his Providence: to reach the upper light, we must follow blind affections; and to realize the lower kind of good, we must forget it. The astronomer, in search of a missing star, looks away from the field in which it lies, and by side-light it steals into his eye; and thus the Christian, with vision directly fixed on one region, seizes the brilliants of another. While we are intent on divine things, God accomplishes the human. We are always planning how we may govern and mould the world according to our will: but he has made us susceptible of affections more powerful than our will,—passions beneath us that deliver us captive to Satan,—aspirations above us that lift us to Christ. These it is that surprise and disappoint our calculations, and snatch us off to ends other than our own. These it is that so often seem to deny the race to the swift and the battle to the strong. These it is by which God rules the world and leads us in a path we have not known. These are the trembling strings of our nature on which his Spirit has but to breathe and play, to change the rhythm of history and deepen the music of humanity.

While this remains the constitution of the moral world, it will defy our boastful predictions, slip through the fingers of rulers and diplomatists, and the Eternal Father will reserve the times and seasons in his own hand. It is of the very essence of these deep faiths and affections through which he appeals to us and lives in us, to produce the most astonishing and incalculable results. When Christianity began to spread through the cities of the empire, it was pronounced an "unsocial superstition," and was supposed to threaten the dissolution of all human bonds. The disciples withdrew from the resorts of gaiety and ambition, and looked with passionless and neutral eye on every game in which others lost or won their life, their all. The Master seemed to let go his rights, and abdicate his pride; for he would take of the bread broken by his bondsman's hand, and chant "Amen" to his impassioned prayer. The Slave emerged from all that was servile, and walked as a man set free by a divine captivity. The Woman, repelling the approach of the frivolous and vain, betrayed a deeper life; and by a certain queenly dignity recalled the matronly images of better days, though without the matron's patrician pedigree, and patrician scorn. No doubt, a new feeling had taken possession of the little flock scattered over that mighty world; a feeling which in one sense could not but have a *levelling* effect on the inequalities of men; viz. the consciousness of each one's personal responsibility to a Holy God, and immortal relation to the self-sacrifice of Christ. Nothing certainly can so sanctify the individual, and lift him into integral importance, as this sense of lonely, secret, eternal intercommunion opened between the soul of each and the Spirit of all. Yet what has been its working in human life? Has it separated each man from his fellow, and planted him in an insular region of his own? Has it rendered Society impossible, and pulverised the moral fabric into human atoms? On the contrary, the Christian individuality has created the intensest social cohesion; and of all the combinations of this world, the churches of Christendom have presented the examples of greatest tenacity and profoundest faithfulness. Nothing else has so conquered the egotisms and exorcised the selfishness of men, and kindled in them the living enthusiasm from which self-sacrifice must spring. No machinery of party, no sectional interests, no compact organization, has ever bound, or will ever bind, a fabric of human elements, like the power of Christian reverence and Christian love. Thinking of no union, planning no framework of incorporation, the true disciples find themselves in mutual relations of unspeakable sympathy, from the deep intentness of each separate eye on a heaven and a God overarching all. The profoundest union sprang direct from a spiritual individuality. These Christians contemplated no such thing as a Christendom: they only sought to take the next step truly on the way to their everlasting Zion: but, putting themselves into the hand of an unfailing Guide, they, like all that will trust him, were led in paths they had not known; and the blindness to them was turned into light for the world. His greatest things are ever born of their own opposites; the highest energy emerges from the lowest self-surrender; secular progress, from spiritual aims; social cohesion, from lonely dignity of soul.

It is the same in all memorable times. If the greatest crises of history are full of surprises, it is because the Providence of God betakes itself to other channels than the elaborative will of man. For the control of events and the governance of the world *we* resort to what in truth is our only leverage,—the dominant wish, the collective purpose, of our community. In stirring up and organizing this, we cast out from it, in order to arm it with its greatest power, all that is special to any section of the whole,—all that is too high for mediocre thought and level feeling; and obtain for our end a general support by reducing it to the measure of general apprehension and interest. A vast area of opinion is thus secured for the furtherance of our aims. And if these aims should also be ancient and familiar, conservative of what exists and is known rather than new and experimental, they win the guarantee of long time as well as large range, and would seem to present an irresistible front,—whether it be to march aggressively forward and seize the next station in advance, or to lie defensively intrenched upon the ground and sweep all the approaches of assault. Yet, with all our resources, there is that behind with which we cannot reckon. Human will, in order to have wide extent and long institution, must dispense with high elevation; you cannot keep the general host or the linked generations of mankind on the strain of any rare and noble vision; and the force they lend you is that of consolidated mass rather than of keen intensity. It never rises into the light which catches the loftier minds and kindles their enthusiasm; and on these it is that each new Divine illumination is shed,—some greater thought, some deeper faith, some fresh compassion, which carries its flash into waiting hearts and changes for them the whole aspect of life. The inspirations of a single soul, at first flung into the winds without an echo, find their way ere long by elective affinity into responsive natures, and, creating them anew, send them also forth with the fire of prophecy: so that the lonely "dreamer" comes to wield a power of conversion which the hugest "Propagation Society" may have reason to envy. It is in the free play of these surprises of insight and affection that the world is lifted to higher stages, and led in paths it had not known. Seek not to organize these revelations of individual minds. Fix them by consent and vote,—turn them into a school,—and their ethereal penetration is gone; they fold their wings and perish. Let them fly as the wind that bloweth where it listeth; and as they impinge on this and that, they will wake up consonant tones, wherever possible, and fill the measure of their harmonies. Let your own heart also lie for ever open to their claim: expect them not; refuse them not; only guard their inward springs with reverent heed,—the secret misgiving of customary wrong,—the dawning love of a more perfect right,—the incipient glimpse of purer truth; for such graces are harbingers of the Divine approach. Follow them simply, when they visit you, though they should draw you from the trodden paths and cherished plans of life. Turn not to the right or left to see whether others are on the track: for the call of God must be submitted to no second voice, but must suffice to take you on your course alone. And then, if some long-laboured purpose should pine away unrealized, it will only be that diviner issues may arise instead: if His way is hid from you even when your feet are on it, it is only that he may make the momentary darkness into more glorious light before you.

XV.

The Finite and the Infinite in Human Nature.

ROM. viii. 19.

"The earnest expectation of the creature waiteth for the manifestation of the sons of God."

AMONG the deep yet neglected hints which lie beneath the surface of Scripture, there is none more searching than the distinction here assumed between the "*creature*" and the "*son*" of God. The "*creature*" is simply the fabric of his skill, related to him as the texture to the hand that weaves it, indebted to him for its existence, carrying in itself his purpose, but only as a *thing*,—a tool,—an article,—in the outfit of his world. The "*son*" is the partaker of his essence, the repeater of his life, related to him as the child whom the parents cannot hinder from being like themselves; growing up therefore into his image, and betraying, even in exile and servitude, an irrepressible sympathy with his affections, and yearning towards him as the everlasting home. In man, both these characters are united. As a product of nature, born to take a place and pass away among the organisms of this earth, he is a creature no less than the cattle on a thousand hills, and God is his *Maker*. As a vehicle of something above nature, as lifted into the freedom of *personal* existence, as sharing in the life of the Eternal Spirit, he is a son of divine lineage, and God is his *Father*. Observe how the apostle Paul regards these opposite features in our nature, and connects them with the person and the life of Christ. Each of the two characters has its trace within us and makes itself felt by desires and sufferings of its own: the consciousness of the natural, ever sinking on the finite, and the consciousness of the spiritual, ever rising towards the infinite, coexist and wrestle in our nature. In that pathetic strife, the weight of self and sense would have borne us down, would even have erased the conception of anything beyond, had not the very spirit of our Sonship taken human form in Christ, and claimed us by the appeal of his divine life, his sacrifice of death, his conquest of the grave. Startled by that perfect vision, the sleeping ideals wake again within our hearts: caught up into the current of his filial surrender, we recover our affinity and cry, "Abba, Father!" and as soon as we have courage to live as sons, to trust the faint longings that bear us homewards, and float away whithersoever they lead us, we find a sudden witness of hope and spring of power. Not that we escape our lower thraldom at once: the outward oppression of nature weighs upon us yet,—the panting breast, the bleeding feet, the dimness on the way, the shadow on the mind. But there was darker eclipse than this on Calvary; and *that* we have seen clear off into an immortal glory; and with the conscious foregleams of the Spirit within us, we can wait, through the time of earnest expectation, for the manifestation, still in reserve, of our sonship to God. Not risen as yet from the outward cross and burden of humanity, we nevertheless bear his mark upon our brow; and carrying the holy secret with us as we toil along, we find whatever is grievous sweetened and what is humbling glorified.

In thus associating us with the divineness of Christ, and expanding the term "Son of God" from a Personal to a Human designation, does the apostle speak to us in an unknown tongue? or does he wake some faint response, some half-heard solemn tones, as from immeasurably distant corridors? Are there any real vestiges in our humanity of something transcending the fabricated creature,—of some living relationship with the Parent-spirit,—some real communion with his holy nature, some melting of our finite life into sympathy with his infinite? Surely the depth and significance of life must be half missed by those who do not find such vestiges in all the higher endowments and experiences of our being.

Look, for instance, at the *Intellectual instinct;* and consider whether, in its direction and its range, it is just what you would expect in a "creature" planted only amid earthly and secular relations and computed to be worked out in threescore years and ten? What is it that men most love and long to know? If you see them in multitudes hushed in eager attention, unconscious of the ground beneath their feet, and lost in an ideal world, what interest, do you suppose, thus holds them in mid air? Is it some truth that lies nearest to them in time and place, and is most in contact with their lot?—the arithmetic which will help them to buy and sell? the sanitary rules, which will keep them clean and wholesome?—the economic laws, which distribute the produce of their toil? On the contrary, these things, with everything that is pursued as the outfit of an art or livelihood, are looked on as a sort of drudgery and learned in obedience to a necessity; and to find these very topics pursued with any enthusiasm, you must usually go to a circle of enquirers where their interest is not personal and practical. The true secret thirst of the mind is never reached by offering selected draughts of "useful knowledge": the dietary of Prudence may adopt and recommend them: but Wonder finds them dry as ashes to its lips. What is learned with an express view to its gainful result is spoiled, by this dominating purpose, of its generous flavour, and is scarcely a mental enrichment at all.

It may be skill: it may be capital: it may be power: but, in the noblest sense, it is not knowledge. Scorning the narrow measure of individual wants, human curiosity flies out,—and with wing more eager as the air grows strange,—into fields remotest from the homesteads of personal and social life. To go forth and see where the stars are and how they lie; to get round them and dive into the fountain of their light; to frustrate their eternal silence and make them tell their paths; to pass from station to station and gain assurance that there is no end to their geometry; and then to drop back on the grass-plot of this world, mentally sublimed by the sense of physical insignificance; has ever had a solemn charm for human intelligence. Nor are we less subject to the spell of incalculable Time than of immeasurable Space. What is it that rewards the geologist for his laborious penetration into the earth's crust, his dim gropings among archaic forms, and all the patient steps of his induction? Mainly this: that he elongates the pendulum of his time-piece till it slackens to the rate of races and the organic pulsations of a world; that in the field or brow beneath his feet he reads the depositions of a million years and the denudations of a million more; and, setting aside the seas and continents and even atmosphere of today, can ride upon the glaciers or peer through the tropic steams or face the grotesque monsters of the planet destined to be ours. How is it that the intensest interest hangs around these far-off sciences?—that we cite them as among the greatest triumphs of human research?—what concern so deep can *we* have with lines of thought that scarcely keep within the limits of the finite? why do they strike in upon us and stir us in the very seats of intellectual romance? Tell me not of their indirect utility, though it is indisputable: does a Herschel live for the sake of the Nautical Almanack, or a Murchison and Lyell for the sake of Californian mines? It is because we love to be spoken to in tones from the borders of the infinite, and feel them to have a native sound. Carrying in ourselves secret relationships with universal space and unbeginning time through Him that fills them both and lives in us, we know the tidings which come furthest from them to be nearest to us: they remind us of our augustest kindred: they free us from our momentary prison: they show us the white sail, they breathe on us with the very wind, that shall take us out of exile. Their awful fascination bespeaks a nature mysteriously blending in its affections the finite and the infinite, and standing on the confines of both.

The same mixed character is still more evident in the constitution of the human *Conscience.* Here too we are well furnished, but at the same time strangely *over*-furnished, for our immediate work. Moment by moment, the way of right is never left in the dark: temptations and duties, taken one by one, are always inwardly known for what they are: definite guidance is ready for us, which, in each case, it is quite practicable to follow. Yet, though *each* fidelity is possible in detail, it would seem impossible to be true to all: to the most constant and devoted mind their call will sometimes come in moments of deadened affection or of weakened will, when their accents cannot pierce the deafness of spiritual sleep; and as soon as the waking hour returns, the eye opens on a lapsed opportunity, and droops in shame. Who but the dull and blind is free from this sad burden? What face is always uplifted to the light of life, and never darkened by the shadow of death? Is there one of us to whom the pure law of Christ, so lovely to see, so deep and musical to hear, lies realized in the past? or, does it yet look down on us from the future, through sad and heavenly eyes, as a distant "Counsel of perfection," and still call us, after all these years, "Come unto me, ye heavy laden, and I will give you rest"? Were the human Conscience, like human Prudence, the mere product of experience; were it the reflection of the world's opinion; were it given only for our temporal guidance without significance beyond; why should we not get rid of our sins as we do of our mistakes,—commit them and have done with them,—and let the Dead Past bury its dead,—and leave no ghost behind? This is actually the approved wisdom of hard and driving men whose ethics are but instruments of external work. But where there is a deeper insight, where the outer *doing* is looked on as the symbol of the inner *being*, where affection, character, will, have any life and drama of their own, this discharge of old compunctions, this cheerful erasure of bankrupt accounts, is quite impossible. Only when evil is regarded as a transitory mishap, can it be thus forgot: once let the consciousness awake that it is disloyalty to the Spirit of eternal Holiness, and there is in this a conservative power which will forbid its awful shadow to depart. And hence, strange as it may seem, it is not the guilty that know the most of guilt: it is the pure, the lofty, the faithful, that are for ever haunted by the sense of sin, and are compelled by it to throw themselves upon a love they never doubt yet cannot claim. To thoughtless observers of human nature this always seems the paradox of piety;—that none burst into such passionate confessions as those who apparently have nothing to confess; that the more faithful they become, the less assuredly have they peace with themselves; that the further they retreat from the power of evil, the more does its sorrow sit upon their brow. Why do you hear from a Fénélon words of humiliation that never escape a Richelieu? why are the prayers of prophets and the hymns of saintly souls so pathetic in their penitence, so full of the plaintive music of baffled aspiration, like the cry of some bird with broken wing? It is because to them the truly infinite nature of holiness has revealed itself, and reveals itself the more, the higher they rise; because in its secret breathings to their hearts they recognise, not any romance of their own, but the communing Spirit of the Living God; because they can no more measure evil, than you can measure hurt affection, by any scale of external magnitude, but, like all violated love and honour, by the inner intensity of its unworthiness and the sanctity of the personal claims which it insults. And the more they surrender themselves to the inspiration which calls them upward and become identified with the infinite sympathies, the wider grows their spiritual horizon, and the deeper their yearning for the everlasting hills that lie folded afar in visionary light. That the blindness of conscience shuts us up in finite comfort, while its kindled sight throws us open to infinite unrest and precipitates us on a mingled world of penitential shadows and brilliant aspirations,—would be an unintelligible contradiction, were it not that our life and nature are more than sentient, more than rational, more than ethical;—and that then first do we find in what a universe we stand, when we gain its spiritual key, and pass the veil that hides us from the Living God.

But if this be the meaning of our sense of sin, what hope, you will say, that it can ever leave us? If holiness be infinite, and we are not, is it not an awful thing to have the susceptibilities, without the powers, of infinitude? And was it not the work of Christ to give us rest from the strife and sorrows of compunction? Yes: not however a rest *within ourselves*, as if we either ceased from sin, or could see it with other and less saddened eyes; but a rest *out of ourselves*, a pure and perfect *trust* in Him whose spirit draws us from before and whose pity supports us from behind. It is an unfaithful attempt, to escape from the burdens of self-reproach otherwise than by completer surrender. Shake them not off: ask not to have them taken away: crave for no peace which they deny: go with them all, go as you are, to Him of whose light they are the shadow; and say to him, "I am a sinful man, O Lord: in my short-comings, whilst I live, I can never acquiesce; but, whilst thou livest, I can never despair." This is the condition of an immortal nature within mortal bounds, of the "son" blended with the "creature" of God. In a nature like ours the vital beams of the divine essence must ever shoot and struggle in their gulf of darkness, and make no white effulgence, but break into the colours of a stormy glory. Do the awful splendours terrify rather than inspire you?—fill you with personal fear lest the whip of lightnings start forth from the cloud and fling its lash upon your guilt? Do you want ease and self-content on any terms? You can sink back into the "creature," and stifle the sighs of the "son" of God within you. But if you will claim your divine heritage, if you will take the type of being which it gives you, you must be satisfied, now and for ever, with something else than self-repose: you must be content with mourning at home and rest abroad: you must so love God as to be willing to resemble him in all except his joy; and then his answering affection will be more to you than all you have renounced, and give you an unselfish "peace that passeth understanding."

On every side then, the relation of our life to the supernatural which penetrates and enfolds it, betrays itself in our consciousness. The intellect, which seeks to transcend the finite in space and time and truth; the conscience, which owns the infinite in duty and stays itself on the infinite in love; indicate the scale of our affinities, and attest a nature that liveth not by bread alone but by every Word of communion with God. Moulded of perishable and imperishable elements, we sink and rise, we sleep and wake, we faint and struggle on; toiling outwardly for transitory wants, pining inwardly with everlasting thirst. Be it not in blind unconsciousness that we carry in us the seal of the Eternal. Shall God's Spirit plead with us every day, and never reduce us to a sweet and holy mind? Because our feet are in the dust, shall our heart never go up into the mountain to pray, and our thought never pace the heights of meditation? Shall the years sweep by and take from us all that is mortal, without waking the immortal life within us from the winter in which it sleeps? Shall we wait to die into the surprise of God, instead of taking his dear and solemn converse now and for ever? Shall we dream of a future eternity, and be blind to that which surrounds us every instant,—which brings its judgments to our conscience, its present God to our trust, its mighty company of saints to our affection? Ah! let the film of the carnal mind fall from our eyes; and yielding ourselves to be led by the Spirit of God, let us claim our divine Sonship and enter on its glorious liberty. There will be no sadness then in the flow of life and change: time will take nothing but our delusions away; will enfold us in a warmer light of divine affection; and clear the everlasting air, till we see even as we are seen.

XVI.

Time to Nature, God, and the Soul.

Ps. lxxxix. 47.

"Remember how short my time is: wherefore hast thou made all men in vain?"

WHETHER or not a man is made in vain depends however very little on his allowance of time. "Long life" may be needful to "satisfy *him*,"—to prevent disappointment of a natural instinct and give a certain completeness to his existence on the personal side; but is far from necessary to God's purposes in creating him, or to the intensest and fullest action of his being on the sphere into which he is born. The divinest life that ever took the form of humanity,—the life above all others least "in vain,"—hung upon the cross ere half our proverbial term was spent; and with a few months of love and sorrow profusely sowed the whole seed-field of human history. The cravings of ease and comfort may dictate the prayer for protracted freedom from disturbance: the passionate cry of desolate affection may protest against the abrupt quenching of its familiar lights, brilliant and unexhausted still: but, by the measures of the Spirit, moments may often suffice for years; and many a soul, though not outwardly stricken, yet inwardly weighed down by the cross of too great a life, is so far from desiring "length of days," as to have no lingerings but for others' sake, and to stand ever eager for the vioce, "Lift up your head, for your redemption draweth nigh"!

Nothing indeed is more wonderful to think of than the different values of Time to different orders of existence. To mere physical natures it is nothing, except the element that contains their successions;—the element that is always there, and always uniform; the empty receptacle of their changes; producing nothing, destroying nothing; the mere open door of all possibilities. The heavens and the earth are insensible to their own vicissitudes, and have neither pride nor fear at their longevity. They measure time for others, but know nothing of it themselves: they move in order to render its march perceptible, but are blind and deaf to the rhythm which they beat. To the rising sun it is nought what day in the world's calendar it glorifies: the transit of the stars is calm alike, whether they look down on the young Paradise or on the trodden latitudes of guilt and sorrow: the clock in the sick chamber does not stop to listen to the parting breath, but ticks on, whether to count the pulses of life, or to sharpen the silence of death. The particular objects in creation have indeed their period: they pass through various stages of a career, all lying between a beginning and an end; and if you come upon them to-morrow, they are not the same that you would find them to-day. The difference however is for you and not for them; and is lost when you restore them to their place in the great organism of nature. The universe as a whole is always sure to be; and to its life, which has all space to roam in, it matters not whether the pulsation be due here or there. To the physical elements, history is nothing: the young oak, if its roots be only fed, is indifferent, whether its sap is from the juices of the new earth, or drawn from the falling foliage of ten thousand years; and the full moon would as soon look down on a Gethsemane as on an Eden. In the fields of creation every hour is equally full, with neither more nor less than what is due: indeed it is this very evenness that makes and counts the hours and gives them equal length; and we set off its constancy against our contingent and passionate existence, because assured that we can rely on its relentless neutrality. Nature, in short, as a phenomenon *in time*, serves only to *mark* it for higher beings; and neither makes it nor minds it. Duration, already on the field, does but use the cycles of Nature as its ministers and interpreters.

If Nature is below any perception of time, God, at the other extremity of being, is above it. He is the great "*I Am*": his verbs have no tenses: his experience is never past; his knowledge never future: with him nothing fades away and sets: nothing dawns and brings surprise. Whatever enters into his being is not phenomenal, but real; not transient and finite, but permanent and infinite. Truth, the expression of what unchangeably *is;* beauty, the conception of a fixed ideal; holiness, the love of voluntary perfection; these, which meet in his personality, are not historical and incidental, but unsuccessive and spiritual, the ground-thought of the universe itself, the law and life that underlie the course and determine the drift of its development. He is the essence of all the eternities: before his eye the accidents of being fall away, and the inner significance alone is present to his view. Only that which is *always* true and fair and holy belongs to him; not learned by him afterwards from the form of its manifestation, but known beforehand in itself; not read off from the face of the world by his perceiving eye, but created into the transitory universe by his everlasting thought. His intellect is not like ours, that climbs upward from fact to law, from law to cause, from cause to the abiding ground of all; but, inversely, meditates downwards from its own infinite essence into specific and multiform expression; and out of its still ocean volatilizes the clouds, and keeps alive the running waters, of all earthly good. For him, who embraces the ages, they can bring nothing, and take nothing away.

God, then, includes time without being affected by it, and time includes Nature which is unaware of it. *He* too completely transcends it, *his works* are too profoundly subject to it, to be otherwise than indifferent to its lapse. But *we* stand at an intermediate point and bear affinity with both extremes. We are akin to nature, inasmuch as we are born and grow and die: we are akin to God, as we bear the stamp of living thought, and wield the power of creative will. As natural products, we pass through time and suffer all its seasonal changes: as supernatural souls, time passes through us, and becomes tributary to a life beyond change. It is in a mixed being like ours,—in the meeting of the physical and the spiritual, the touch of the divine upon the human,—that duration ceases to stand and begins to flow; that the hours count themselves off aloud, and mingle with grief and joy, and ring out by turns the chime and the dirge. We cannot pretend to be mere organisms, to which each period comes alike; ready to bloom in the spring or wither in the wintry wind; or to be passive and unconscious, like the sea, whether glancing in the moonlight, or sweeping wildly under the darkened sky. We cannot pretend to be "as gods," lifted above the reach of change, exempt from sleep and waking, and lost in constancy of light and love. Life has its perspective for us; bright forms and slanting gleams and soft shadows in the past; a haze not without its glory in the future; both, looked at with a sigh from thorny ways and wasting heats in the present. In relation to lower existence, our human consciousness of time is a prerogative: in comparison with God's life, it is an infirmity, or at least a limitation. And according as we use or abuse it, we may verge towards either extreme, sinking ourselves into nature or merging into God. Do we use change, or does change use us? Do we drift into the currents of necessity, or keep the open sea, where, with the good winds of heaven, a course may yet be steered? Do we surrender the eternal in us to the temporal, and yield the soul to the seasonal pressures of life? Then do we go over to the side of mere nature, and claim our slave-lineage with pride. Or do we convert the temporal in us into the eternal, and appropriate all change and loss to feed imperishable love and glorify divinest truth? Then do we draw nearer unto God and humbly own our heavenly filiation.

It is with good reason that we are accustomed to put a high estimate upon *experience;* to give heed to men who have it; and expect from them counsels rich in wisdom. But experience, in any high and comprehensive sense, is the rarest, as it is the choicest of human qualities. More must go to make it than we are apt to suppose; not habit and opportunity alone, which can only give a narrow dexterity of hand or mind; but some breadth of faculty to seize relations, and depth of conscience to read life truly, and quickness of affection to sympathise with it largely; and a cultivated reverence of mind to know its own ignorance and find the way to others' wisdom. The materials and occasions of experience may often abound; and yet may remain without moral result, for want of the living mind and moulding love to elaborate and shape them. Some men there are whom no lapse of time seems to soften or expand; from whom whole floods of experience will flow off and leave them dry; who pass through events, and remember them, and like to call back their outward image again, but are just the same as if the events had been different; who reproduce in age the very sentiments and prejudices they had looked up in youth, and gather nothing from the past but a mood ungenial to the present. They repeat the story of their early days, not as a poem, but as an almanac; can give you the dates but not the meaning of the changes they have seen; and of the men they have admired can tell as much as the register and the coffin-plate. To such natures, case-hardened against the elements, time and the seasons come in vain: winter and summer, not a crevice opens in the rock where a green thing can push its root. Wanting susceptibility to appropriate what is given and work it up into the organism of the personal existence, they can only by an abuse of terms be said to have "experience" at all: they want its diviner conditions, though supplied with its natural vicissitudes; and were life to come over again, they would do and be essentially the same. Nor is this hardness of mind, this resistance to the solicitations of time, at all peculiar to the rough and working world. In the intellectual as in the practical sphere of human affairs the same fact may be observed. To some minds knowledge itself seems to come, not as a nutriment, but as an incrustation: they take it up and keep it, yet are scarce wiser than before: they let themselves serve as mere organs for its elaboration; and when the honeycomb is ready, the insects come out as they had gone in. It is amazing to find how few there are whom knowledge enters as *living truth*, and moulds to higher beauty; how often it proves but a Satan's promise to those who taste the fruit, "Ye shall be as gods." The littleness that may stand in face of the widest field of thought, the insensibility that hears no Saviour's voice when tender griefs stand at the door and knock, the self-will that can hold its stiff footing and deny its prayer when God is waiting for the surrendered heart; too clearly show how many, of all that are born, yet remain to be born again. It would almost seem that, for different souls, there are different periods for opening, and different rates of ripening; and that while some welcome the first breath of spring, and strike their eager fibres into the mellow soil, others never in this world burst the capsule of their self-enclosed humanity; or at least make only such tardy and reluctant growth as to stint the glory of God's natural year, and reserve for another clime its grace, its foliage, and its fruit. Not always however are we doomed to fear that the heavenly birth is thus delayed. There are some to whom the tearful atmosphere of this world early brings the dew and sprinkling of regeneration; and to whom, thenceforth, no event is simply physical, no experience chiefly external; but an inner fire takes up and kindles whatever is offered, and is sure to be nurtured by it into a purer and diviner flame. To such souls every element of life is sacred, and every momentary change is rich; and the transient brush of sunshine that but touches the grass and flits away, will show them more than the longest and the most staring summer-day can give to the shrewd open eye. Whatever happens to them or passes before them becomes a part of them: their tablet of the past is not the memorandum-book of business and affairs, but the illuminated calendar of the affections, where the names are holy and the days are bright. The legends they have to tell are not superficial anecdotes that fools can understand as well as wise; but snatches from the great drama of reality, strophes flung out from its chords of joy or grief, moving and significant to those only who know it as a whole. Where there is in the soul this living mood of watchfulness and response, it needs no large knowledge to give the finest wisdom, no length of days to enrich the heart with the deepest experience. Let the mind be only pure and tender with the love of God, large with his presence, and free in the quietude of faith, and its faculties move upon the slightest hint, and find more in an ordinary year than sharp-sightedness and sound-headedness alone could discern from beneath their knitted brows in half a century. I know not indeed which is the more marvellous;—the frequent ripeness of the young, where their nature is well directed, in moral and spiritual wisdom; or the apparent failure, equally frequent, of the longest life to awaken the most elementary sentiments of religion. In either case we learn how little mere Time has to do with things divine; how, when we keep near to God, the smallest allowance may suffice; and, when we quit him for the mere natural life, the largest is of no avail.

Indeed, that Time is no measure of value in the deeper concerns of our humanity, is apparent from a comparison, not only of different persons, but even of different parts of our own individual experience. No hour-glass, no diary, can estimate for you the "fulness of time": it is the soul that fills it: if the soul lie asleep, it is not filled at all; if she be awake, in the vigils of suspense, of sorrow, of aspiration, there may be more in an hour than you can find in a dozen empty lives. As it is with *place*, so is it with *time*. Often it happens that some one spot, uncoveted by others, visited by no pilgrim feet, may be more to you than all the world besides: it may be but a bit of meadow-land with a path beneath the elms; or an old house that looks upon a street; or a bench in a plain village church. But if it be *there* that your childish steps ran free; if through those windows you looked ere the tint of wonder had yet flown; if at that shrine you knelt in your first deep sorrow; if shadowy forms surround you there with benign and holy looks, and tones are in the air that you alone can hear; the place will have for you a sacredness quite unique and immeasurable; a magnitude of interest that no lines of longitude can define. In like manner may a weight truly unlimited be condensed into a speck of time. In Gethsemane itself it needed but three cries of briefest prayer, and the most pathetic crisis had passed from the sublimest of histories. Less pregnant, and yet of immeasurable contents, was the point of suspense for the Christian confessor, while the Roman tribunal paused on the verdict—"To the release," or,—"To the lions"! And in the private house where, as you gaze up to the chamber aloft, the unaccustomed lamp, the soft-flitting shadows on the blind, and an indescribable look of hushed intensity betray the vigils over some life quivering on the verge, what, think you, would you learn from the pale watcher of those fading eyes, if you asked her how much she lived in the hour ere they closed? The patriot, snatching from his courier the news of the decisive battle lost or won; the widow, when her son's ship has foundered, asking at the broker's office for the list of the shipwrecked and the saved;—these can tell you,—or rather cannot tell,—what may be comprised in the twinkling of an eye. Nor, for this experience, is there need of any startling external vicissitudes; it belongs no less to the purely internal story of the mind. As Newton, in testing his theory, approached the end of his calculations, and foresaw that it would be verified, the rush of thought became too great for even his tranquillity, and with trembling hand he delivered to another the task he could not complete himself. Such a burst of sudden discovery,—the solution of a life-long problem,—comes charged with a meaning in excess of human strength. Nay, even the simple student, who discovers nothing, but only finds the wise whom he may follow, can never forget the hour when first he felt the power of the higher mind that wakened up his nature and revealed him to himself; if by the living voice, the memory of its tones will make all others seem empty; if by the silent page, it will look up with a deep and tender light which brighter genius will never eclipse. Still more marked are the nodal points of the spiritual history; when from our penitential prayers the shell of custom breaks away, and floods the heart with all their meaning; or when, after long darkness on a trackless sea of doubt, the cloud passes from the pole-star of our life, and gives us our true way; or when we are caught up into self-forgetfulness and enter on the freedom of a surrendered will. The magnitude of these moments, their real proportion to the whole story of our days, no dial-plate can show. The pendulum may beat but once, ere all be over; yet that instant may carry in it the burden of years. For the higher regions of our nature, the true measures of time are found, not, as with physical changes, in any ratio of traversed arcs, but in the relation of events to our affections; and in a focus, which is only a point, may burn a light of the spirit greater than you can find diluted through indefinite wastes of dull and hazy life.

Magnitude of life then stands not in mere length of days. *That* is but one of its dimensions; and only "in our haste" can we protest, when it is abridged, that God has "created us in vain." It is not larger time that we want, so much as the more capacious soul to flow through every pore of the little which we have. So long as we shrink within the fence of selfish ease, and see nothing, feel nothing, think nothing, beyond the drowsy range of personal routine, our lot will be so empty, that no amount of it can ever seem enough; and our complaint of its brevity would not be cured by the gift of centuries. While the spirit sleeps, the longest time-piece will be running down, and can count nothing but its own lessening distance from stoppage and death. But to the insight and affections of a mind awake there is no end to the plenitude of things; it overcharges the hours that try to give its reckoning. Shall we forget in what a world we have our place? Ere our pulse beats thrice, the neighbouring air vibrates with the cry of every passion, the tones of every sorrow, of humanity; and sun and moon look down on the incidents of unnumbered moving dramas; and he who dwells in this air with susceptible ear and looks on this stage with open eye may well lose all heed for his own life, while it is multiplied and melted by sympathy in a thousand others. A single instant of the Divine Life, spread over all that is simultaneous, is worth an eternity of ours, which at least begins by taking all things one by one. And in proportion as we emerge from this childhood of the mind, and claim our approach towards union with God, will the contents of our experience enrich themselves, and its area correct its evanescence; till a mere moment may become worth a millennium before; and the Transient may be to the large soul more than the Everlasting to the little: and then whether our Time be long or short by Sun and Moon may well remain indifferent, since the life that is beyond time and nature is vivid within us.

XVII.

Forgiveness to Love.

Luke vii. 47.

"I say unto thee, Her sins, which are many, are forgiven; for she loved much: but to whom little is forgiven, the same loveth little."

In order to appreciate aright the sentiment here meant to be conveyed, we must, I suppose, slightly correct the form of words, and restore to the two clauses their due balance and contrast: 'Her sins are forgiven, for her love is great; but he to whom little is forgiven,—it is because he loveth little.' That is to say, there is a perfect parity of movement between God's receiving affection and our trustful advance; profuse attachment on our part being met by free reconciliation on his; whilst the cautious and frugal heart scarcely reduces its estrangement in the least. In this great lesson lies the whole point of the incident: to lead on to this are the figures,—at the head of the feast and at the feet of Christ,—presented in such elaborate opposition;—the cold politeness of the Pharisee, content to be civil to the Son of God; and the passionate reverence of the woman, who forgets the restraints of usage in her gratitude and tears. The evident intention of Jesus is, to plead her intense devotedness as a sufficient ground for Divine forgiveness; and not, as the historian inversely supposes, to *account for* her attachment by a *prior* act of pardon: for it is not till the last moment of the scene that he winds up with the announcement "Thy sins are forgiven"; and silences all murmurs by again referring to her fervour of trust as the reason of her release; "*Thy faith* hath saved thee; go in peace." No doubt, the same tender and susceptible soul that wins forgiveness by depth of love will also repay it with devoted gratitude: the imploring faith at first, and the resulting joy at last, will be of the same rich tone; and, in his words to Simon, Jesus may have touched on both relations, and spoken of forgiveness as at once the answer to a love spontaneous and the awakener of a love responsive; and with this he may have contrasted the hopeless case of the insensible and formal mind, which for want of love goes without forgiveness, and, unmellowed by forgiveness, flows down in no love. And this double turn to the thought may explain the evangelist's wavering and confusion between the two directions. But whoever will set himself at a little distance from the incident and look at its character as a whole, cannot fail to seize its essential spirit in this truth; that in heaven there is mercy for the reverent and loving, and a strict account for the critical and cold.

Perhaps the historian would have kept this lesson more clearly in his eye, had he not apparently taken too dark a view of the woman's character, and been misled by Christ's words about her "*many sins*" into the inference that she was living a life of outward shame. The appearance of such a person, with attitudes of such vehement enthusiasm, in the dining-room of the fastidious Simon, would present a manifest improbability. And we are relieved of the difficulty by the other three evangelists,* who relate an incident so similar to this that it can be nothing else; an incident in which the entertainer is still Simon, and a woman in devoted discipleship expends her precious spikenard on the Lord, and the guests find fault with his permission of the act. If these are features which could hardly occur twice, we must suppose the same fact to be the common base of all the narratives, and must use them to correct and supplement each other. We thus learn from the other gospels that the scene was in Bethany, and from the fourth evangelist that the woman was no other than Mary the sister of Lazarus. If so, it is no wonder that her act is regarded by the narrators as the simple expression of reverential homage, apart from all *penitential* meaning; and that no reference is made to any *sins* in her that asked

* Matt. xxvi. 6–13. Mark xiv. 3–9. John xii. 1–8.

forgiveness. By taking our stand at a mid-point between the two accounts, we may perhaps discern the truth of both. To the outward eye of the spectators at Bethany there would appear no ground for *contrition* in that gentle Mary who had long sought, and well knew where to find, "the one thing needful"; and they would see nothing in her demeanour but the outpouring of an unsparing veneration. Yet in the *inner* relations of that susceptible soul might there not have been many burdens of self-reproach,—many grievous failures and transgressions which she had longed to confess, and now at length had laid at his feet? Those good sisters, as we know, were not always quite genial together; and the brisk hand and the tender heart, being human both, might well make sins for themselves and sorrows for each other, that needed the eye of Christ to clear them away. But as this would be all among themselves,—private as the confessional,—any words of re-assurance that might escape the lips of Christ would fall upon the hearers without their key; and an expression of forgiveness, repeated to those who knew nothing of the persons or the scene, might be misconstrued to imply that she to whom it was addressed must have been "a sinner" in human sight as well as in Divine. Let us, however, who know that it was Mary of Bethany, not so misunderstand those bitter tears, and the gracious words that dried them at their fountain-head. We cannot penetrate the spiritual confidences which so humbled and moved her at the feet of Christ. But this we know assuredly; that the same eager susceptibility which was so quick to choose "the good part" and follow whither the heavenly thirst might lead, would also cause her to feel as if "her sins were many": for the ideal wing is often broken against the barrier of the real: the holiest light in the upper region of the soul flings the deepest shadow on the ground; and the depth of contrition is proportioned to the height of aspiration. Nor let us dare to call this an illusion: for it is the most certain of all moral laws, that every sin brings a film upon the inner vision and sets the soul more nearly in the dark; that in the heart where evil is faintest, there is it best known; and that none can take the full measure of its shadow but He that sees it from the Light of lights. And what, accordingly, is the consolation which the Saviour offers to her contrition? Does he treat it as a mistake? does he say, she need not distress herself, for in reality there is but little amiss, and Lazarus and Martha declare she is the best creature in the world? On the contrary, he respects her self-abasement; he adopts and repeats her remorseful estimate; he owns the sins to be many, only not too many for the reconciling love of God.

Here then we have the distinctest contrast between two types of mind and character, with a direct verdict from the lips of Christ on their relative nearness to the heart of God. There is the apparently correct and unobjectionable Simon, honest enough to risk the imputation of discipleship by opening his house to the Galileans, and worthy to be on intimate terms with the good family of Bethany. Evidently sensitive about the proprieties, and vexed that he cannot avoid "a scene," he has no insight below the surface,—no sympathy with the hidden source of those silent tears. Cold and even in himself, he has an aversion to the language of intense affection, and likes to see the gloss of decorous moderation spread over all things. His ethical self-management guards the balance of his habits and keeps him negatively right; and, having no real appreciation of sin or sigh for inner consecration, he probably finds the "pleasures of a good conscience" just upon his level. Though self-righteousness can never be without a touch of pride, we know nothing against his morals, his charity, or his outward religion. One single feature,—and *that* a *want* and not an *enormity*,—arrested and fixed the eye of Christ: his *love was little.* On the other hand, there is the devoted and affectionate Mary, known to us only by her contrition, aspiration, and reverence; of whom we can only think as of a face now uplifted and receptive, now downcast and in tears. Her outer life remains for us in the dark: we can only see that that passionate inner nature must have passed through many a strife, and may well have been betrayed into many a fall. We can by no means feel sure that she never was surprised into the sharp and bitter word, or was always punctual with the outward task ; that she did not miss the near duty in quest of a far wisdom ; that, where her love was strong, no golden mist ever dimmed her clearness of eye or purity of conscience. But, whatever her delusions or sins, they were not those of a dead but of a living heart : they had no canker of selfishness : they were the weeds of a vernal nature, so green as scarce to be told from promised flowers,—not autumn spawn, growing where the sap is gone and the rot begun. The upper springs of her soul, however troubled in their later flow, were pure and untainted yet : humility and trust had not ceased to be habitual, or self-complacency to be impossible. The vision of a higher sanctity stood ever at one remove, and kept alive a secret light within the eye, and moulded the very features into reverence. If her will was weak and knew not how to rule, it was not stiff with pride, but could resign itself and serve. Sad and confused as may be the accounts of such a one with God, there is an open hope,—a source of power,—a likeness with himself yet uneffaced,—so long as the *Love is great.*

The emphatic preference which Christ evinces for this form of character above the ethical and self-reliant is no accident, exceptionally appearing in this passage of his life. It pervades the whole expression of his mind. He would not let this same Mary be withdrawn from sitting at his feet : he blessed the wondering heart of the young child: he told how the voice of the contrite publican reached the ear of God: he opened the Divine arms to the prodigal returning and subdued: he sorrowfully saw the rich youth go away, who had obeyed the commandment without joy, yet had not faith to take the cross. It is indeed the one essential characteristic of his religion,—that which distinguishes the gospel from the law, from natural morals, from self-spun philosophy,—that it insists on the doctrine of *reconciliation by love.* To teach the *rewards of obedience* may be simply Deistic: to proclaim *pardon on repentance* is only Jewish: to announce *forgiveness to affection and trust* is distinctively Christian. Short of this truth we have not entered on our discipleship. This thought it is which makes the difference between the new ages and the old, between true churches and false, between Christian and Pagan art, between a Magdalen and a Cleopatra, between a Saviour and a Nemesis. And if the consciousness of Christendom, after passing through Paul and John, through Clement and Augustine, through Tauler and Luther, has not brought this truth home to our hearts, we have yet to lay ourselves open to the benignest breath of a regenerated world.

"Her sins are forgiven; for she loved much":—does the reason seem to you inadequate to the result? Remember what Divine forgiveness is, and alone can be. It is not a rescinding of the appointed sufferings of guilt. It is not a treatment of moral wrong as though it were moral right, or only neutral. It cannot alter the sinful past, or relieve it, by a single shade, of God's disapproval: he can never be brought to see it other than it is. But the act which is evil in itself is also an offence against Him who identifies his will with all that is good. And of this *personal alienation* forgiveness is the removal. Is it strange that it should be removed by *personal love*, and *not removed without it?* How should sympathy and communion be restored, while the offender's face is averted in distrust? How should they fail to be restored, when the inner discordance has now ceased, when the stain on the past looks alike to both, and the same loves and aversions render the human and the Divine mind again congenial? What is it that ever separates us from God? It is simply the unlikeness of our minds to his;—their low tastes and disproportioned desires;—their pride in what is nought to him, their indifference to what is all in all;—their devotion to the perishable *self* amid the flow of his everlasting love;—their slight of the truth he has so magnificently shown, and the holiness he has yet more awfully secreted in the very heart of things. We throw around us the self-evolved clouds of a nature neglected or debased, and then complain that his beams are hid: we plunge into ever deeper shades, and marvel that the Sun is under permanent eclipse. But the light of his countenance is steady and eternal; and it is ready to shine in again upon us, whenever affections go forth from us intense enough to perforate the mist. Nay, He himself, with the breath that bloweth where it listeth, often sweeps mercifully by, and makes inlets for gleaming lights and tender colours not our own. To remove the estrangement, it only needs that, on such invitation, we set our face the other way, and look to him with free response and trust; that we reflect him instead of darkening ourselves; that we let him show us our delusions as they really are; and, stripping away reserve and self-enclosure, pass into affectionate communion with him. The return of sympathy is the removal of ungenial separation; and he that is not separated is forgiven.

Thus and thus only is the *personal relation* which has been disturbed by sin re-adjusted and rectified. As for the *outward penalties* incurred, they yet remain; and it would be a thing furthest from the wish of a restored and purified mind, that any act of oblivion should blot them out. Nay, were they not already there, provided in the legislation of the universe, the regenerate heart would never rest without creating and suffering them, self-imposed. With or without the contrite love, the consequences of our sin have to be borne. Only, *without* it, they come upon us as dry and unrelieved suffering,—a parching fever untended and alone, consuming us in exile, with no tender looks hovering near us, and no home tones floating on the ear. *With* it, they light indeed their fires within us still; but they are cooled and well-nigh quenched in the joy of reconciliation and the floods of living sympathy. Wherever there is a true thirst for God and that thirst is not in vain, hell itself is fresh with water-brooks, and so bursts into green as to be hell no more.

And as it is with the *peace*, so is it with the *power*, of the spirit of awakened love. We are helpless and paralysed without it. The mere *regret* for past and irrevocable wrong only gnaws the mind with unproductive self-contempt, or works upon a feeble prudence that cannot lift itself from its own flat: and even true shame and remorse, while only retrospective and mellowed by no personal trust and present sympathy, rather prostrate than inspire the soul. They are the needful weakness by which we are brought low and made clear, in preparation for the access of a higher strength. It is only in the guise of a deep love that that higher strength enters to possess us. It is only when the force of conscience ceases to be a propulsion in the dark, and stands before us transfigured with the glory of a Divine form,—only when it is discovered to be no mere part of ourselves, but the immediate real presence of the Holiest of all, that we are touched and caught up by its inspiration. Then it wins to itself the transcending power of a personal affection; and the spiritual impulse and the deepest love fall into coalescence. Instead of distant obedience arises near communion:

in place of a precarious and trembling will, toiling on the dust, we find the transporting wing of aspiration, and leave detaining weights behind. As for mere human strength and self-reliance, it cannot hold through this high race. Not long shall even young resolve press on without being weary; and the youthful spirits too often utterly fall. But they that, with trustful love, "wait upon the Lord, shall renew their strength"; "they shall mount up on wings like eagles; they shall run and not be weary; they shall walk and shall not faint."

XVIII.

Life to the Children of the Prophets.

Acts iii. 25.

"Ye are the children of the prophets."

It is an old problem, to determine the characters which most clearly distinguish man from the other tribes that share with him the occupancy of this world. I will venture to add one to the many answers it has received: *he can tell what o'clock it is.* His nature indeed has few more discriminating symbols than that small instrument, *the watch.* Other creatures travel down the path of time: but he alone can count the steps. They too are liable to season and to change: but he only can mark the cycle and anticipate the end. They also bear within them the vestige of the past, and can dream again of some old sight or sound: but in him alone, from knowledge of its source, is it ripened into memory. They belong to duration: but duration rather belongs to him; not indeed to change its empty form, but to mark its divisions, to glorify its spirit, and determine its contents.

He would have no name by which to describe the present moment, were not the past and the future simultaneously before his thought. It is a high prerogative,—this meeting of the three elements in his mind at once: nor does he often appear to me in closer affinity to the Divine nature, than when I hear the church-clock beneath the midnight skies,—man's hour-bell striking on the ear,—and watch God's time-piece of stars gliding before the eye.

Yet how little true to this prerogative does he practically seem! If you place him before you in idea, as the only known being, save God, who can measure the flow of time, and discern the relation of his *Now* to a heretofore and a hereafter; you think his position august and sublime, and expect a nature widened and calmed by that breadth of duration which seems to claim him. But if you turn from his chronometer to himself, if you look for the past and the future in his own mind, extending his sympathy and tranquillizing his passions, the solemnity of your expectation is sadly disappointed: you see almost the same slavery to the moment, the same blindness to all beyond, as in creatures who are aware of nothing else. He seems delivered over from instant to instant, like a helpless tradition moulded by small pressures of the time, and losing permanent truth at every point. He burns away with self-consuming care in the running focus of the present, fusing down his life into drops that no man cares to gather; and shows nothing of that large lustre of the soul which resembles the spacious and unwasting light of electric skies. Nay, his very privilege of seeing fore and aft is corrupted by him into a means of heating up, instead of cooling down, the interest of the moment: his dexterity, his experience, his power of anticipation, are freely applied to deepen his immediate stake, and make the instant game more desperately engaging to his passions; but not to give the quiet heart and steady hand of one who frequents it only as the gymnastic of a divine skill, and is undazzled by its showy prize. Instead of abating the vehemence of his short-sighted wishes by the sense of larger and more enduring good, he directly imports all the resources of memory and the fervours of hope into his momentary desire, and thus doubles his slavery instead of attaining his freedom.

This habit of *living for the moment* is, even in its best forms, narrowing to the mind and withering to the heart. It cannot coexist with the sense of God upon the soul. It makes the difference between the blindness of passion and the long sight of affection,—between the evanescent haste of impulse and the permanent aspiration of enthusiasm,—between the heats of the natural and the intensity of the spiritual man. This is readily admitted in the case of one who lives for immediate *pleasure*. The common feeling of mankind looks with contemptuous pity at his inability to resist the bait that dances before his eye,—his fickle purposes, changed by each bright colour which the prism of life may throw upon the wall of thought,—his feeble captivity to stronger wills,—his quick spirits and his lingering repentances.

Could such a one be persuaded to change immediate *pleasure* for immediate *interest*, it would be more difficult to procure his condemnation from the verdict of men: for the *inconsistency* which most offends them would be replaced by a steady and prudent self-command. Yet the improvement, though fitting him for the competitions of the world, may leave him absolute stranger as before to the love and life of God; nay, may even be the sign of a more hopeless alienation: for I believe there is no hell so far from God, no exile so total, as the cares of sordid self-interest. Under that spell the very language of recall becomes an unintelligible jargon, and, amid the sleep of the interpreting soul, is taken for unmeaning cant. There are men voluntarily delivered over to the work of mere livelihood and gain,—men who, without the sad necessities and redeeming inspiration of affection, dwarf their whole nature to the scale of retail trade, who, instead of withstanding by a noble spirit the littleness of life, fall into it with glee and relish; the paradise of whose hopes is a comfortable business, and the idol of whose admiration is the shrewd neighbour sure to make his fortune. To such a man all the depth and beauty of life are closed. The sweetest relations suggest nothing but shapes in his secular affairs; his daughters are emblems of so many marriage chances, and his sons of so many apprentice-fees; and his charities and his church, an investment in decent reputation. Friends, there is nothing degrading in the humblest and the hardest fate; nothing much nobler in this world than a meek true soul struggling against the narrow bounds of the sphere assigned it, and faithful to cherish the light of God in the inglorious darkness of a bitter lot. But to find the smallness of affairs a relief from any higher strain, to hug the degradation and make ourselves at home with it, to plead it in excuse for the unresisting meanness of our nature, to preach from its low platform a crusade of blind unbelief against the visions of prophets and the breathings of the devout,—this is a direct betrayal of the post of life, and treason against the holy Providence of all. Whoever fixes himself upon the centre of mere prudential interest forfeits thereby his title to speak, because his power to judge, of anything divine: for heaven pays small respect to our poor taste for *plain* truths, and so withdraws from the earthly eye the "deep things of God," that "the natural man cannot discern them."

Nay, this blindness may befall a far worthier class than the votaries of pleasure or of interest: it is the penalty of all who concentrate themselves upon the present,—who live for the moment, even though it be the momentary *Duty*. Conscience also has its narrowness; its scrupulous, microscopic gaze, that looks for the animalcules of obligation till it grows blind to the stars of faith, and the free heaven swims dizzily before it. The anxieties of the merely dutiful mind show that there is yet a barrier leaving it outside the union with God. Those cautious steps betray the deterring fear, and are unlike the free movements of a confiding love. I know at once *whose* steps they are: they belong to one who appreciates religion as the means of good morals, instead of morals as the germ and condition of religion; whose very faith therefore is a worship of prohibition, a conservatism of limits, an apprehension of the escape of some fugitive desires; and can never fling itself in pure enthusiasm and with fearless trust upon a large career where no rule can guide it but only love impel. The small scale of affection in these honest and rigid minds shows itself in censorious thoughts: they cannot see beyond the circumference of their own rules: they have no sympathy for other types of life,—no large eye for good if God should hide it under strange costume: and so, as the world will grow into unexpected shapes, they are amazed at the perverseness of the world; treating it indeed with no greater rigour than they would severely apply to themselves; only forgetting that the Lord of Omniscience gathers himself not into their centre, but rather calls them out into his circumference. In short, the soul which foregoes its privilege of spreading itself out on past and future, and lives for the moment, whether of pleasure, of interest, or even of duty, suffers a dwindling in its nature. In helpless irritability, in miserable egotism, in ungenial rigour, in uneven spirits, does the exaggeration of the present betray itself. By continuance in it a man inevitably becomes ever smaller in soul, while, by losing sight more and more of anything beyond him, he feels as though he were greater; till at length he becomes incapable of *learning*, of *trusting*, of *looking up* at all; and exhibits all the littleness of the child, only without the child's tenderness and faith. Nor is this result at all prevented by any magnitude in the mere scale of a man's outward and personal life. It is as true of master as of man, of merchant as of clerk. Be the outline and circumference of occupation large or small, the contents, taken one by one, are not dissimilar; and while the minds that penetrate them remain alike, the only difference will be between a taller and a lower stature of the same type of character.

There are times, I suppose, to every thoughtful man, when the impression of this littleness in his actual life comes upon him with a startling force. A touch of sorrow which wakes the faded forms of old affection,—a poet's strain at which some high enthusiasm vibrates in the heart again,—a night upon the mountain or the ocean where a Presence greater than the whole field of worlds is felt in the rush of the waters and the silence of the air,—or the sight of some secret sufferer who meekly bears a cross unknown to us,—surprises us into the humbling discovery, that we have been dead to the sublimities that lie as a cloud of glory around us and within us. Something deeper than the senses show or the hand can touch gleams upon us everywhere,—an expressiveness behind the features of life and nature which we had never seen before; and scenes quite often looked at now seem to *look at us*, and with the living light of a Divine eye. *Something* that was eternal we had always supposed that there must be; now we find that there is *Some One* who is eternal; and the drawing near to him, the penetration to him through his universe, the saying of a true word, the lifting of a clear face, to him, appears to have a meaning we did not suspect. Compared with this meaning, how poor seems all that we had taken to be most real! how empty the contents of our busiest day, too troubled about many things to leave any opening for the one thing needful! Yet what is a day, but a sample of the eternity in which we are and are to be?—If this arousing of the soul is not faithfully followed up, habit will reassert its power, and contradict the divine call by a positive relapse; and an utter scepticism of everything infinite will ensue, and the mind will look back on its only waking experience as a brilliant dream. But if, by perpetuity in the change, this proves to be a true regenerative hour, the opposite effect will follow.

Finite things will be despised and disbelieved; will suffer vengeance for their long tyranny, and be spurned as mere deceptive shows; and the more intense their despotism has been, the more thorough will be the renunciation of their sway. When the scales first fall from the eyes of one who has been living for the moment, that which lies before his astonished view is the eternal depth of God, towards which the currents of a resistless spirit appear to draw him. If he have a strong impetuous soul, like Augustine or Luther, he plunges in and loses himself in quest of the everlasting point of view. The conversions of such minds from the life for the moment to the life for eternity are facts to be treated with a hearty reverence. Nevertheless, the sweep at once from egotism to God is too vast not to bring some giddiness, some loss of equilibrium, into a nature like ours. The sudden transfer from the exclusively personal point to the exclusively divine is not free from the illusion of vehement contrast. Finite things are too absolutely quenched, and sink away from even their just rights. All that is human is dwarfed and slighted; and every mild and gracious light, of natural pity, of domestic affection, of cultivated art, is put out by the intense splendours of the beatific vision. Hence, periods distinguished by a rapid burst of religious consciousness have rarely been unmarked by wild and tragic features, by a life deepening into vivid colours and shaping itself into gigantic forms. A taste and feeling for greatness unsoftened by beauty has developed itself. The immensity of the divine ends pursued has swallowed up the scrupulous care of conscience about the means employed. The curbs on human passion, the respect for human life, the rights of human thought, have given way. And breathing in a region of transcendent air, men have lost the gentleness and warmth of a kindred and considerate heart. The new-born soul, carried aloft by the fiery steeds of præternatural affection, is apt to be stripped, in the mighty wind of its ascent, of the mantle of its humanities, and let it drop on less glorious prophets, still toiling on the level of this world.

Behold then the opposite dangers between which we stand. He who lives for the moment never finds his soul and is alien from God: he who springs out of this darkness to live straightway for eternity wins a giddy height which only the most balanced minds can safely hold, and whence the lesser graces and charities are apt to pass out of sight. Have we nothing then to mediate for us between these two,—between the simply natural and the simply spiritual,—between the purely personal and the absolutely Divine? Are there but these two foci of position for our nature, the solid darkness of self, and the ethereal effulgence of God,—the one blinding from its gloom, the other from its brilliancy? Far from it. There is an intermediate realm, or rather an interposed path spreading from the one to the other, with stages of sweet rest for weary souls, and many a loving help on the way from earth to heaven. For those who cannot take the whole distance at a bound, God has prepared, between the natural and the spiritual, the heroisms, the martyrdoms, the sanctities, of *History*. If we cannot live at once and alone with him, we may at least live with those who have lived with him; and find, in our admiring love for their purity, their truth, their goodness, an intercession with his pity on our behalf. To study the lives, to meditate the sorrows, to commune with the thoughts, of the great and holy men and women of this rich world, is a sacred discipline which deserves at least to rank as the forecourt of the temple of true worship, and may train the tastes, ere we pass the very gate, of heaven. It is an exercise which neither permits us to remain in self-idolatry, nor yet plunges us into self-annihilation. It strengthens what is weak in our souls by the sympathy of ages: it supports us against the derisive face of living fools by the sublime gaze of whole centuries of the wise: it relieves the sense of our life's littleness by showing us the possibility of greatness. Above all, it corrects and inverts our delusive estimates of what is solid and powerful in this world. In our own individual experience we are ever tempted to think nothing real, nothing positive and practical, except our material business, the visible produce of our pains, the outward administration of our life; while the inner and ideal life is deemed so unsubstantial a dream that those who speak of it are supposed to be beating the air. The experience of nations and ages reverses this. The glories of the past are not in huge trades, or fine properties, or even in laws and rites and institutions which in their day kindled the passions of party strife: these, chafed into dust by the mouldering hand of time, successively fall away with the earthly conditions from which they come; while the mere impulses of expression, through which affection and admiration pour themselves forth and heart appeals to heart, mould themselves into imperishable Arts, though asking only for the most perishable of materials,—forms and tones, colour and language; and precisely the most ethereal and interior of thoughts, which visit us only in evanescent gleams,—of something terrible in sin, of something infinite in duty, of a possible union with God through love and a mastery of life through entire surrender,—prove the most permanent realities in history; constructing themselves into faiths which have been the cradle of nations and the divine nurse of the most vivifying individual minds. The ink of Virgil on its thin leaf outlasts the Roman walls and aqueducts: nay, the *unwritten* words of Homer survive the cities where they were sung, and are our only guide to the rivers and plains which he has made immortal, but which nature and history could not keep. Of nothing does the aspect change more with time than of that wealth and station for which such sacrifices are made. Who now cares for all that Kallias *had*, in comparison with the least part of what Socrates *was?* or would save the banking credit of all the Fuggers at the cost of a table-talk of Luther's? Who would envy the pontificate of Leo, if he could have the pencil of Raffaelle? And in spiritual things, when they steal from their true retreats and dare to speak, it is the simplest truth and love that are surest to endure; and ages that can no longer yield the heart to the ceremonial of St. Peter's or Notre Dame or Westminster, will still surrender to the persuasive piety of a St. Francis, a Fénélon, a Leighton. Next to the judgments of God himself are the estimates of the human mind exposed to the long tests of history. And the pure insight of religion, if not intuitively present, may be reached perhaps by a silent circuit through the élite of generations gone.

Shall it then make no difference to us,—except to our accumulated capital,—that we live in an *old* human world, rich in the memory of ancient dynasties of thought? We are "the children of the prophets"; and are fond of owning it by rebuilding their tombs or raising memorials of a century's gratitude and honour. Shall the record of their genius and graces be fixed on the marble or the bronze, and tell no story except when there is sunshine to show it and an eye to read it? Shall it have no transcript on "the living tables of the heart," to be ever with us and gleam by night as well as day? We forfeit the chief source of dignity and sweetness in life, next to the direct communion with God, if we do not seek converse with the greater minds that have left their vestiges on the world. Rather let us keep a constant eye upon the light of their spirits, and never quit our hold of the shadowy hands, of which the nearest is almost at our door and the furthest feels the touch of Christ and disappears in the effulgence of God. If it is not given us, with the inspired apostle, to reach "the third heaven" in the twinkling of an eye, or, with the rapt mystic, to spring aloft on the wing of prayer and float straight into the arms of the Infinite Love, *they* will draw our feebler spirits upward by insensible attraction, and bring us to the same end at last. This blessed dependence, this holding on of link to link, of soul to soul, of age to age, is the true "communion of saints," which bridges the waters of death, and embraces its opposite banks in one City of God.

XIX.

The Godly Man.

PSALM xii. 1.

"Help, Lord; for the godly man ceaseth."

WITH many a bright child, many a high-minded youth, restive under Puritanical guardianship, it would seem, I fear, no bad news that "the godly" were ceasing; and his suppressed feeling would be that they could very well be spared. For the phrase has become appropriated to a type of character far from lovely in even its best aspects, and so adverse to natural joy and dreary in its idea of perfectness as to repel all large and genial minds. It is the standing infatuation of divines, first to spoil the poetic depth of religion by reducing its speech to technical use, and then to charge on human corruption the repugnance which the dismal product excites. The kind of person to whom they would award the epithet "*godly*" is familiar to us all; —the man of evangelical piety, whose life is ruled by gratitude for unmerited salvation and desire to rescue others from the perdition which he has escaped; who can glibly say the creeds without a pause of doubt, and is duly shocked with the superstition that adds anything to them or the heresy that takes anything away; who looks on his Church as the great agency by which God is in contact with the world, and measures by its rule all men and things, all history, all life, all progress; who pours his gifts into its treasury, and makes it the almoner of all his bounty. That a character of this form is compatible with many excellences,—nay, is even a pledge of them,—we need not deny: but the selection is narrow and peculiar; it carries with it grave deformities and faults which it consecrates as sanctities; and it omits, as if profane, many human characteristics which must for ever remain objects of admiration and trust.

Even apart from its abuse in the religious dialect of a school, the word "*godly*" has come to mean something vastly more limited and less certainly significant of nobleness, than it once denoted. It marks only one special aspect of character,—one order of feelings and habits,—viz., those which are directed towards God. No doubt these *ought* to carry in them all else that is pure and good, and to refine and perfect every other side of the moral nature. And wherever God is present to the thought as the everlasting life of beauty, truth, and goodness, and kindles their faint authority with the glow of personal affection, there, to live in conscious relations with him will sustain the whole action of the soul at its highest, and be equivalent to righteousness all round; and secret communion with him will take the mind to the very well-spring of every better love, and revive the aspirations drooping in the heat and dust. A spirit always rightly disposed towards a perfect Being can neither be in disorder within itself, nor be wrongly disposed towards any other. But then religious susceptibility is often keen, where the conditions, intellectual or moral, of so manly and comprehensive a piety are wanting; and a worship may be paid which sanctifies the discord of the passions and confirms the confusion of the conscience. And, on the other hand, there are secular forms of character, undeniably high and noble, which seem to have no sympathies on the spiritual side, and are unconscious of light from above. It would be a monstrous and a monkish rule to measure men in our time by their devotions; to admit to the glory of godliness every assured intimate of heaven, and exclude from it every one from whom the living presence of the Most High is hid.

It may check this overbalance of our estimates on the side of piety to remember that the word "*godly*," in its primitive intent, means only "god*like*." It expresses, not the personal affections which have God for their *object*, but the characteristics which may bring a human soul into *resemblance to him*. To the strong and simple builders of our speech he was a *godly* man who drew *their* reverence, not whom they found constantly expressing *his own;* with whom they felt themselves in the presence of something divine; whom they trusted as a rock of righteousness; to whose shelter they could fly in every storm of wrong. Such a one they would doubtless take to be "the Friend of God"; but the sign of it to them was not in his devotions and private demeanour towards the world above; rather in this, that he stood to them in the place of God, and was the chosen Organ of eternal Right. If, with this clue, we seek for the central essence of the character, we shall certainly not rest with the pieties exercised in conscious worship. For precisely here it is that we stand on purely human ground, and are disposed of by affections which the Supreme Spirit cannot share. To look up, to aspire, to adore, to weep the tears of failure and breathe the sighs of hope, are the pathetic privilege of finite natures, planted on the open borders of the infinite. God lives without personal relations above him: He has no prayers to say, no creed to repeat; and the beauty of holiness in him can have no fitting emblem in the uplifted eyes and patient looks of the true saint. Of his perfection we can think only as of a spontaneous conformity with an inward righteousness and a pure preference of the best; as an inherent love of planting out the germs of this moral order in other minds;

as an ever-during sympathy with its growth there, bringing them nearer to himself. If, then, Goodness, in its culmination, is something other than devotion to a higher nature, and is divested of its character of personal affection, how can I disown it as the Divine in miniature when it appears under the same aspect in a human mind? If I see a man living out of an inner spring of inflexible right and pliant pity; if he refuses the colour of the low world around him; if his eye flashes with scorn at mean and impure things which are a jest to others; if high examples of honour and self-sacrifice bring the flush of sympathy upon his cheek; if in his sphere of rule he plainly obeys a trust instead of enforcing an arbitrary will, and in his sphere of service takes his yoke without a groan, and does his work with thought only that it be good; I shall not pry into his closet or ask about his creed, but own him at once as the godly man. Godliness is the persistent living out an ideal preconception of the Right, the Beautiful, the Good. Wherever this is dominant, it ensures—

1. A certain *perfection and thoroughness of personal work.* There are two ways in which all human achievements may be carried out, according as you elaborate them from within or from without. It is the boast of the practical man that he adapts his operations to the external conditions which shut him in, takes accurate measurement both of his exigencies

and of his possibilities, avails himself of opportunity and evades difficulty; and never permits himself to be run away with by impracticable aims; and he perpetually confirms his opinion of his own adroitness by his visible success. Life, thus administered, is like a game of skill, in which every move is computed by balancing the values of surrounding contingencies, and making it an advance or a retreat according as there may be a better chance to win. On the other hand, it is the habit of a creative mind to spend its chief labour in the field of thought, to clear its designs, to fix its standard, to mature its projects there; and not till then, except by an unconscious tact seldom absent from such a nature, to take account of the allies and foes encamped upon the outer plain; and when baffled in the struggle, as it often is, to withdraw with quiet and abstracted look, unaware of the obtrusive laughter which proclaims the enthusiast's defeat. Life, thus administered, is like a poem or a meditation overheard; which finds a deeper meaning for what else were shallow noise, and haunts the world that *is* with the spectre of what *ought to be.* These opposite methods have no doubt, to a great extent, their separate spheres; the one prevailing in works of adaptation and convenience, the other in works of genius. But neither can afford to dispense with the other: and, above all, there is no human function so purely mechanical, no task so poor and common, no drudgery so dry, as to admit of being performed at its best by manipulation and arithmetic, without a directing idea in the mind and zeal in the heart. Take this away,—let there be no image in the thought of the perfect product as it should ensue from the hand,—no sense of shame if it be inferior, no joy if it transcend; and industry is bereft of its very soul, and, in the selfish attempt to shirk its obligations, sinks into veritable slavery. Once measure your diligence by mere outward necessity, with no anxiety but to get passably to the other side of it, and the root of all dishonesty has struck within you, and will bear its fruit. If you build, the hidden stones will be rubble; if you plead, your language will become suggestive of falsehood, and your ingenuity degenerate into tricks; if you rule in public affairs, you will learn the arts of shiftiness and evasion, and will lapse into that shrinking from responsibility which is the modern form of treason to the State. The one security for personal fidelity and effective achievement lies in the ascendant habit of working from within; from the native love of order, beauty, right; from faith in them as the mastering powers of the outer world; from reverent allegiance to them, which makes acquiescence in their defeat impiety. As God eternally thinks out his universe into a perfection more divine, so does the godly, shaping the scene around him from the life within, turn it into a completer kosmos, as his time flows on.

2. This godliness again it is, this inward stay upon

the right and true, which gives *authority over dependent natures*, and most wins obedience, while most frugal and tranquil in demanding it. It is sometimes said, that the gift of command goes with strength of will; and certain it is, that from weakness of will it passes entirely away. But it is little that can be effected in the affairs of men, and nothing in the higher departments of human life, by mere driving force of purpose, and intolerance of personal defeat. It was never meant that in this world, or any other where responsible minds are found, the pleasure of one should be the law for all; and wherever that pretension is set up, we all turn rebels on the instant, and the push begins of will against will; and, submit as we may, it is with protest, and keen watching to slip the tyranny. In the armed pleasure of one mind there is no natural authority over the unarmed of another; and if the helpless yields, it will be as the captive, to work in chains, and plan revenge in tears. It is not stronger Will, but higher Right, that bears the title to rule in the societies of men; and only he who visibly forgets himself, and becomes the organ of a law he did not make and cannot alter, whose will is firm because it is *not* his own, but is backed by a divine adamant that cannot yield, can win a loyal and glad obedience. He is not enforcing his personal preferences, but vindicating the just and good, which he at once embodies and obeys. This total retreat of self, this advance to the front of an august and invisible moral necessity, is the secret of that quiet dignity with which effective authority is invariably exercised. Rebuke itself acquires a solemn weight where it falls with impersonal gentleness, spoiled by no heats of fluttered egotism, and tinged only with the sorrow of disappointed trust. Whoever lives out of any inward faith in good, is involuntarily disposed to presume it in others even while it is yet latent, and is the first to see it when its incipient expression comes; and in dealing with them he addresses himself to it, and confides in the response. The very light of his eye kindles into life the spot on which it falls: he looks for the conscience, and it is there. All who come into his presence learn to feel that they have more than justice done to them; that the best they have is seen in them, and the best they can is expected from them; and under this warmth of appreciation every promise of good hastens its growth, opens into the upper air, and is nourished into strength. Yet, if they even fail, they know it is a part of the same faith which led him to expect the good, that he will make tender allowance for the ill, and not surrender the hope baffled for the moment, but true for ever. No induction of experience, no life computed by the outward look of men and things, would ever attain this mingled authority and sweetness. They are the natural expression of that godliness which works out of an inward faith in beauty, truth, and good.

3. The same principle carries with it a grace which at first view might seem to contradict the claim of natural authority over dependent natures;—a certain *deference* towards others which refrains from self-assertion, and rather becomes receptive of their good. Where there is no deep faith in the spiritual bases of human life, in the revelation and the power of Right in the conscience of mankind, there is in the heart no certain source of "honour towards all men," no patient hope of future nobleness for them to soothe the disappointment at their unworthiness. Unsustained by moral trust and reverence, the gentle respect, the gracious amenities of life are left to rest only on the personal affections; and scarcely go beyond the private circle, except when misfortune startles compassion and wakes the generosity which the sunshine sends to sleep. In how many a family may you see the most loving interior relations, the quick discernment of each other's good, the modest self-estimate, the mutual sacrifice of personal desire, the joy in opportunities of help; yet, towards the outer circle of the world, a critical attitude from which every line of tenderness, nay, every look of justice, has disappeared; the censorious talk, the malignant hint, the suspicious prophecy, the mean construction, the eager tale of some shame at which the heart might weep! All this would seem to contradict the first impression of that gentle home. It is simply that the affections are near-sighted, and have

no faith; they are ready, clear and true, so far as their vision goes; every soft light arrests them, every blossom of beauty charms them; but where the distance lies beyond their organ and the mist closes round, they believe only in darkness and all that it may hide. They are unconscious of their strange illusion; that in a world all human, a world which in its breadth does but repeat their little plot, they should see so much that is lovely at home, and believe in so much deformity abroad. God save us from the bitterness and scorn of the cynical spirit, by giving us the faith of the godly in the secret springs of good! For him, in his intercourse with men, the presumption is always on the side of simplicity and rectitude; he does not believe in knavery till his keen search has been pushed through all the title-deeds of good repute; he recognises a provisional claim in humanity itself, and allows his respect to enter into possession, until some fatal flaw compels its retreat. As it is the theory of habitual distrust, the perpetual need of exceptional vigilance, that makes the City vulgar, so it is the natural ease of a pure and confiding mind which imports true refinement and composure to the person in whom it dwells. Surrounded by those whom he respects, if not for what they are, for what they may be, he is drawn out towards them on the lines of genial appreciation; he converses only with their good; the egotism possible to us all sleeps and never stirs within him ; its insolence of thought, its rudeness of speech, its selfishness of act, are impossible to him ; and the dignified stability of a mind that lives from within is naturally clothed with the modest grace of reverence and charity.

Wherever these lineaments of character appear, we look upon the face of righteousness, and cannot join in the desponding cry "Help, Lord, for the *godly man* ceaseth." If they do not reflect the Divine likeness, I know not where we are to seek it. Shall I then say a strange thing if I affirm that, nevertheless, the picture is not perfect? Its features take no notice of God, and mould themselves as if he were not. They would complete the human lines of excellence and beauty, if Man were the highest of beings and stood upon the world as its god ; but does *not* complete them, since they leave without trace his relation to the Infinite Mind, whose love he unconsciously shares and whose trust he blindly executes. To live "like gods," when we are not so, is a condition which no virtues or affections can redeem from distortion and mistake. And were we really "gods," yet embraced in the empire of a "God of gods," it is plain that to ignore or forget this feature of our position could only weaken and mutilate our moral nature, leaving it without the energy of loyalty and the graces of confiding obedience. To consummate, therefore, the adjustment of our character to our place, we need to own the Divine Spirit above us as well as to have it within us, and to let its brightness in ourselves be the reflection of our communion with him; to transform what was before a self-asserting impulse of right into personal reverence and love; to learn what it is to lean on an invisible support, to find a living Guide in every darkness, and to hear an inspiration that is not carried on the wind. He who thus recognises his human position, and takes its new affections into his heart, is not weakened, but incredibly strengthened by his conscious dependence; and will the better serve as a stay to others, when his own feet are planted on the Rock.

XX.

The Inner and Outer Kingdom of God.

Rom. x. 14, 15.

"How shall they believe in him of whom they have not heard? and how shall they hear without a preacher? and how shall they preach, except they be sent?—As it is written, How beautiful are the feet of them that preach the gospel of peace, and bring glad tidings of good things."

Ever since Civil Society has been an object of study and reflection, it has affected thoughtful minds with a strange mixture of admiration and compassion. It seems at once the glory of our nature, and its shame. Other races are rendered gregarious by various wants and common affections; but man alone balances yet deepens the mutual dependence by the arts of exchange. Other races submit to be led by the strong, and combine their toil for co-operative works; but with him alone does Law ascend from force to Right, and union pass from blind instinct to conscious self-devotion, and the mere nest or hive is replaced by the City and the State. To detect any clear improvement in other creatures, you must take your survey by geologic time; but, for him, the little span of history suffices; and while the swallow, the beaver, and the ant build and live as they did before he began to note their ways, he needs but a few centuries to move with accelerated pace from the rudeness that keeps no record of itself to a civilization crowded with material resources, and rich in its jurisprudence, literature, and art. A *human commonwealth* with its hierarchy of mutual service, its army of tamed passions, its invisible guard of ideal restraints, its traditions of heroism, its hopes of greatness, its sympathy with the moral life of the world, is the highest product of the Providence of God, and the most impressive witness to the possibilities of Man. Yet within this glorious product, as it grows and spreads, there lurks a canker that feeds on its exuberance, and perforates its substance with misery and decay. The expansion and consolidation of the State, which give a grander career to genius and power, leave no shelter for the maimed and weak, but turn them out into a battle where they are sure to fall; and in some form or other,—the slave-quarter,—the serf-village,—or the poor-house,—the sign has never been absent, from any nation that has a history, of a crushed or unreclaimed humanity. It seems as though the distances widened as the education of the world advanced; and while our nature at one end moved on a vaster scale, at the other it shrivelled and rotted away. Only in a ripe community can the statesman, the poet, the philosopher, the artist, appear, or any product of the Mind go forth that shall be "a possession for ever." Yet the great cities which they immortalize hide, behind their temples and their courts, a thousand festering ills; they are the birth-place of new diseases, the nursery of hateful vices, and afford in their densest parts but a crowded solitude of unpitied miseries. This contrast of brilliant resource with humiliating failure, of a society blossoming at the head and pining at the root, has always affected thoughtful minds with a "noble discontent." The joint spectacle of high capabilities and mean sufferings is intolerable to every generous heart: the light of inward hope conflicts with the darkness undeniable without, and tries to penetrate it and touch it with some colours of ideal promise. From this impulse have sprung all social theories;—philosophical republics, Eutopias, socialisms, kingdoms of heaven; all aspire to realise the ascertained possibilities, and exclude the saddest disappointments, of our human union.

No relief, said Plato, will ever reach the ills of men, till either statesmen become philosophers, or philosophers assume the government of states. This saying indicates the direction in which the Greek mind sought the solution of the social problem. You must deal, it was thought, with the commonwealth as a whole, and put a reconstructing hand upon it from the place of power. The *scene* is all wrong on which you plant men, and where you train them: you leave it open to unprincipled competitions: you make its bribes to private selfishness too great, its demands on public sacrifice too small: you place its supreme interests at the disposal of incompetence, setting over its tribunals those who have no knowledge of justice, and over its schools those who have false notions of education: you let the poets tell mischievous fables about the gods, and the orators talk flattering sophistry to the people: you foster the taste which admires successful ambition, and scorns the abstinence of incorruptible rectitude. You must sweep all this away, and rebuild the theatre of life; permitting none to come upon it who do not bid fair for manly strength and virtue; assigning to each his place and career, and precluding him from functions for which he is not fit; and so disciplining all for the character possible to them,—the workers for industry and temperance, the soldiers for bravery and obedience, the rulers for wisdom and integrity,—that the whole may exhibit a partnership and equilibrium of goodness like the unity of a single harmonious Soul. Schemes of this kind for mending the world rested all their hopes on arrangement, and computed simply the forces of environing influence. In dealing with the problem, men, as they were found in experience to be, constituted the immutable factor, which was to be let alone, and made to yield a new result only by being worked into new conditions. A revolution in the world was required, to change any individual man.

The method of Christianity appears the very opposite to this; and has at all events become so in its administration now. It is not, with us, a theory of reorganised society, the dream of a new Polity, through the establishment of which character is to attain its true proportions; but a direct appeal to the individual conscience, which aims to redeem men, one by one, and bring them, just where they stand, into inner harmony with God. And it is true that, in its origin also, Christianity left the existing constitution of the world alone, and, unlike the philosophers, propounded no projects for modelling it anew. This however arose, not from any better opinion of it, but from a worse; not from indifference towards it, but from despair of it; not from retreat into the citadel of the inner man to defy the enemies without, but from the vision of a City of God in which already the disciples were enrolled, and which, without aid of theirs, would soon replace the Empire of the seven hills. It was not for want of the old dream of a divine commonwealth, but because that dream, as they believed, God would realise for them, that they were neutral to the existing State, and wasted on it neither zeal nor enmity. They too had their image of perfect life, their sacred allegiance, their society swayed by eternal justice and secure of righteous order; and, possessed by the faith and expectation of it, they so lived in it as to become "*dead*" to this world, and carry all their thought and heart into the relations of "another country, even a heavenly." Their despair of the actual and historic scene of things was thus deeper than the philosopher's: for they never thought of mending or reconstructing it: they simply left it to perish. And in withdrawing from it, they meant to retire, not into a mystic inward life of individual piety, much less into any Stoic strength of personal isolation, but into the citizenship of a better community, soon to be realized, and blending in itself meanwhile the seen with the unseen, and animating the posts of duty below with the living inspiration of Christ and God above.

This death to the actual world, this life in an ideal which replaced it without conflicting with it, incidentally brought into existence the highest characteristic of Christian civilization. The image of a holier life, of a kingdom of God where wrong and sin should never come, touched the sleeping springs of higher affection and spiritual power in the heart, and lifted men into a new birth of character. New tastes, new love, new hopes broke upon them from depths of their nature never reached before, and delivered them from the thraldom of outward things and the strife of the passions they had served. Snatched from themselves, and carried off by a spirit diviner than their own, they see their own past which was hid from them before, and hear and answer many a call of God that had come to their deaf ear in vain. A consecration falls upon the walks of daily duty and the place of nightly rest: a beauty enters for them into the simplest task that only has a better and a worse; and there is a Presence that allays the troubles, and puts a sweetness into the discords of life. Looking away from the scattered and broken fragments of goodness among men to the perfect natures of a supernal sphere, the disciple was carried clear past the ancient standards of piety and moral strength; and, leaving behind him the piece-meal distribution of virtues among classes and ranks, rose to the great idea of *One Righteousness*, realized in heaven, approached on earth, alike possible, alike necessary, for all minds. This is the true and indestructible ground of Christian brotherhood and unity,—this recognition of a common capacity for resemblance to God, a common liability to fall away from it, a common trust to press into greater nearness to it. And this was found in the fervour of that first age, when the Christians died to the fermenting world around them, and flung themselves into the affections of an ideal state, and tried the tender ties of mutual sacrifice, and rehearsed the life of a holy and perfect world. And the experiment, once tried, vindicated itself by the permanent elevation which it produced in human thought and character. The accidents of the conception fell away, the essence remained: unsuspected depths of the moral nature were revealed: indefinite possibilities of the spirit burst the bounds of expectation, and showed where the living germs of good were lurking unseen; and it became the settled experience of Christendom, that humanity and God are never hopelessly estranged from one another; but that, if the true congenial point of any single soul can be reached and touched, even the dead will be alive again, and the lost will be found.

Thus, from the lonely life of the first Christians, which could only work internally upon itself, came to light the great truth that, without waiting to reconstruct his world, man in himself may become a new creature, and take the initiative at home in introducing the kingdom of heaven. Renouncing the maxims of prudent despair, —that you must take men as they are, that you must suit the scene around them to their proved weakness and make the best of their inevitable sin,—Christianity has ever charged its missionaries thus: "Go forth to this people, and speak to them from the level, not of what they are, but of what they ought to be: take with you the measure, not of outward existence, but of the inner sanctuary: abate no claim of God upon them, but tell them all his righteous will: remember that you are his, rather than theirs, or theirs only for his sake: fling yourself on the tide of his love, and fear not that you will be borne in upon some hidden inlet of their nature: nay, his compassion in your heart will make a way where there was none before, and shake the dull souls till they start up and prophesy."

This faith in the spiritual possibilities of every individual conscience has passed, as an inseparable constituent, into the permanent life of Christendom. Only, it now acts on a world which is no longer expected to perish, which we cannot dismiss from our attention as delivered over to Satan, which we are not permitted to escape as foreign to us; but which, as the abiding school of our humanity, we are bound to set in order and to recover for God. So that the *scene of things* is returned upon our hands, and the social problems of the old philosophy renew themselves upon a larger and more complicated world. The two rival proposals, which Pagan wisdom and Evangelic zeal divided between them,—to redeem the *life of persons*, and to amend the *scene of things*, have lost their enmity, have fallen into partnership, and devolve upon us together. In dealing with them, however, there must still remain a division of labour; seeing that, in spite of their unity at last, the agencies and faculties that are needed for the one are seldom qualified to serve the other. It must ever be the function of the *secular State* to readjust the *things* that furnish forth the theatre of life, to settle institutions, economy, police and laws, and see to it that they constitute a fitting school for just and righteous habits. But to the *spiritual agency of the Church* it must be left to address itself to *persons*, one by one, to reach the secret springs of better life, and speak for God to the languid but undying conscience of humanity. Of this divine work we must never weary, and never despair; but carry into it the eternal patience of God; who, age after age, solicits with his grace every soul of man; and now here, now there, stands at the door, and knocks, and would lift the latch on the first hospitable hint. With one and another, nay with multitudes, the Christian appeal may seem to be made in vain: but, if only the true beat of the heart goes with it, it will find some hiding-place in many a mind that for the moment owns it not; and, like a phrase of forgotten music or the snatches of a perished dream, will steal forth in some tender twilight hour, when there are none to see the tears of compunction, or to mock at the returning tones of prayer. This trust in the living Spirit of God, which finds some crevice still open in the hardest heart, this persistency of appeal that cannot listen to despair, is the true prophetic gift, without which the Church is a pretence and the preacher had better hold his peace. It is the first requisite of Religion, the primary inspiration of all Faith, that the witness to the higher life must never falter and never cease: if once it grows ashamed before the face of unawakened men, and, like the timid poet, shrinks from the laugh of the dull and blind and can only nurse itself in solitude, it is living faith no more; and is equally unlike the apostle, who, amid the splendid idolatries of Athens, remonstrated "daily in the market place with such as met with him"; and the Son of Man himself who, even in the retirement of the hills, when he saw the multitudes "as sheep without a shepherd," had compassion on them, and poured forth to them his divinest words.

To reach the springs of inner life where they are sealed up, and keep them clear where they are flowing, the one great agency is, the personal power of an earnest and sympathetic mind, living itself in a higher order of ideas, and above the danger of being dragged down to the level where they are lost. There lies the true pastoral gift; deep faith in God, deep pity for man; and strength to carry the vision of a divine order into the clash and confusion of the world: and wherever you meet with any good measure of this gift, thank God that the prophets are not dead: arm it freely with your outward help, and confide in it from your inmost heart. Send it,—better still take it,—as the messenger alike of humanity and God, into the City recesses, where the struggle of life is fiercest, and brightened least by either physical or spiritual light. There is nothing like the living breath of conviction and trust, for fanning every latent suspicion and healing compunction that else would die. Tell me not that the weight of ill is too heavy to be lifted; the greater the burthen, the more elastic force is needed to heave it off. Do you say, the material conditions of our poor neighbourhoods are too oppressive to give encouragement? then are they too oppressive to permit desertion and neglect. The more they stifle the spiritual possibilities, the more must they be counterbalanced by persistency of culture, and intensity of appeal. Would you really plead the density of the darkness as the reason of withholding the sparse and only light? Be assured, if we speak thus of our poor, they are no darker than we. It is all a fancy that, even in their lot, different as it looks, they are much other than ourselves in their temptations, in their affections, and in their victories. Who that knows them, in their troubles and their strivings, would dare to give the counsels of hopelessness? Are there not, there as elsewhere, inequalities of character, ranging over every grade, from the mean to the heroic? marvels of unselfishness, fortitude, and temperance, attesting the noblest force of conscience, as well as the yielding habits by which indigence itself may rot away in luxury? From such a field, at once of sadness and of promise, would you recall every reminder of higher obligation, every aid to struggling goodness, every nurture of divine hope and love? Can no father be sustained by self-sacrifice to prolong the education of his children? no mother be helped to make her sons and daughters truthful, brave, and modest? no youth be braced up to manly self-government amid the temptations of the City? The more tainted the atmosphere around, surely all the more need is there for a loving friend of every righteous effort to pass, as a breath of moral wholesomeness, through the unventilated courts of life. Nor is it true that this personal dealing with men, one by one, stands in the way of any larger reform of the field on which they live. On the contrary, it justifies the reformer's enthusiasm and accelerates his work; and brings to every problem that minute and practical insight without which it cannot be wisely solved. Indeed every religious mission that carries the cleansing spirit of Christ where it was unknown before, reforms its own field in little, and rehearses the experiments that must pass on to a greater stage. Not till the outward and the inward agencies understand each other and go to their work together, will men be relieved from the pressures which keep them in their littleness and sin and suffering; or their nature expand in all dimensions together, and justify the ideal hopes of Christian faith. But in this partnership, it is and must ever remain the peculiar function of Christian societies to deal, not so much with the things that surround and influence human life, as with the living persons themselves that constitute it; to see them in their individuality; to hold them in presence of sympathy which feels not only for them but with them; to find in them, by searching appeal, the higher capacities and lovelier features of that humanity which Christ sanctified for us all. The Church which abdicates this office or turns it into a pretence is in the eye of God a Church no more; and in abandoning its divinest function will soon discover that its own life is withering away. Some sincere and natural intercourse with the poor and suffering, some vivifying contact with struggles and sorrows not our own, is indispensable to the discipline of character as well as to the fulfilment of duty; and the frequent tendency to substitute, for the real compassions and executed labours of love, the fictitious griefs of the drama or the tale which genius fetches from scenes of misery to fling into the lap of ease, will be found, if it lead to no personal action, not a source of strength, but an enervating delusion. Not so, but by standing face to face with the injured natures and grievous lot we would redeem, by meeting them eye to eye and speaking to them in the vernacular language of the true heart, can we vindicate the communion of all orders and ages of men with one another and with God, as kindred branches of the great family of souls.

XXI.

Religion in Parable.

MATTHEW xiii. 34, 35.

"All these things spake Jesus unto the multitude in parables; and without a parable spake he not unto them; that it might be fulfilled which was spoken by the prophet, saying, 'I will open my mouth in parables; I will utter things hidden from the foundation of the world.'"

THE parable, then, is a mode of uttering "things hidden"; of bringing to the light the deep-buried secrets of the heart; and drawing forth into consciousness those divine and primitive truths which have been set from the beginning in the firmament of the soul, but, for want of an interpreter, have been taken for sparkles instead of suns. All the critics in the world, with their learned disquisitions on allegory and apologue and metaphor and simile, can never mend the prophet's idea of a parable,—so brief, so exact, so profound,—as a way of indicating realities hidden from the foundation of the world. The critics will tell you that the use of this mode of instruction in ancient times was a consequence of the oral teaching then prevalent; that printing being unknown, and writing uncommon, it was necessary to strike deep into the mind at once the lesson which vanished on the lips; that so, the prophets in the palace or the street, the seer in the desert, the man of God on the beach or the hill-side, borrowed hints from the scene around, and painted sacred things in visual and dramatic forms on the imagination of monarch or of multitude. But now that art has clipped the "winged words," and memory betakes itself to books, we are more elaborately and precisely taught by argument and precept; and human nature, emerging from its childhood, exchanges its love of fable and similitude for moral and religious philosophy. I rather suspect a different cause for the phenomenon in question; and doubt whether, even if Jesus of Nazareth were living among us now, amid all the advantages of cheap tracts and daily journals, he would teach us much otherwise than after the old fashion,—not with the dead page and laboured disquisition, but with the living voice, and the artless parable. For, I take it, different conceptions of the work to be achieved lie at the root of his method and of ours: ours assuming that religion is to be *put into* the mind; his, that it is to be *brought out* of it; ours aiming to teach the truth by intellectual judgment; his, to inspire it by moral sympathy; ours speaking with didactic baldness, as to the ignorant; his, with mystic hints and deep suggestions, as to a fraternity already taught of God, and needing but a new touch of holy light to re-awaken trust and wonder from their sleep. He who instructs by indirect and figurative methods, and, avoiding literal statements, delights in allusion and analogy, supposes one or both of two things; viz. that his subject is incapable of direct presentation; or, that his hearers possess its fundamental ideas, and require, not its form within their thought, but its spirit in their souls. Both these assumptions appear to me to pervade the whole ministry of Christ; to have opened his lips in parables, as the natural speech of religion; and to explain in part, why "never man spake like this man."

The essence of parable obviously consists in this; that its representations are typical and mediate, not literal and direct; special and picturesque not abstract and philosophic; moral in their unity and movement, not logical. Hence it will be found the fittest instrument in religion for the expression of Belief, of Worship, and of the sanctities of Conscience.

Religious belief is obliged to resort to the language of emblems, simply because its objects are all infinite in their nature, and respecting infinite things the *literal* truth is unattainable and incommunicable. God, heaven, responsibility, are beyond the measure of our experience; vast as the atmosphere to the bird or the forest to the child; regions whose circuit we cannot make, but which embrace us always, yet never shut us in. We were created in their midst; we dwell within them now; we can emerge from them no more. Our souls are subjects, and not lords within this realm,—permitted only to do its appointed service, and obey its nearest law. Not unless they transcend the confines of our experience can any objects of thought become religious. If we could discover the country of departed spirits,—hold daily converse with the sainted blest, and grow familiar with the everlasting hills, the reality of the better land would so far cease to be a religious truth, and be transferred from our faith to our geography. And when we ourselves have emigrated thither in death, be its experience what it may, it will become our earth; divine perhaps and holy, but, if so, only through a discernment equally possible here, of some invisible sanctity, some secret awe within its scenes; while this world, as it falls into the retrospect, will sink into the celestial hues; and we shall live between one heaven of reminiscence, and still perhaps another of hope. So again, if the work of life presented itself to us only as an external and mechanical task,—a routine of dry and calculative habit, there would be nothing devout in duty. It is the boundless depth of obligation,—the infinite beauty of holiness, the sigh for a sinless devotion of heart and will, that fling the conscience into penitence and prayer. And were it not that obligation enlarges with capacity, and the tension of the will must maintain an everlasting strife, and the ease of living well bids us begin to live better, there would be no permanent sacredness, no heavenly allegiance, in the moral ties that bind us. Nay, God himself is adorable in his perfections, in that they are unapproachable. Behind their visible splendour they pass into the deeps and hide themselves in mystery. From the outlines of daylight he seems to vanish away; and he made night on Sinai's top ere he could appear: and though on the mount of transfiguration it was a bright cloud by which he overshadowed his servants, yet cloud there was to veil his glory still. We are not indeed to suppose that there is any piety in mere ignorance, or anything but impiety in withholding attainable knowledge: but assuredly only *that* can permanently remain venerable to us which is above us,—which puts forth power, and life, and light upon us: and so wonderful is the universe that lies before the worshipper's thought, that the more he knows, the more seems the province left unknown, and every new world that he detects appears to deepen the abyss in which it floats. Religion, in truth, in all its forms, announces a series of realities surpassing experience and conception: all its terms, in every language, are so contrived as to denote this. At one time it describes divine things in *negatives*, venturing only to say what they are not, and confessing the inadequacy of our ideas; speaking of the *immensity* of God, that is, his transcending all our measures of thought; of the *immortality* of man, that is, his outliving all our limits of time; of the *immaculate* sanctity of Christ and the spirits of the just,—that is, their maintenance of an ideal perfection. At another time it has recourse to *superlatives*, and turns to God as the Best, the Greatest, the Most Holy. And it is clearly impossible that things transcendental and superlative can come before us in literal definition: they would then belie their own character, and become determinable by the formulas of experience. They can only express themselves symbolically; and how truly they then present themselves will depend on the vastness and grandeur of the emblem, and the wealth of the soul among whose thoughts and affections it runs with suggestive power. At best, our approximation is humbling enough. By the law of our mind, the natural perfections of God seem to elude our distinct conception. For we are obliged to assign to all objects a position in time and space: we cannot speak of the Divine existence without assigning to it a when and a where; yet are assured by reflection that this is an illusion of our own; that these relations belong only to our perception, not to Him whom we perceive; before whom duration and dimension are nought; and in whose Absolute Being dwell all things in a universal *Here*, and all events in the everlasting *Now*.

Nor is it in mere *magnitude of scale* that the immensity of God consists. We cannot coldly satisfy ourselves with the mere physical belief which diffuses his being among the stars, and perpetuates it through the courses of eternity. In this kind of sublimity there is nothing truly divine: the atheist's mechanic force, or dead dumb nothingness, might have the same; and it were heathenish thus to confound the gigantesque with the godlike. God is a Spirit: and, besides this boundlessness of dimension, is infinite also in moral intensity; not, if we may say so, in quantity merely, but in quality too. Wisdom, beauty, holiness, are immeasurable things, which are appreciable by pure perceptions, but which no rule can gauge, and no argument demonstrate. That the blush of morning is fair, that the quietude of grief is sacred, that the heroism of conscience is noble, —who will undertake to *prove* to one that does not see it? Nor can you say in terms of measurement *how* good and right it is to pity the wretched, and maintain fidelity and truth. In everything which we profoundly revere and love, there appears a certain infinitude which fills us with untiring wonder and draws us into perpetual aspiration. What unfathomable depth of sanctity and sorrow in the features of a Madonna! What exhaustless sublimity streams upon the eye that gazes devoutly on the crucifix! What fields of unspeakable freshness and purity lie open in the full eyes of a thoughtful and loving child! and these things reside not in the mere material form or colour, or size, or in anything that knowledge can estimate or words define; but in a spirit gleaming with mysterious expressiveness through them all. It is in no mere hyperbolic sense that we speak of the infinitude of the moral perfections of God. And to feel this is to feel that there is a profundity entirely beyond our present view; that the thoughts of him we now possess are significant of more than we can reach; that to set before us whatever is most perfect is, for the time being, to approach him nearest; and that still our musings are always in parable; a symbolic presentation, perhaps logically false, yet most divinely true. Religion is the manifestation of the heart's indestructible faith in perfection; and so it must ever dwell at the summit; and that which ceases to be *our highest* belongs no more to our religion, and yields to the conception that transcends it. In no slight sense, therefore, the superior truth of a religion consists in its greater majesty and loveliness; and he who best awakens the sleeping perceptions of the conscience and the heart and penetrates their actual life with a quickening ideal, reveals the most of God and heaven. And what has ever wrought so effectually for this end, as the tales of inimitable beauty, by which Jesus melted the soul of nations and of ages?

Worship too, as well as belief, naturally frames itself into parable. It instinctively avoids the vain and harsh attempt at literal speech; and abandons to a petty rationalism that critical precision which, in dread of the forms of error, wanders altogether from the spirit of truth. At best, when we try to speak to God, religion sinks with the utterance, and seems to become poor: the pure celestial thoughts, the deep and solemn wants, the sad and lowly confession, seem to come with intolerable friction from our rough human voice; and the inner skies of meditation, so vast and clear in silence, becloud themselves in speech. When Jesus loosened the imprisoned tongue, the noisy praises of the healed man were less expressive than the dumb looks with which before he had gazed up on the face of Jesus. Language hides too little and defines too much, to bring forth truly the things of God within us: so that spoken religion is apt to pass into theology; and those who have it most upon their lips are very apt to have it least within their hearts. Its constant external exposure to the petty commerce of words destroys its vastness and ideality within. Hence it is not surprising that the shallowest religion has been usually the most voluble, and the deepest has maintained the greatest frugality of speech; has resorted rather to the worship of signs and emblems, beneath whose vagueness the sanctities of faith find quiet shelter. The stately minster, whose vault overarches the dead, and whispers the sighs and plaints of the living; the picture of sacred story, giving to the present the silent beauty of the past without its familiarity; the gestures of holy men bending low in prayer; the organ's chant, contradicting no man's thought, and praying for all hearts with a sweet and mighty voice; these have been spontaneous creations from the soul of Christendom, heaving with the inspiration of God, and labouring to speak, without spoiling a love so holy. These symbols have the breadth needful for the affections, and cover far more than any words. They commit no one to thoughts that may not be true to him; they speak, not to him from others, but from himself to God, taking up his own emotions more faithfully than he could tell them. They awaken within him his own highest, without taking it out of his hands, and shaping it precisely for him. It is the same with all the deep affections of our nature. Who can dare to speak to sorrow bowed to the earth, or to penitence in its inconsolable shame? The lips seem to insult the heart; and, after vain attempts, we give up to silence, and are content to grasp the hand or kiss away the tears. Of death too we feel that we cannot fitly speak; and the flowers upon the grave, or the sculptured emblem in the church significantly hint at cherished memories and griefs sharply graven on the soul; or if words are used, we love to take the consecrated phrase of Scripture, or at least the unsoiled and hidden beauty of an ancient tongue. All which may show us clearly, that there is no *prose religion;* that it demands an ideal beauty as its native and rightful dress; and cannot purely worship except in emblem and in parable.

Nor can even our *Moral Life* dispense with reflected images and similitudes. In its first and unspoiled simplicity indeed, the intuition of conscience is direct and true, and in the competitions of impulse never mistakes the better for the worse; nor does it need, ere it can rightly judge them, to see them thrown into an external picture, or dramatised upon a foreign stage. We cannot meet, standing face to face in our own mind, compassion and anger, or the prompting to truth and the gain of a lie, without knowing their relative claims upon our will. And so long as this insight is healthily followed, and character unfolds itself with unstained purity, this immediate discernment of the right will continue unimpaired, and grow in clearness and in range. Nay, it is not even lost by the first sin; for what is the remorse that follows it but the straight and true vision still, only of the shadowed instead of the illumined side of the reality,—the sorrowful eclipse of the same glorious and hopeful light? But just here is the crisis; it is the last chance of the simple unperverted vision. Will you throw yourself open to all your compunction, and go back with it at once, though with bare feet and over thorny ways, to the station you have left? Then shall you retain your direct perception of the good, only with enfeebled power to act on it. But if, as must be feared, you haste away from your sorrow and smother the keen shame, you will shift from the moral to the sentient and selfish point of view, and, bribing your better feeling into silence, will dress up your case in such false lights as to deceive yourself.

And thus it is that by unfaithfulness we are delivered over to self-justification, and forfeit the native capacity for looking eye to eye at the presence and proportions of our duty. The clear discriminative apprehension once surrendered, we are at the mercy of the accidents of emotion; till, swaying to and fro as the waves may swing, we lose our count, and measure our. course no more, but drift upon the current, we know not whither.

When the moral order has thus fallen to pieces in the mind, the ruins choke the avenues of direct entrance to the conscience, and self-deception resents the very approach of remonstrance. Who does not know the blinding power of pride? who will undertake, by mere onset of rebuke, to carry the entrenchments of egotism? It is rare indeed that others' righteous indignation draws the tears of penitence from the wrong-doer; so quick is the demon of self-excuse to leap in between and freeze them at their fount. But, while it is the curse of sin that it spreads a film on the eye turned inwards, and works in the darkness it has made, it leaves the outward gaze of moral discernment for a longer time undimmed: so that fallen men can still be critics of the upright, and the conscience, blind to its own wreck, can mark even a slight deflection in another. Shall we be angry at this, and forbid the worse to pronounce judgment on the better? See rather to what happy use you may turn this feature, if only you have the ingenuity of love and the clearness of the prophet's insight. You can avail yourself of the offender's remaining perception to make him judge himself. Instead of dwelling on his own individual case, and so touching the springs of vanity and resentment, you can withdraw him from the personal point of view, and let its confusing disquietudes sleep. You have but to set up before him the portrait of another personality, into which you weave the colours and adjust the relations of his character; and in that mirror he sees the deformities he had not felt, and abhors himself at secondhand. The child who yields to a burst of anger or a seduction of selfishness without a twinge of reproach will be rivetted by the tale from which the same passions look at him from another's eyes: his cheek will flush, his sobs will quicken, with the thrill of a true moral sympathy; and when at last it breaks upon him, as the terrible resemblance deepens, that for that picture he might himself have sat, the inward wave of retributive justice is beaten back upon his own conscience and floods it with repentance. Every wise parent is led by the tact of love to discover the power of such dramatic presentations of life, and acquire the skill to place them on the stage of the child's fancy. And when, in Jerusalem, the poet-king, wrapt in a cloud of passion, added crime to crime without a touch of shame,—treachery to license and murder to both,—the prophet, with ready insight into that rich ideal nature, drew the picture of the poor man's ewe-lamb that grew up with his children and drank of his cup, only to be slain for the rich man's table; and by the tension of indignant pity shivered the crust of guilty illusion, and flashed conviction home upon the conscience with the words "Thou art the man!" Thus may the parables of the moral life beguile us out of our darkness, and force us once more to be impartial witnesses of our own character. They fix in a secondary image what we had let slip in immediate feeling. They plant us clear of the fierce crossing rays of the momentary position, and serve as optical purifiers to ward off all except the light we need; and show us again, at visual distance, some of the "things hidden" from us by their very closeness to ourselves. Their function is thus like that of experience itself; which is never a present, but always a posthumous teacher; and delivers its lesson by changing the position which misleads us, and in parting us from the past reveals it more distinctly to the view.

XXII.

Neither Man nor Woman in Christ Jesus.

Luke xx. 35, 36.

"They who shall be accounted worthy to obtain that world and the resurrection of the dead, neither marry nor are given in marriage; neither can they die any more; for they are equal to the angels; and are the children of God, being the children of the resurrection."

In the representations of Christ by the great masters of sacred art, it is seldom that you complain of any preponderance of manly strength. The fault is rather of the opposite kind; an excess of feminine gentleness and grace; a fineness of feature and clearness of brow and soft-flowing hair, that give too much to beauty, and leave not enough for force. It is far from being true, indeed, that this prevailing character carries with it of necessity the impression of *weakness*. It is redeemed however from this danger by the infusion not of *manlike* but of *godlike* elements; intellectual majesty, heavenly serenity, spiritual depth. Even in the portraiture of his sufferings,—the Ecce Homo,—the garden, and the cross,—it is usual to find an intense passive susceptibility, immediately combined with a divine repose; without any intervention of wrestling energy and personal power. It is as if a kind of slight was put upon the special attributes of men,—the moral solidity, the resolute will, the strenuous fidelity to trust, which are the noblest of their more distinctive marks;—as if these, however justly held in honour in human society as the main reliance of the world, were incapable of being worked up into the type of sublimest life.

Nor can we fail to trace the same peculiarity of Christian ideal in the legends of his birth and the doctrine of his double nature. Whatever was human in him was his heritage from Mary; and could be nothing but the pure, the gracious, the tender and trustful, the suffering and patient. And the higher attributes that mingled an ineffable dignity with these and turned them from weaknesses into powers, belonged to his celestial nature, and proclaimed him Son of God. What is this but to say that in him the love and pity of the woman's heart were straightway blended with the thought and holiness of God; passing by and omitting the more voluntary energies and self-asserting personality of men? The Christendom which invented these legends must evidently have been wearied with a world of violence, passion, and selfishness,—of masculine ambitions and grasping resolve; must have sighed for some form of strength which might consist with reverence and affection; and have felt that only He who, while consciously at one with the Highest, was touched also by sympathy with the frail, could escape the self-idolatry of an age that had hardened itself against both. In a world trodden down by Roman legions, and ruled by competition of corruption, a world where all the force seemed Satanic and the refinement enervating and impure, it is intelligible that refreshment should be found in an image of humanity carrying divine insight and resource into the domestic retreats of sorrow and affection.

The picture which has thus set itself in the Christian imagination, though owing some of its lineaments to after-touches of grateful thought, is legitimate and historical in its outline. Even Paul, who otherwise knows nothing of the personal portraiture of his Lord, appeals to the disciples "by the meekness and gentleness of Christ"; and though the gospels are not without examples of authoritative energy and terrible invective, still it is not these that we feel to be half so characteristic as the blessing on the child, the call to the weary, the look upon the guilty, the lesson of the field-flower, and the forgiveness on the cross. When he corrects the morals of his time, it is to render them passionless and self-denying; when he ascends to the springs of its devotion, it is to make them overflow with more copious love and clearer trust; when he opens the contents of human hope, and lets us see his image of final and perfect life, it is a vision of natures pure as the angels, and not called to die any more. Himself the Lamb of God, meekly led away to sacrifice, he has so endeared and consecrated the forms of affectionate and self-forgetful goodness, that the old Pagan and even Hebrew notions of God's character have become uncongenial to a Christian mood: we feel it cold and hard to speak exclusively of "*virtue*,"—(the right life of *manhood*),—of justice, of rectitude,—and require to ascend into the higher and warmer conceptions of sanctity and holy peace,—of faith, and hope, and charity.

This gentle, feminine type of religious character owes nothing to the Jewish parentage of the gospel; and it is in proportion as you take your impression from John and Paul rather than from the Judaic records of Matthew and Mark, that the ideal disengages itself into clearness. It is the general tendency of strict monotheistic religions to bring out the force, but overpower the finer susceptibilities of our nature; to make zealots of firm will, to bind hosts together by a conquering purpose, to form brotherhoods of intimate fidelity, rather than to melt the soul with comprehensive pity, or inspire a tender reverence for even the weak and wandering. The monarchy of God in heaven repeats or realizes itself in a theocracy on earth: he *commands* rather than *inspires*, or inspires chiefly to command: his prophets are always *men*, and their message is *political:* nature and mankind are his fabric and his instrument, detached from his being, but subject to his sovereignty, and constrained to do his will. The relation of man to God is one of obedience more than of communion: its sentiment is founded, not on their nearness and kindred, but on their distance and contrast: far as the heaven is from the earth, incapable of blending as the East is with the West, are the thoughts of the human spirit in respect of the Divine. The Hebrew imagination is ever on the strain to put an infinite space between the majesty of the Creator and the subjection of the creatures; to magnify him and humble them; to seat his presence above the circle of the sky and spread the inhabitants of the earth "as grasshoppers" beneath him. Nor is this conception of *natural distance* contradicted or removed by the closer and tenderer images with which prophets sweeten and diversify their song. They all imply, not inward congeniality, but outward protection; the father of the son, the mother of the nurseling, the husbandman of his favourite vine; and all are founded on the feeling of *interval between* two natures, not of resemblance; affinity itself being used to express not so much the identity of *kind* as the affection of *individuals.* Quite in harmony with this consciousness of natural distance, is the belief that God's communications with our race are always through some *mediation,* of angel or prophet, empowered to bridge the chasm, and open a way into nature from the realm beyond. The Arab learns of Mahomet, and Mahomet of Gabriel, and Gabriel alone of Allah. The Catholic listens to the priest; the priest to the apostles; the apostles to Christ; and Christ himself to Moses and Elijah, who come to him from the Lord and world of life. Special *interposition* implies ordinary *separation;* and only in the absence of *immediate* communion can *mediate* messages find room to pass to and fro.

This Judaic conception, of perfect distinction between God and man, as of two individuals existing quite apart, unless by exceptional provision for meeting, is favourable to strong moral conviction and masculine resolve. It is of the very essence of the sentiment of *duty*, to feel that we are charged with a *trust* from God; and a trust can be devolved upon us only from one who is *outside* of us, and knows that we have an isolated power of our own. He gives the law, for us to execute: he is there, and we are here: he leaves us a field whose tillage or whose barrenness is ours; and conscience, in every utterance of self-reproach, confesses the power of self-command. This consciousness, that he is *lord* of something, inspires a man with self-asserting energy; quickens his sense of obligation; and makes him aware, as he casts his eye over that which is committed to his charge, that he has much to answer for in the good or evil administration of this world. His sphere of *duty* is his sphere of *power:* in ruling it, he holds a kingly attitude towards all that it contains; and whether it be a household,—a business,—a tenantry,—or an empire, that is given him to keep in order, it lies beneath him, subject to his will, trusting to his fidelity, appealing to his affection. The delegate of a law above him, he has to give and be a law to those beneath him; rendering it flexible to their nature and capacity, yet ever true to the measure of eternal right. This is always the peculiarity of the purely *moral* view of life: man, deputed for his separate work, it sets apart from God, and each man, as bearing his own burden, from every other. It produces the sense of inalienable, lonely responsibilities, giving infinite importance to every soul that carries them. It sees around it a universe of detached persons, to no two of whom is just the same shade of sentiment and action due. It is founded on the *differences* of beings and of things, and directs a discriminating regard to each according to its nature and character. The conscientious, turning the eye within, feel distinctions and scruples which others slur; and, directing the gaze without, perceive moral lights and shadows hid from less fastidious vision. It is ever their tendency to remain at a critical distance, just and self-possessed; severe to themselves and not tender to the world. Or, if God has given them, not only the pure conscience, but also the gentle heart, they will perhaps have pity to spare for sin as well as sorrow; provided however it be sin deep and dark enough to look like misery, and baffle all estimate: for an ethical benevolence will often spread a profuse compassion on the lowest wickedness, while habitually censorious to the slight faults of neighbours, or, it may be, to the mere divergent tastes of a younger generation.

That this temper of mind and mode of regarding life is rather Stoical than specifically Christian, and more properly Jewish than either, must be felt by every one whose gospel is defined by John or Paul. It gives us simply human morality, with a divine sanction:—a noble gift, truly; but still securing only half our life, its manly vigour, its self-regulation, its clear justice and fidelity; and leaving as yet untraced the other half, its feminine dependence, its tact of love, its flush of enthusiasm, and whatever is characteristic of Him who opened his lessons with the beatitudes and closed them with the legacy of peace. To fall into any harmony with these, the soul must assume quite another attitude, and enter into quite another thought of God;—an attitude, not of lordship over the duties beneath, but of captivity to the divine solicitations above;—a thought of God, not as sending instructions through an outer medium, or from afar in time or place, but as our immediate living Light, as the holy Spirit of our spirits, the everlasting ground of grace and beauty and love. In contrast with the *moral* impulse of the mind which looks at the *differences* of things, is the *devout* which seeks their *unity;* which ascends beyond all diffracted or intercepted rays to the primal light that flings them ; and, instead of remaining outside spectator of other beings, delights to lose itself in the embrace of the All in All, and become the organ of the Eternal Will. We sigh for a conscious *union with God,* which is far from being implied in mere *obedience* to him ; nay, which is excluded till obedience gives place to a freer and less reluctant harmony with him. To know that we belong to another, and that other, God; to hear him ever claiming us in low, near whispers, dissolved through every silence and still shooting on us amid the voices of men; to see him gleaming on us, not only in the exposed places of solitude, but through the thick foliage of events, like the horizontal sun, flooding the open desert with crimson, or piercing the forest with a patterned glory ; to read a meaning that is his in every aspect of life and nature, and go forth to meet it when it is hopeful and reconciled, or droop our eyes before it, if it be sad with a shade of pity; to feel our whole being dipped in his spirit and imbued with the sacred tincture ever more :—this is the surrender to him that makes the life of holy communion,—that completes and balances the soul on its diviner side, and that gave that feminine depth and gentleness to Christ. Without this mood of contemplative oneness with God,—this genial melting of our life in his, there may be in us no want of masculine sense and energy, of clear truth and honour, of faithful constancy under temptation; but there will also be a Jewish hardness and narrowness of mind, a dry unmellowed temper, an egotistic and critical irreverence for all that will not submit to our survey. If aspiration is not to die out from our religion,—if affection and self-oblivion are not to fly away and leave it empty of all diviner habitant,—if the love of God, as a passion and a power, is not to be insultingly dismissed among the romances of the past, we must open a more hospitable heart to the gospel of the Spirit, and more deeply enter into the life of the living God. It is a significant fact, that in all religious systems which, instead of representing God chiefly as *moral Lawgiver*, are fond of dwelling on him as the *Holy Spirit*, there the prophets are, or at least may be, *women*. So was it among the Phrygian Christians of old, who developed the doctrine of the Paraclete. So has it ever been among the Society of Friends, who keep silence till the Spirit speaks. So is it when the Catholic estatica attests the supernatural grace that still penetrates and consecrates the organism of the visible Church. If the fact shows, on the one hand, the dangers of a faith overbalanced on this opposite side, it shows, on the other, that the view of God most cherished by a tender piety, and most cherishing it again, is the mystic rather than the moral,—that which envelopes us in communion, rather than sends us out on errands of obedience,—which takes up our personality into a higher sphere instead of detaching it for separate work in a lower. Morality defines downward the duty of each; lives in the midst of human and natural details; attaches itself to the particular persons and concrete businesses of life. Devotion opens its arms upwards to the Source of all; merges itself in the divine and supernatural Infinity; sighs after the universal spirit of all reality and ground of all appearance and secret tincture of all good and beauty. For neither the masculine concentration of the one, nor the feminine diffusion of the other, is our nature exclusively designed; to neither can it be given up without one-sidedness and perilous excess. If they are rarely harmonised, it is not for want of a visible ideal or of a fitting capacity. In Christ, at once the Son of Man and Son of God, they were blended without discord or interference,—the majesty and the meekness,—the force for this world, the tender mingling with another,—the percussion upon human evil and the melting into divine communion. And in the higher mind of us all the possibility exists of similarly blending all the seeming opposites that make up the equilibrium of goodness, and drawing into one nature the fair and happy contrasts that begin with distribution, only that mutual fascination may help them to union. What but our own low ideal is to hinder the moulding of our defective and broken humanity into more Christ-like completeness? Shall we never rise to an inflexible moral enthusiasm, untainted by personal passion; to an indignation at wrong, kindled only by reverence for the right, and made persuasive by sympathy with the wronged; to a transparent simplicity unspoiled by the deepest insight and the largest intellectual view; to the fusion of quick affections with unconquerable will; to a passion for beauty so loving as to labour in the midst of deformity; to such inward union with the Highest as shall brace the soul to undismayed compassion for the lowest? Are the graces of character never to have any vigour, or its vigour any grace? Are the heroes to be for ever rude, and the saints for ever sickly? Not unless the cross is to be forgotten, and its very shadow to vanish from the earth. So long as it stands visible and fixes any venerating look, no poor fragment of spiritual good can ever content the conscience: without aspiring to the whole, we fall at once from the disciple's place; and when our all is done, we must still feel ourselves a great way off. To have neither restlessness nor apathy, but pass freely between energy and repose, at the call to act or the need to suffer; to bind the wounds without indulgence to the sins of men; to have no tears but those of pity,—to utter no reproach but as the true interpreter of conscience,—to send forth no cry that does not soften into prayer; to mingle with the beauty of the world, yet find it but the symbol of a more transcendent glory;—only brings us somewhat nearer to that marvellous life in which the contradictions of thought and the conflicts of feeling formed the very harmony of a nature lifted into perfect peace. His own picture of the kingdom of heaven is the unconscious reflection of himself;—the finished and all-blending sphere, where the differences are not indeed lost, but separated no more, between the woman and the man, the elder and the child; and all are as the angels of God, that serve him with the wholeness of a balanced nature. So conceived, that kingdom is neither distant nor future; in its germ and possibility, it is already within us. And when, in realizing it, we have "risen from the death of sin to the life of righteousness," we shall have passed, through that resurrection, into the singleness of spirit which belongs to the "children of God that cannot die any more."

XXIII.

The Powers of Love.

GAL. v. 22.

"The fruit of the Spirit is love, joy, peace."

IF these be the fruit of the Spirit, they cannot be mere matters of temperament. They have a higher origin than a physical frame happily moulded, or even a will dutifully disposed. There is something in them of more heavenly fire; lighting up our human nature, but not entirely kindled there; leaving with us the blessing, but rendering back to God the praise. When philosophy gives an account of the human soul, it can find only *constitutional propensities* and *voluntary acquisitions*. When we interrogate Christianity, we are told, besides, of *communicated sanctities;* states of mind which inheritance cannot give, or resolution command; which need some touch of God to wake them up; which are above us, and yet ours; which do our work, and yet are better than our will; and seem to lie on the border-land of communion between the finite and the Infinite spirit. That this language, which has approved itself to the deepest and devoutest men in Christendom, should be all a senseless mysticism, is an opinion which modest thought will be reluctant to maintain. There is something strange and unintelligible in the anxiety of a pretended rationalism to get rid of the inspiring God, to make sure that our nature will be quite let alone, to environ it with an impassable ring-fence, and plant sentry-boxes of argument all round, to exclude the possible encroachments of anything Divine. If the apostolic language expressed no other truth, it would at least describe, with simplicity and faithfulness, the complete transformation which religion effects in the original instincts and feelings; how, by conquering, it glorifies them; and turns them from animal impulses into moral and spiritual powers. To a mind uplifted in divine conversion, and, through past toil and patience, dwelling in a light above the storms of sin and sorrow, a new being seems to have arisen; a thick dream to have broken away; a drowsy pressure to have flown from the head, a sultry leaden cloud to have been swept from off the freshened heart. Its old affections, though called by the same names, appear but counterfeits of those which are ascendant now; poor masks, serving for the mimicry, but mocking the reality, of life. How indeed is it possible to disguise from ourselves the pretences of which, till the spirit wakes to the inner truth of things, we are half-willing dupes? how much society there is without communion, and laughter without gladness, and quiet without escape from care! The acts and habits which should flow from the affections of the soul, spring often only from its misery. The good fellowship that seems so cordial, warming the lips and brightening the eye,—how often is it a flight from self rather than a quest of others, the opiate of conscience rather than the wine of Love! The mirth that rings with so genial a sound, and seems to flash from heart to heart, is it all like the true glee of childhood? or can you not discern a false and eager heat, as though something were thrust down that the gladness may leap up? And the composure and self-possession of men, is it not sometimes a mere negative tranquillity,—the calm of them that sleep?—and at others, a triumph of intellect smoothing the troubled fancy, and of will refusing to betray?—in neither case, the serenity of inward affection and living content? The retreat from secret thought, the restlessness of wasted power, the suspicions of injured nature, the aching of unsatisfied capacity, are always at work with silent free-masonry among men; hurrying them about to clasp hands with one another in conspiracy against themselves; and leading them to mimic the look of things that would appear, were they a world of faithful souls. The disguise is transparent to the eye of purity;

which looks on the drama as on children acting the wedding and the funeral in the nursery; occupied with the scenery and the pageantry, heedless of the meaning and the pathos.

Even the genuine instincts and healthy sentiments of men, freed from all corruption of pretence, undergo a complete and noble change, when living in the atmosphere of a religious soul; and always fail of some portion of their grace and power, till breathed upon by this, their natural air. We are glad enough indeed, in a world like ours, to welcome a loving heart on almost any terms. When the sickness is at its height, we do not ask the physician for his diploma; when the bleeding lie so thick upon the field, we must accept any nurse that will bind their wounds; and of him that lifts the faint we demand not whether he be a Samaritan. It were ungracious to complain of such charity as can be found to soothe the grievances, and shame the selfishness, of life. Only, the gentle mind is ever open and docile too; they that love well are thankful to love better; and in precise proportion as the spirit of affection is elevated, is its work more surely achieved, and its experience more truly peaceful.

There is a *humane* love, which constitutes the humblest and most frequent form of unselfish feeling. It finds its objects among the miserable, and attaches itself to them in proportion to their woes. In human pity there is a strange combination of repulsion and attraction, which it is the paradox of philosophy to state, and the mercy of God to ordain: it cannot endure the sight of wretchedness, and yet can never leave it. To no ear are the cries of anguish so piercing; yet it hovers within the circle where they wander, and flies to the centre whence they come. To no eye does manhood struck down in its strength and wasting on its bed, or the child decrepid with hunger and neglect, or the wife deserted and broken beneath the burden of life, present a sight so sad; but it is fascinated to the spot, and lives amid the haunts it dreads. To stop that ear, to shut that eye, would seem to give an easy promise of relief; nor is there anything to hinder except that they would cease to be the organs of humanity, and would be degraded into the instruments of selfishness: and so, it is no more possible to get them closed, than to persuade the sobbing child to put aside the story that draws forth its tears. It is needless to say what we owe to the soul of compassion; of how many infant ills it has rocked the cradle till they fell into the sweet sleep of recovery; of how many a cruel passion it has stayed the uplifted arm; what old and giant oppressions it has challenged to the lists, and laid low with the sling and stone of its youthful indignation. It is indeed an emotion, to be incapable of which were to be less than human. It is the great power which lifts the heavy mass of mankind above the gross interests, the unworthy sloth, the heartless indifference, towards which they are else continually sinking. And just when the low temper of society and greedy negligence of men have brought us to believe in self-love alone, some sudden outbreak of this passion breaks through the crust of our philosophy, and proclaims the hidden fires of our nature that fuse the cement and shatter the structures of our selfishness. Pity certainly fulfils one of the conditions of all the noblest love: it is not a lonely and unproductive feeling: it cannot pass (except through imaginative abuse) into an empty luxury. It looks a brother in the face: it puts a consolation into his heart: it fans into a flame the embers of dying hope; and thus, it awakens a grateful return. In place of an affliction that looked up, and a sorrow that looked down, there is a reciprocal sympathy standing eye to eye with a mild and manly brotherhood. But, with all this, there is work ordained for us which this impulse will not suffice to do. Fastening itself on suffering alone, it sees nothing else. It looks on man exclusively as a being capable of pleasure and pain; and until it perceives the trace of pain, till it is roused by the sigh from behind it, or moved by wringing hands before it, it remains at rest as if all were well. Yet suffering is not the only or the greatest ill: beneath the smooth and glossy surface of easy life there may hide itself many an inward disease which the mere glance of pity does not discern. Flourishing iniquity that gives no seeming pain it lets alone: invisible corruption may spread without arrest. Even suffering is commiserated by quantity rather than by quality, being estimated by the scale of the sentient nature, more than by that of the rational spirit; and a blind instinctive treatment is administered, destructive of the higher discipline,—like that of the ignorant nurse, who, at any price of indulgence, hushes the cries of the wayward child. Any way, the character of animal impulse clings too much to this feeling, to allow of its satisfying the demands of a good heart.

In minds of a higher culture,—at the present day in the minds of an immense class,—there is a very different order of affection, for which great claims have been advanced, as though it might assume the empire of the soul, and wield the very sceptre of religion. I refer to *imaginative or æsthetic* love, which attaches itself to objects in proportion as they are beautiful, kindles the enthusiasm of Art, and completes itself in the worship of genius. Let us not be provoked by the exaggerations of others to think slightingly of a power which is of a very high order in the combinations of our world, and owes its sickliness only to its isolation. Our life would be but a poor affair without it,—a miserable succession of present instants, with no landscape sleeping in the past, no perspective enshadowed in the future; with light to cut our corn, and fell our timber, and steer our ship, but not to play upon the waving fields, and paint the forest stems, and glance upon the sea; with an intelligible task before us, and worthy neighbours near us, but no solemn expressiveness in the one, no feature of inspiring heroism in the other; with a kindliness at heart, that would not stand still and see a creature die, but with no eye to see further than the suffering flesh, or ear to catch more than the uttered words; so that the plaint of deepest pathos is reduced to prose, dumb sorrows are uninterpreted, and the light hand of a graceful love is but a dull prehensile limb. In this affection there is a feature, not found in our compassion, but never absent from the noblest love. It makes us *like* and more like the object that engages it. The rays it sheds upon us touch our features with transformation, till the countenance of the soul glows like that of the prophet who has been with God. This assimilating power cannot remain involuntary in a self-conscious being like man: it is not a blind tendency, but a confessed desire, an intentional effort, wherever realization is possible. No one can admire without wishing to resemble, and tracing in his spirit the lineaments that transfigure him "into the same image, from glory to glory." Hence, to this feeling for what is beautiful we owe the temper of aspiration, the pressure towards a perfection that, with our ascending nature, ever rises and recedes. What more, you will say, do we want than this? the tact of love below, and the urgency of desire above, seem to complete the graces possible to our limited souls. Yet is this affection very barren, until thrown into the midst of others, to harmonise and glorify them: by itself it is but as the spread of colour without design, which may turn the canvas into atmosphere, but represents only the airy conditions of a scene that might be or that is to be. No reciprocal sympathy is requisite to this sentiment: that which is admired as beautiful, does not admire in return. And, above all, there is a direct tendency to turn with indifference or even merciless repugnance from what is unlovely in human life; to stipulate for interesting objects of compassion; and to shrink from the harsh tasks, the mean cares, the repulsive sights, the obscure dangers, which patient goodness encounters without a word. The early Christians were very sensible of this, and left a curious proof how profoundly they distrusted a feeling which has since attained unrivalled energy in Christendom. They interpreted with literal severity the words which they accepted as prophetic of their Lord: "He hath no form nor comeliness; and when we shall see him, there is no beauty that we should desire him;" and they consistently made the first images of Christ objects frightful to behold. Whence an enthusiasm so strange and barbarous? It was a violent reaction from the Pagan worship of beauty, which had ennobled Art, and corrupted nature; extracted wonders from the quarries of Pentelicus, and horrors from the populace of Rome and Corinth; perfected the marbles of the temple, and degraded the humanity of the worshipper. Heathenism had brought into monstrous combination physical beauty and moral deformity: the Christians retaliated by reconciling moral beauty with physical deformity. But the union was not permanently possible to the human heart. For, that ugly Christ of the early disciples was also most sacred and beloved; the hiding-place of a divine grace, the covered centre of whole galaxies of holy light; and *that* was a secret which human nature could not for ever keep: some gleam would fain shine through to rebuke the scoffing eye of the profane: the features must now and then be touched with a holy radiance: the divinity, enclosed in so inadequate a cell, would conquer the feeble humanity at last, and by the perseverance of inward sublimity, change it into visible and undisputed glory. And thus, as in nature, so in faith, love becomes the source of beauty; and so refines the forms and deepens the expressiveness of things, that matter grows transparent, and earth is but the transitory film veiling an eternal heaven.

There is however a higher mood of affection than this idealizing thought. We are conscious of a *moral* love, which has reference to persons only, not to things; which attaches itself to them, in proportion as they are *good;* judges them by the standard of an internal Law; and expresses itself in tones, not of tenderness as in pity, or of admiration as in the trance of beauty, but of grave and earnest *approval.* This it is that first sweeps with a healthful and invigorating breath through every other sympathy, turning it from a consuming excitement into a productive faculty. But for this, life would be only piteous as an infirmary, or fair as a gallery of art; not a theatre of strenuous action, where conflict gives birth to noblest deeds, and to many a sorrow too glorious for compassion. This it is that makes the world a drama of deep and often breathless interest; that forces us to take sides in every struggle and stretch forward with looks of suspense and prayers for victory, as the hosts sway to and fro in the thick fight; that draws out our favourites and heroes in history, and makes of them a perspective of great spirits through the past. But for this, the martyr would be only a man burnt; and the confessor on the rack of inquisition but as the patient on the surgeon's table. This puts a mighty courage into the woman and the child, and turns the gentlest nature into heart of oak; and even fills us with a tempestuous glory at the sufferings of the good. Inspired by this, we can stand by and see the prophets sawn asunder; can cheer on the apostles hunted from city to city; can feel, as we watch the Christian maidens waiting for the tiger's spring, the defiance of a dreadful joy; can cling to the robe of Stephen and say, 'Hold on, Brave heart,' while they shout 'Stone him to death,' and lay bare our head, "that we also may die with him." The moral affection unites the separated excellencies of the others; at once creating reciprocal sympathy, and exercising the strongest assimilating power. To be approved by our brother is to hear the trembling hope of conscience confirmed, to know that there is another nature like our own, to feel that our vows and prayers are lonely no more; and we are conscious of that mutual intelligence, which is at once the secret and the solace of affection. And to approve a being as good is to acknowledge a claim to become like him: and the claim implies desire; and the desire pushes itself into tendency. I know not indeed a more serious thing than the responsibility thus incurred by all human affection. Only think of this: whoever loves you is growing like you! neither you nor he can hinder it, unless at the cost of alienation. Is the resemblance worth creating? should you be pleased to see in your own friend another self? would he appear to you with an added light of excellence, or with a duller shade as of disappointment and saddened hope? O, if you are not a desolate being in this world, if you are grateful for but one creature's love, if a child's trust or a parent's shelter, a sister's pride or a brother's manly joy, rests upon you, rise to the height of so pure a blessing: reverence the sanctity of those dear souls: drag them not down by the very embrace with which they cling to you; but, in requital of their faithful cares, strive, if it be possible, to lift them to a mood they will rejoice to reach, and through their gentleness secure their consecration.

Even this moral love, however, is not without imperfections, leaving something still to be supplied. Its characteristic sentiment of Approbation has always in it a certain *patronizing* air, not welcome to the mercy of a true heart, and more like the rigour of a Zeno, than the grace of Christ. True it is that the eye of conscience penetrates readily to inconspicuous excellence, and lifts the poor out of the dust, if he be but a struggling saint. But, should he be a lost sinner, it puts him, with severe justice, by the side of rich and gaudy wickedness, as a creature joined to idols, that must be let alone. Nor can it admire anything but efforts of the will, the battle of resolution with temptation, the strife after a harmony of spirit yet unattained. Transplant it to a scene where that harmony is already won, where evil shows off its attraction all in vain, where angel-minds find nothing to resist, but love and do with one accord whatever is fair and holy and sing at their work the glad strains of emancipated natures, and this feeling finds itself in a strange land, where its plaudits would be a coarse intrusion, and die away upon the sainted air. Nor in any of the forms of love which we have named, is there adequate provision for suppressing the discords, and quieting the troubled passions, of mankind. Pity grieves over the suffering they give; but, not going to their heart, can only hush them up, and charm the delirium to tempcrary sleep. Imagination dislikes the jar, and evades it by escape into its dreams. Conscience disapproves, and scolds the uneasiness into sullen silence, but cannot exorcise the demons of the heart. This is a kind of human ill that goeth not out except by the voice of prayer and in recompense of faith. Not till we call down the Spirit of God himself, can we find the consummate fruit of love, and joy, and peace. There is an affection higher than we have named;—a *Divine Love*, directed first upon God himself, and thence drawn into the likeness of his own love, and going forth upon other natures, in proportion to their worth and claims. This is the crowning and calming term of all prior affections; presupposing them, and lifting them up from clashing and unrest to harmony and peace. Who can show us any grace or power which it does not include? One who lives in converse with Infinite Perfection can neither be without the sympathies that ennoble minds on a lower level, nor surrender itself to any as tyrant over the rest. The springs of his tenderness and strength are ready to be touched by whatever has native claims upon a human heart,—by suffering, by beauty, by goodness; nay,—*so* ready, that the fitting love will not be driven back though the suffering be ugly, and the beauty wicked, and the goodness narrow and unattractive. He is not insensible to the shadows of imperfection, but is carried with intenser feeling to the lights of character; for they alone are the soul's realities, and there it is that the promise lies; and as they brighten and spread, the shadows will flee away. This faith, which naturally flows into him from contact with the All-holy Mind, saves him from the bitterness of cynicism and the despondency of romance. No preferential love, it is true, —not even the Divine,—can be without its aversions; but when they fall upon remediable and perishable ill, while the heart is engaged upon an everlasting good, their harshness is softened and their dejection relieved. He that is taken up into true love for God dwells at the fountain-head of perfect life, and has there, not only an ever-present Refuge from his disappointment in partial natures, but the goal of hope, the purifying and penetrating force, whither the most distant wanderer tends. The higher his conception of the Soul of souls, the less is his surprise that in our humanity the image is broken and the resemblance faint: he stands at an elevation where impatience is impossible, and from the consummate end of all good a joy goes forth to greet its smallest beginnings. Yet, quick as his sympathy will be to detect the germs of every grace, he will no more be carried away with enthusiasm for detached and limited excellence than be flung into despair by the uncancelled wrongs and grievous sins of men; for he lives where he can be shut up with neither, and both are transcended and seen only in their true relations. Entranced with the vision of the Supreme Good, he can never fail to recognise and embrace its broken reflections everywhere; also he can never cease to demand the missing features that are yet withheld; and so it is that this love of his is generous and exacting too; meeting the achievements already made with refreshing response, yet pressing for all that yet remain behind, with a grave arrest of sympathy and an expressive silence till they come. This highest form of love is as well proportioned and discriminative as it is quick and copious; and while flowing freely in to cherish every actual grace, still fixes an asking look upon the possible, under which no earnest conscience can ever sleep. It is a *prospective* affection, grateful for the present, but thirsting towards the future; and is thus, if not the source, at least the foster-parent of all progressive righteousness. It will suffer no slight to the little child, and casts a tender eye on the rudimentary heaven of his nature; yet will give no rest to the noble youth who had kept all the commandments and yearned for something more. When I am contemplated by this Christ-like spirit, I know that I am regarded with an interest measured by the capacities of my being; and with a love which is in perfect tune with my inward character and has no reservations but from my own unfaithfulness. In proportion as the conditions of my life-problem are fulfilled, as my powers put themselves forth in adequate and fitting activity, as I promptly and truly respond to the demands upon my will, am I animated and upheld by support of the divinest sympathy. And just as far as my nature fails and flags, as I forfeit strength by unresisted temptations and incur shame by degrading compliances and shrink from required sacrifice, do I feel upon me a look which deepens all my guilt and doubles the sadness of my infirmity, and yet silently pleads with me to re-assert the rights which I have impaired, and overtake the march from which I had fallen away.

Thus, from this highest term, of divine love, there is nothing omitted: it covers, it blends, it modulates, it dignifies, it sweetens all the rest. Hence the chief religious minds have a largeness of their own which, as history shows, gives them a mysterious grasp of other and minor natures, and lifts them, in the moral world, into the same relation to partial forms of character, that, in the intellectual world, the philosopher bears to the specialist, and, in the sphere of Art, Michael Angelo bears to a pattern-designer. The soul in which this commanding affection remains silent may breathe out this or that rich tone, and even its snatches of broken melody; but it is as a lyre without its chief string, or an organ with its central octave dumb; and it can never be adequate to deliver the great masterpieces of human creation, which tax all the powers of performance and comprise all the resources of harmony.

The humane, the beautiful, the right, remain only scattered elements of good, till they are gathered into the Divine, and blended into one by the combining love of God.

XXIV.

The Discipline of Darkness.

JOB xiii. 24 (part), 25 (part).

"Wherefore hidest Thou thy face? Wilt Thou break a leaf driven to and fro?"

As the Book of Job and Lockyer's Astronomy lay together on my table, I could not help contrasting in them the genius of the ancient East and of the modern West. Only the Mediterranean longitudes lay between the authors; yet in the face of how different a world did they live! To the one, as he looked up on the heavens from the Arabian plains, the vault of night seemed written all over with mysteries: to the other, scanning it from his observatory, it is inscribed with diagrams that may be worked and periodic times that may be registered. The Patriarch (if we may substitute him for his poet) had never, it is plain, been lectured to at any Royal Institution, and looked with superfluous awe at many things in nature which we 'perfectly understand.' Orion and Pleiades above, the forests and the torrents below, the wild creatures of the mountain and the floods, the speed of the ostrich, the flight of the bird, the neck of the war-horse, the scales of Leviathan, are marvels in his eyes,—the speaking fragments of an almighty life behind. From us, the wonder of these things is gone. That "He hangeth the earth upon nothing" is no less a matter of course than that the stone flies from the sling. "The way for the lightning of thunder," far from being "hid from the eyes of all the living," we may see on every church steeple. Since our lessons in geology, we know it is the "raised beaches," instead of "the Almighty," that have "set bars and doors to the sea and said, 'Hitherto shalt thou come and no further, and here shall thy proud waves be stayed.'" We have "measured the breadth of the earth," and ascertained what a trifle it is. We have "entered the way where light dwelleth," and can name the incandescent chemicals from which it comes. The "wild ass" and the "unicorn,"—are they not stuffed in our museums? and in the nearest Zoological Gardens may you not see Behemoth in his reeds, "moving his tail like a cedar"? We have got so familiar with the place and plan of things, that nothing looks in upon us with a quickening eye, and our wonder is all used up.

This habituation to the order of the world, the result of long and large experience, satisfies our natural desire to see into the *Law* of all that is and happens. We do not like to be taken unawares: we prefer the track clear and open into the distance, and gladly escape the starts of the thicket which hides we know not what: we deem it a gain to reduce the surprises of life, and stand on a field where nothing is unforeseen. Nor is this the mere craving of our sentient nature, seeking for repose. It is no less the ambition of the intellect to unravel the seeming tangle of events, to lay out here and there the many-coloured threads, and trace how the parts make up the pattern of the whole. If Science ever indulges an Elysian dream, I suppose it is to live in a scene where all can be predicted for the future and interpreted in the past; where the intricate shall be only a cluster of the simple, and the mysterious a forgotten haze that once veiled the plain; where no duration can hide anything and no distance dwarf it; and from the perspective of thought the shadowed glades, and the curving sea, and the dip of the horizon, shall take themselves away.

With this ideal, in its application to the work of our hand and the range of our research, there is no fault to be found. To be out of gear with the system to which we belong, is to be displaced from its movements, or to feel them only as a shock. The more insight we can obtain into its rules, the more shall we fall in with its power, as if it were our own; and be prepared for its certainties, as if they lay in our design; and be saved all struggle for what is not to be, and all anxiety about what is sure to come. In proportion as we grow into the scheme of nature, making our understanding its copy and our will its servitor, do we extend our knowledge, secure our action, economise our strength: no error, no waste, no frustration, confuses our career; and, suffer as we may, it is the quiet endurance of calculated ill, with no added pang of horror and alarm.

Wherever then we can push our conquests over the darkness of the world, it is not for us to pause in the advance: wherever the way is open, we are free and bound to go. But it is another question, whether we have reason to complain of the many paths we *cannot* enter, and of the impassable limits that baffle us and turn us back. Must we deplore it as a spoiling of our life, that not all its elements are uniform; that the date of death hovers over four-score years, and alights now here now there; that the birth of children, the incidence of disease, the specialities of mental constitution, nay, even such outward things as the shipwreck and the fire and the missile's flight, defy our foresight, and, though intensely affecting our well-being, hide themselves in the inscrutable order? That in one sense we feel a grievance in such irreducible uncertainties, is evident from this; that by the method of *insurance* we endeavour to get rid of them, and find an equivalent for the prescience we cannot exercise. The advantage we thus win is still of the same kind. We secure ourselves against a shock, and establish a base to make our reckoning safe; and though we cannot steady the uncertain sea on which we ride, we place in equilibrium a compass that shall direct the helm. And so, if all our life's interests could be reduced to rule, if everything human could be predicted like the phases of the moon, we should doubtless become completely adapted to a world without alternative; every hour would find us ready; our place might depend upon us with the certainty of fate; no step would ever have to be retraced; habit would be perfected with us. But then, *Habit would become supreme.* We should be worked up into the mechanism of nature, and what else would be our *Personal* powers would be yoked into the same team with the weights, and damps, and winds. Wherever such a state is approached, we turn out more work, but exercise less Soul; inasmuch as Rule in nature becomes Routine in man. If, to perfect this, and make it all in all, fulfils our ideal of humanity, and the largest outer product gives the greatest life, then we must lament that an uncertainty remains to strain the cords of our hearts, and fling forth music from the swaying air. But if our life have another measure, taken from within, if it may be judged, not wholly by what it successfully *does*, but in part by what it intrinsically *is*, if moreover it has other attributes than it takes from the intellect and the will, if, with rights transcending these, it have a trust of duty, and a pleading of pity, and a flood of great affections, then we must see, in the irreducible uncertainties, the very school and discipline of this side of our humanity, where its glory and its sorrow blend.

In truth, for the birth and the freshening of human Love, the conditions most essential are just the conditions we most resist:—the *inequalities*, and the *uncertainties* of life. It is because we are not all alike, but a great mixed company of weak and strong, of men and women, of young and old, of bright and sad, nay, of ancient and modern, of native and foreign, that our dull souls awake into sympathies which carry them out of themselves in all directions, and that reverence, trust, compassion, rise and spread through all the spheres. And it is because, thus taught to love, we cannot see what will befall, that we are driven to love the more. There are times, no doubt, when we forget that anything is precarious, and for the moment accept the unbroken health of things as if it were a pledge that so they would always be; and these are apt to be bold and wanton times, when the voice is loud, and the laugh is rude, and the words not free from insolence. If ever, in such an hour, we have borne hard upon a friend, let but an illness stretch him before us, and his life begin to look frail, how instantly we know that we have too little prized it, and all the harsh tones disappear! Wherein lies the magic of that look of his? Whence do those pale features draw the persuasion they do not mean to speak? If we knew for certain that in a month he would be on Change again, and that the bell would not toll for him till after thirty years, would the turn of his eye equally smite upon our heart? were there no *crisis* sitting on his face, no suggested moment of trembling between life and death, should we move around him with the same reverent step, and speak to him with the same meaning in the voice? No: it is not from what we see with the outward eye, but from the questioning visions of the mind, the haunting dread, the half-ready tears, the shadow of the morrow behind the light of today, that the thoughtful tenderness all comes; and a rigid certainty would soon crystallize upon the soul and bring the hardness back again. And as it is when fears are deepening, so is it when they are waning too, yet not forgot. Let the crisis pass, and the days of convalescence come, when the faint glance grows bright, and the languid cheek begins to glow, and the feet are planted firm again, and the sunshine and the rustling leaves, and the children's merry voices, are charged with a new joy; why do we linger near our friend, as if a sacred fascination held us? why gaze at him with an insight we never had before? why feel an old weight lifted from the heart, and spring to him with the trust and promise of a fresh vow? It is because the trembling scales have turned, and we are purified by the wonder of deliverance; snatched from the compunctions of inadequate affection, and placed on the threshold of better hopes. It is ever the secret background of possibilities we cannot read, which invests the forms in the front light with mellowing tints of mystery, and a veil of unearthly beauty; and did these never reach us with their appeal, we might know the actual, and do the palpable and safe; but we should aspire to nothing, and venture nothing, bear nothing with high trust, and take no vow of self-devotion.

In trying then to eliminate uncertainty, we strive, through the instinct of the understanding and the will, to destroy the very discipline appointed for the conscience and affections; and as, morally, we conquer in our intellectual defeat, and repair our defects of knowledge by nobleness of love, it may well be believed that we shall never push our lines of foresight to the further limits of our human world, but, in the last days as in the first, find ourselves on the bounding shore of the seen and the unseen, with our nature competed for by the finite light and the infinite shadows, and wrung into its glory by the conflict and its sorrows. Had not Life the interest of an ever-opening plot, with catastrophe preparing every instant but hidden to the last, with how little care should we see its curtain rise, with how little sympathy watch its actors play their part, with how slight a sigh perceive its drop-scene fall! Why, as you look upon a group of children at their play,—why does the ringing laughter bring you, along with the response of happy affection, a graver and a tenderer mood ? It is the contrast of the thoughtless present and the hidden future : you know there is a drama writ, but with invisible ink, and reserved in the casket of each young life ; and the images throng upon you of the countless moving vicissitudes of our humanity ; and upon the ear of thought, the peal of the happy marriage bells, or the toll for the early death, rings out ; and you wonder *which* is on the first step of manly faithfulness or womanly devotedness, and *which* on the slippery incline that descends into untraceable ruin. And so in every emergency of later years, in the last embrace before the long voyage, or in the parting before the war, it is the alternative images peering in upon the mind, of happy greeting, or of a silent spot for ever sacred in the far waters or on the foreign field, that deepen the moment with a meaning it cannot speak ; and though the voice perhaps is cheery and the heart beats firm, the strength of each friend is only in the other, and in the high trust they carry into the dark. If you take the danger and the doubt away, where would be the gentle reverence of the surrender ? Let there be no arrow by night, no malady by day, let the three-score years and ten be assured to the last hour, and the eyes fall punctually asleep with the setting sun entered on the calendar ; and would anything tender and divine hang around this death by the clock ? No watchful love could hover round the invulnerable : they might go forth on their enterprise alone, and be forgotten; followed by no musing fancy, that is flushed with their triumph or anguished at their fall. Between *us and God* it may be true that "there is no fear in perfect love"; for the Eternal is for ever safe: the All-holy is for ever good: but *among ourselves* it would be a shallow love that was without its fear; for the very goodness and sanctity to which we look up are noble because secured by no necessity; and the lives that are the joy of ours would shine with a drier light, were they less precarious; and it is the refraction of tears ever possible, that breaks the rays into colours soft and beautiful. If we are faithful to one another in our onward march, it is because there is not one who may not fall: our road lies through a perpetual ambush; and whoever has a friend to keep step with him on the way will try to place him on the sheltered side. Of our moral nature it is the very essence, that it is given to meet alternatives; of our affections, that they have to live in the actual with eye upon the possible; and the whole wisdom and magnanimity of life consist in a will conformed to what is, with a heart ready for what is not. Unless all *character* is to perish, the contingencies must stay. The tacit mutual dependence, the secret suspicion that here or there the ground which looks so solid is undermined, the constant possibility of a total change of parts in the drama of our life, and so the silent wonder that mingles with every scene, these are the freshening powers breathing on what else were common or unclean, and meeting and startling us like angels encountered in the street. Whatever depth there may be in our poor love, whatever reverence speaks in our rough voice, flows into us from that world unseen.

All our private experience goes to soothe our complaints of darkness, and reconcile us to the conditions of a precarious existence. The witness of history is on the same side. In the education of mankind, what races have played the most quickening and effective part? Is it the industrial and gainful, that, in the interests of prosperity, have cultivated isolation, and have evaded the conflicts of honour, lest they should raise the rates of insurance? Phœnicia, who treated the world as an Exchange, and crowded every port with her ships, could not even hand down her maritime discoveries, and died without a bequest, except of her colonies, her superstitions, and her crimson dye. Egypt, by the very uniformity of her physical fertility, remained in moral barrenness: and, with a monopoly of the arts and sciences, sat for ages, like her own Sphinx upon the desert, placidly gazing on an unfertilized world. Her stereotyped civilization aimed, not without success, to reproduce in society the inflexible order of natural law, and to bar out the contingencies of affairs. If you would estimate such stationary periodicity, compare its fruitless longevity with the brief flash of the Hellenic States, which still lights up the thought and thrills the hearts of men. And in lands where freer and larger play is conceded to human capacities, is it, do you think, the safe and quiet times when risk is absent and ease secured, that cut the distinctive lines into their character, and give them a physiognomy in history? On the contrary, it is in the days of peril, in the crises of anguish, that the force of character steps forth and constitutes itself, and under some high and daring guidance, finds a footing upon the rock and retakes the citadel of hope. Had Thebes never been humbled, she would have found in Epaminondas no deliverer to illuminate her page in history. Had Athens never been abandoned to the Persian invader, there would have been no magic in the names of Marathon and Salamis: her writers would have been without their most telling allusions, her orators without their most kindling appeals; and her people would not have risen to that ideal type of life which makes them the wonder of all time. Had Rome seen nothing but an Augustan age, she might have had historians, if there had been any history to tell; and poets, if they could dispense with great admirations, and sing without the material of great actions; and philosophers, if the problems of the world had ever agitated the sleepy experience of men. But it was the tyranny of Tarquin that created the Republic: it was from the cloud of Carthaginian invasion that Scipio emerged: it was amid the shame of spreading corruption that the noble protest of Stoic virtue arose, and mingled a melancholy majesty with the empire's fall. Nor is it otherwise with any State that has earned a remembrance of itself. Of every great City, the memorials of fallen heroes and the trophies of dread strife, are among the chief works of art. Every legislative hall is guarded by the figures of those who once braved the dangers of their country's darkest hours. In every national tradition, the popular favourite is the captive king, the chained patriot, the unflinching martyr.

And if it is the great crises of peril that, as they are passing, train a people's character, so is it their reflection in literature that, ages after they are gone, still spreads and perpetuates the ennobling influence. The inspiration that descends on us from the Past, and makes us heirs of accumulated thought and enriched affections, —from whom chiefly does it come? Is it from the uniformly happy and the untempted good? from those who have most realized the lot for which our sentient and intellectual instincts cry aloud? No: but from the central figures of the great tragedies of our humanity; from the conquerors of desolating monsters; from the creators of Law and tamers of the people; from love beyond death, that carried its plaintive music to the shades; from the avengers of wrong; from the martyrs of right; from the missionaries of mercy; from the pass of Thermopylæ; from the Milvian bridge; from the fires of Smithfield; from the waters of Solway; from the cross of Calvary. A world without a contingency or an agony could have no hero and no saint, and enable no Son of Man to discover that he was a Son of God. But for the suspended plot that is folded in every life, history is a dead chronicle of what was known before as well as after; Art sinks into the photograph of a moment that hints at nothing else; and poetry breaks the cords and throws the lyre away. There is no Epic of the certainties; and no lyric without the surprise of sorrow and the sigh of fear. Whatever touches and ennobles us in the lives and in the voices of the past is a divine birth from human doubt and pain. Let then the shadows lie, and the perspective of the light still deepen beyond our view; else, while we walk together, our hearts will never burn within us as we go; and the darkness, as it falls, will deliver us into no hand that is Divine.

XXV.

Rest in the Lord.

PSALM xxxvii. 7.

"Rest in the Lord and wait patiently for him."

IT is difficult for the young, and not less so for those who yet remain children in soul, to believe the startling assertion, by religious writers, of the universal misery of men. The sad music of the prophets, the passionate outpourings of an Augustin, the plaintive meditations of a Pascal, and even the tender voice of the Man of Sorrows, appear to them pitched in too deep a key and to wander over notes too far from the brilliancy of joy. The impression is thus very prevalent, that devout persons take melancholy views of things, and throw the unreal shadows from their own minds on the outward scene of their existence. Yet if you will but turn over the page and consult the expression of the same mind in another mood, you may find words transparent with an infinite depth of peace, or dashing on in a torrent of rejoicing. The same Paul who now wrings his drooping hands and cries, "O wretched man that I am," ere long flings them aloft to exclaim, "Rejoice in the Lord always; and again I say unto you, Rejoice!" The same Wesley who now deplores his "vain repentances,"—his life grown "fruitless at its end,"—in lines that bear the trace of tears, then bursts into the triumph of his watch-night songs, and glories in the awful joys of death, in strains that make the passing bell appear to ring with victory. To the inexperienced, both the sadness and the joy seem strange and unintelligible,—vehement and opposite outrages upon truth and reality,—the alternations of a tumultuous and ill-regulated mind. And yet they not only co-exist without any tendency to mutual exclusion; but are found in men most remarkable for their calmness and constancy of soul, for the clearness of their purposes, and the force and patience of their will.

The fact is, the childish and the saintly mind form different judgments of life because they look on it from opposite mental stations; the one from a condition of *unawakened aspiration*, the other from that of *aspiration that has found its path and touched its limits*: while the great mass of men on whom their observation is made fill an intermediate field, of *uneasy and neglected aspiration*. The child, gazing at the grown world, and seeing men's outward possessions and not their inward wants, thinks admiringly of their lot, regards it as a powerful and cheerful thing, and longs to press into it. The saint, discerning an inward want beyond all the measure of outward possession, pities the infinite thirst that feeds only on ashy and juiceless fruits. And in this deep compassion, with which he looks on life, he from time to time includes himself; for though he has reached the head-spring of ever-living waters, he is not always there: he wanders from them and often becomes as he was when he knew them not, and is then not less parched and sick at heart than all the rest. The three stages of character are not so separated, that when we have emerged into the higher, we cannot relapse into the lower: we cannot ascend, till the atmosphere of God is spread around us; but to descend in its very midst, we have only to droop the wing. And so it is, that those who have touched the summit know the sunshine and the cloud of every elevation; while they who are yet below listen, as to strange tales, to the glories and the terrors of the height.

The great secret of all peace lies in the ascendency of some strong love. Love,—the admiring or reverent direction of the heart on some object,—is the positive power of our life; and on its free action, on its due match against the problems it undertakes, depend the tranquillity and unity of existence. The child is happy, because his love is well proportioned to its ends: it ranges over the little circle of good before his eyes;

and goes unanxiously forth to embrace and realize its aim. He is checked by a venerated control from without, not by shameful hesitancies within: he sighs for little that is out of reach; and he lives ever pursuing and ever winning his pursuit. The man, at least of the present and all similar ages, is unhappy, because in this he has ceased to be a child. The balance of his nature is destroyed. He has more understanding, and has no more love. The great motive energy of his soul is overchecked,—regulated by exacting scruples into an uneasy incapacity. He can no longer surrender himself freely into the possession of a great truth, or plunge into the tides of a glorious passion. He has the wish to take the right course, and the discernment to avoid the wrong, but no impulse to bear him hither or thither; and so he sits, like a pilot in a calm, with infinite skill to direct his helm, but not a breath to swell his sails. The office of the intellect is purely regulative, that of the conscience mainly prohibitive: they speak to us in negatives;—"not this way, for it is foolish"; "not that, for it is wrong." They supply no power, but, assuming it to be there, prevent its waste and its abuse. An age that develops them to the neglect of all else, and attempts to live by them alone, finds itself therefore wise in the cure of all diseases, yet without the freshness of natural health, poising its existence on dietetic niceties and not breasting the winds of the mountain and facing the driving of the snow. We have surely fallen on such a time of feebleness and unrest. We have the critic everywhere: the lover nowhere. Nothing so cheap as the intelligence which suffices to contradict and the conscientiousness which prompts to object: but the heart-wisdom that can light us on our way by the lustre of sweet and earnest affection, the holy zeal that can melt our doubts away and make our duty a march of common joy instead of a skirmish of individual scruples, are little less than obsolete. Disintegration is at work in every church: irresolution marks every party in the state: isolation enfeebles every man apparently fitted to lead in thought or action. Sects keep together by external repulsion rather than by internal attraction; and the only fervours that appear seem to be the inspirations of antipathy. In private life the lines of care are deepened: a certain anxiety of mind, a visible susceptibility of temper, the absence of a genial and trustful spirit, betray the unsatisfied nature and the dearth of guiding sympathies within. Thought, grown too quick and active for love, becomes a painful restlessness. It is incapable of any flight of steady aim that shall enable it to migrate from clime to clime of truth; but is like the swallow that has lost its nest, wheeling in idle circles through the air, sweeping the grass or tipping the water with its wing, still hovering round its place of loss, with a cry that proclaims it desolate.

Wherever this source of unrest exists, there is no remedy but in restoring the lost proportions of the soul:—by disciplining the affections into a greatness suitable to the control of so critical a judgment and so scrupulous a conscience. In the absence of anything of nobler scope, limited loves, particular enthusiasms, mere fancies of the mind, be they only innocent, are a great good; breaking the threads of detaining hesitations, and in one direction at least delivering the heart from contempt. The active votary of any harmless object is better than the passive critic of all; and the dullest man who lives only to collect shells or coins is worthier than the shrewdest who lives only to laugh at him. And if his pursuit, instead of fastening on a mere dead product of nature or history, attach itself to some *human* object, if it be the pride of a father in a child, or the guardianship of a mother by her son, it redeems life from the curse of sterility, and enriches it with many spots of gentle beauty: it turns the soul out from its own close centre and gives it the free air of disinterestedness: it imparts strength for wholesome self-denial; and smooths out the hard lines upon the features with the softening touch of pity and of joy. In these days it is a wiser and more difficult skill in education to preserve the enthusiasms of nature, than to regulate them by the artifices of reason; to save the moral admirations from false shame at their own earnestness than to restrain them from rash excess.

Let the fresh dew lie undisturbed upon the young child's soul: only by drinking it eagerly in during the early hours can it bear the noonday heats and lend an unwithered smile to the evening shades.

But it is only in contrast with *no love* that we can thus accept *any love* as a good. It cannot be morally indifferent *what* the object of affection is. It would be a weak and sentimental abuse of Christian doctrine to suppose that, because "love is the fulfilling of the law," any sort of feeling that carries us out of ourselves satisfies the demands of divine obligation and completes the conditions of a holy peace. The objects offered to the heart are very variously worthy of its attachment; and only when each has its just share and place and, however dear, recedes before more venerable claims, can we cease to be among the weary and heavy-laden, and find the true disciple's inner rest. It is the vice of amiable fanatics to treat love as in itself the supreme good, the end of the Christian life; to pray always and only for the melting of the stony heart; as if, when this were done, all was surely right, and nothing remained for vigilance and aspiration. Love is a good, not on its own account, but on account of the excellence to which it clings; not because it sets the heart at one with *something*, but with something noble, true and holy. Nobleness, truth and holiness must therefore be higher than affection, being that to which it ought to spring. Where they are not made supreme and paramount, wherever love stays with mixed and lower objects and intercepts the clear view of these, wherever it learns to be satisfied with its tenderness and heedless of its purity, not only is its influence tainted, but its peace is spoiled by utter instability. A heart entirely surrendered to its human and earthly relations, without throwing around them the hallowed atmosphere of faith, is indeed redeemed from the dry pining of a bark-bound and unmellowed nature; but has no security from the sorrows and sins of impulse, no shelter from the storms of tumultuous anguish. The domestic love which is a mere enlargement of instinct, without moral appreciation, without reverence, providing the tender care, but unconscious of a holy trust, is detained with the earthly form, and never catches the heavenly spirit, of its lot. No sacredness mingles with the daily task: no angel-hand wipes the tears of weariness away: no treasured hope beguiles the bereft and mourning heart with visions sweet and calm. For want of a supporting reverence, the truest affection loses its clearness and misses its proper end. The parent, for instance, loves his children: nor was there ever perhaps a country or an age in which this relation had more power than with us. Too often, however, he loves them with no tincture of *respect* or restraining sense of sanctity; but more and more with the tenderness of indulgent instinct; less and less with that quiet strength to deny them and authority to guide them, which springs from the consciousness of a trust and the presence of a Divine eye. Hence, the natural distance between souls,—the very thing that makes the beauty of life's perspective and the wholesomeness of its discipline,—is disappearing from recognition: young and old, wise and foolish, are brought to the level of a kindly but prosaic equality; and the hoary head turns coward, whilst the young child grows bold. Hence, too, a spectacle more and more common, especially in the families of the affluent, which a thoughtful observer finds it sad to behold. Often you may see the earliest years of children cared for with a studious conscience; not merely a well-adjusted physical management, and a steady mechanism of habit and good instruction; but a nice vigilance over the temper and dispositions, a scrupulous regard for truth and purity, an anxiety to train the moral taste aright; giving you every hope that the parents know their sacred trust, and feel their house to be a shrine of devout service. What fairer sight can there be than the children of such a home?—the open brow, the clear confiding eye, the gracious ways, the artlessness moulded into beauty, present a frequent picture which it is a joy to behold. Thus far the purest desires of the home, the prayers that the children may be *good*, have no hindrance: they regulate the hours, they choose the instructor, they form the speech, they determine the companions, they select the tale. But the nursery does not last for ever. The time comes when its threshold must be passed, and from a distance the hum and murmur begin to flow upon the ear from the great halls of life; and how often does that dizzying sound act with a fatal charm and confuse the native religion of the parent's heart! He no longer offers these young souls only to goodness and to God, but now limits his higher wishes by the conditions of fashion and success. That his sons should be pure, manly, noble; that his daughters should be guileless, modest, and of loving earnest heart; that both should be so true to their best aspirings as to meet any Christ-like eye and lie open to any holiest spirit;—these wishes are qualified now by the resolve that no disadvantage shall be suffered in the hot race of life, and no unskilfulness endured in the usages and ideas of the surrounding world. And so, from that moment, the tyranny of custom intrudes upon the serious sanctities of parental choice; and on the minds hitherto so protected a thousand influences are permitted to pour which shock their purity and bewilder their veracity and, with a false dazzle of frivolity, put out the earnest stars of heavenly contemplation. It is of all things the most melancholy to watch the moral clouding over of life's early dawn; to trace the dim veil stealing over the artless look; to notice how the earnest tone begins to leave the voice, and every worthy enthusiasm dies away into indifference; how it comes to be thought a fine thing to speak coolly of what is odious for its vice, and critically of what is awful for its beauty. Thus to see the young that had filled us with love and hope growing out of their simplicity and intuitive clearness instead of maturing into depth and enlarging into greatness, is like the disappointing passage from the fresh spring to the mid-summer in the precincts of a large town instead of in the open country and amid the breezy hills; the brilliant foliage, the joyous grass, the sportive light, fading in the one case into a dingy grimace of nature, ripening in the other into a massive fulness and splendour. Where this spoiling takes place, I believe it is because we mingle no *reverence* with our affection, and accept without awe the solemn trust of a child's conscience. Were there a deeper reality in our cares for religious training, we should feel committed to us a soul new as if born in Paradise, and should watch to see the divine features come out; should fear to quench any aspiration, to contradict any protest, to hurt any sacred instinct, of a spirit nearer perhaps to God than ours. Do you plead the necessity, urged for so many questionable things, of giving the youth betimes "a knowledge of the world"? Aye; but of *what* "world"?—for that is a large name, which covers several different things. Do you mean the crowd of contemporaries on the same level with himself, his equals or inferiors in principle and character, who by their tendencies and habits vote into existence the customs amid which he is to live? If so, you propose to bring him down to the average standard created by the mixed multitude of good and bad, to kill out every higher expostulation of the soul, and undo as he advances the hopeful work of earlier years. No: be not afraid to scorn so poor an ambition. Let him grow familiar with an elder and a better "world" than this; with the men of grander stature, who constitute the honour and lustre of history; who will rebuke in him all mean enclosure in the present and make him conscious of high communion with the past; who will kindle him with veneration for the nature given him to adorn; who will detain him in the company of the wise and holy, and touch him with shame, if he be not worthy of their society and kindred. The minds above him, the spirits of patriots and saints, martyrs of truth, apostles of righteousness,—these are the "world," in the "knowledge" of which it is ennobling to excel, though it gives no passport to the assemblies of fashion, and supplies no key to the slang of frivolity.

As with domestic love, so is it with every affection that can separately possess the soul: if it escapes the grasp, and is not taken up by the glory, of a devout Faith, it is never safe from becoming wavering, wild, or tyrannous. If frustrated,—its disappointment is without rebound, falls with crushing blow and then lies still as a dead and irremovable weight. If satisfied,—the joy of success, spoiled by self-gratulation, becomes a mere exuberance of spirits, and has none of the serene dignity of a thankful soul. Where there is no quieting perception of a Divine Presence in the world, the sense of justice, the indignation at wrong, sinks into a revolutionary passion, fantastic in its speech and reckless in its ways, instead of a grave and considerate obedience to the eternal Law of God. All human enthusiasms, permitted to become ultimate and disown their divine subordination, invariably degenerate into restlessness and precipitation; fret and chafe impatiently against the obstacles that stay their course; and where they cannot win a happy way, waste and corrode themselves with inner scorns and vexations. A vehement temperament may no doubt be *externally* subdued by considerations of policy, or the discipline of good taste and intellect. But how paltry is this decent self-control, compared with the real internal calm when the Christ-like spirit has walked over the wild waters of the soul! No sublimer spectacle do I know on earth, than the faculties of a grand and passionate nature, as in a Socrates or a Paul, falling into stillness before the face of God, and by the awful light of his countenance turned from a stormy nobleness into a loving and working power. It is a spectacle which emerges painfully and rarely from the battle of the will, spontaneously and often from the repose of faith.

In thus seeking a divine transfiguration for all our natural impulses, I am far from wishing to set up, like our older divines, the love of the Creator in opposition to what was called "the love of the creatures"; as though the mind intent on God must find every other sympathy absorbed, and feel itself alone and without relation amid the Infinite. This fancied antagonism between the human and divine yearnings of our nature is a cold metaphysic sublimation so false to reality that the gentlest spirit, we may safely affirm, will ever come more gentle and loving from its prayers; and the first trace by which God marks his path across the soul is the new tenderness in every tint of pure affection, and the quicker movement in each work of kindly service. But this I do profoundly believe; that all finite loves are only *half-born*, wandering in a poor twilight, unknowing of their peace and power, till they lie within the encompassing and glorifying love of God. Where there is no reference to him, our pictures of the moral universe become as much mere local distortions as the systems of nature which misplace the stationary Sun. The soul, drawn out by filial sympathy into his infinitude and blended by aspiration with his absolute perfection, sees the inner orbits of dependent good precisely as they are, fair and true in themselves, but borrowing a more solemn beauty from their relation to the whole. Held to their centre of equilibrium, and facing his light from their several distances, the lesser affections observe their proportions and do not fly from their tracks. How can they ever look away from him? He is the element in which they live. Though they were to perish, he would endure. While all else rises and flows by, he *is* and ever stays. Amid the fleeting shows and disappointed promises of good, he abides with us, the inexhaustible Essence and reality of all. In him alone, but in him for ever, there is Rest. In evil days, when just men strive in vain to beat back the hosts of wrong, and mad tyrannies gall the heart with shouts of triumph, the Sentinel of every world is on his sleepless watch, and knows how to protect it from surprise. He is the continuous thread of all our years, and his love throws in each pattern of beauty woven into their texture: and when the images of the past, the distant fields, the dear abode, the gracious forms, the vivid hopes, the earnest heroisms, of our young days, gleam with a fairer light through the sorrows and failures of maturity, it is his breathing spirit that dissipates the cloud of time, and sends his reviving sunshine through. Only let us be at one with him, and our life gathers down upon it the strength of his infinite serenity. The simple thought, that 'God is here,'—that the august Ordainer of our trust and supporter of our faithfulness is present in the very hiding-places of the soul,—contains within it the most powerful agencies of religion. Warning, sympathy and rest are treasured in it to inexhaustible amount. Amid the fatigues of life's incessant struggle, under the sense that we can never sleep or all things will go wrong, refreshment is instantly gained when we ascend to the fountain of all affection, and touch the parching lips with the draft of life. In temptations to unfaithfulness witnessed by no human eye, let us but say, 'Ah! Lord, but thou art here,' and the failing purpose springs to its feet again. And under the encroachments of fretfulness or despondency from the frequent perverseness of men, what can so soon check the hasty thought, soothe the unquiet passion, and put a music of patience into the soul, as the look of that pure and loving eye from its depth of infinite calm? In the trembling of age and the stealthy approaches of the last sleep, the dear presence of an Almighty Guardian, to whom age is as childhood and who unites the future with the past, fills the deepening shadows with a mild and holy light. Let him only be near; and the obscuring veil of mortal ill that sometimes seems to shut us in, and tempts us to believe in nothing but the sad rain, is soon withdrawn, like the cloud lifting itself from out the glen; and the sunshine first glorifies, then dissipates the haze; leaving the mountain-range of immovable goodness and beauty clear against the everlasting sky. So pass the storms away, so deepens the heavenly view, to the soul that will but "rest in the Lord and wait patiently for him."

THE CHRISTIAN IN THE WORLD. By Rev. D. W. FAUNCE. 16mo. Price $1.50. Contents: The Statement; The Method; Principles; The Christian in Prayer; The Christian in his Recreations; The Christian in his Business.

From the Boston Cultivator.

It will be remembered that by the will of the late Hon. Richard Fletcher a fund was bequeathed to Dartmouth College, from the proceeds of which should be offered biennially a prize of $500 for the best essay on the importance of holy living on the part of Christian professors, and to the author of this admirably written work has the prize been awarded. This earnest, practical appeal for a higher standard of Christian living comes fresh from the heart, and we think must reach the heart and bring forth fruit in the lives of those who read it. In its wide application it comes to the Christian in his business and social relations, his daily duties and recreations, telling him how in all these varied relations he can be a "Christian in the World," and a blessing to his race.

From the Christian Era.

But *the* characteristic of the work, one which will attract to it a class of intelligent, spiritual-minded Christians, the unorganized fraternity of the inner and the outer life, is its lofty, uncompromising, exhilarating idealism. It exhibits the perfect man in Christ, and to that picture it points with the calm earnestness of conviction, though with the humility and sympathy begotten by the consciousness of sin and the remembrance of divers stumblings in the way of life.

From the Syracuse Journal.

Mr. Faunce is a clear and forcible writer, whose name is familiar to readers of the Baptist press, and in this essay he has most powerfully and practically developed his subject. He first impresses the practicability and positiveness of Christian duty, demanded alike from Christians and busy men in the world. The first five chapters are devoted to the Statement, Method, and Principles involved, devoting the remaining chapters to the duty of the Christian in Prayer, in his Recreations, and finally in his Business. The full, rich, practical suggestions contained in this essay, the earnest spirit which inspired it, and withal its pleasant, flowing style, render it one of the most desirable of books on kindred topics, and we bespeak for it at least a place in every Christian library.

Sold everywhere by all Booksellers. Mailed, postpaid, by the Publishers,

ROBERTS BROTHERS, BOSTON.

SINGERS AND SONGS OF THE LIBERAL FAITH; being selections of Hymns and other Sacred Poems of the Liberal Church in America, with Biographical Sketches of the Writers, and with Historical and Illustrative Notes. By ALFRED P. PUTNAM. 8vo. Price $3.00.

From the New York Independent.

The service which has been done by Dr. A. P. Putnam, of Brooklyn, to those communions usually called Liberal, by compiling his beautiful book entitled "Singers and Songs of the Liberal Faith," is one not easily exaggerated. . . . As literature, these hymns have a high value ; but they signify most as expressions of religious sentiment, as devout utterances of trusting and aspiring souls. . . . There is, as Dr. Putnam reminds us, very little heresy in hymns. And we pity the bigot who could read this volume through without feeling some drawings of Christian fraternity toward the people whose deepest life is here so nobly expressed.

From the Liberal Christian.

It is very creditable to the editor that he has embraced so large an area and reaped the fruits of fields lying as far apart as the utmost extremes of our Zion. We find no evidence of any partisan or school prejudices in his selections ; indeed, we know no work from which personal biases have been more successfully or creditably excluded. In this respect, Dr. Putnam's volume is a true Irenicon, a peacemaker; sweetly reconciling the discordant voices of denominational polemics, in the harmony accordant of *song*. We cannot doubt that the assembling of so many and such dissimilar thinkers, in one chorus of praise, is a long step towards a union in higher sentiments of those temporarily divided by intellectual diversities.

From the Christian Union.

The literary value of Mr. Putnam's collection is unusually high, when we compare it with that of other volumes of religious poetry. To our minds the most convincing evidence of the existence of religious feeling among the people is the immense circulation of books of religious verse. We speak from actual knowledge when we say that certain compilations of religious poems have sold in greater numbers than the works of the most popular poets. These pious verses have, as a rule, been entirely devoid of poetic expression or sentiment, but their subjects have reconciled readers to all literary defects. Admirable as is the spirit which accepts such books, we cannot help believing it would be improved and elevated if the same thoughts were presented in language more poetic; for spirituality is, practically, the poetry of devotion. We hope, therefore, that Dr. Putnam's book will be largely bought and read.

Sold everywhere by all Booksellers. Mailed, postpaid, by the Publishers,

ROBERTS BROTHERS, BOSTON.

THE PERFECT LIFE.

In Twelve Discourses.

By WILLIAM ELLERY CHANNING, D.D.

Edited from his manuscripts by his nephew, WILLIAM HENRY CHANNING. 12mo. Price $1.50.

"The pulpit of the present day is in great danger of losing its dignity. For this, as well as other reasons, we welcome these Discourses of Dr. Channing. They are written in a fresh and pure style, and express lofty thoughts in simple yet noble language. We marvel that they have not been previously given to the public." — *Bibliotheca Sacra.*

"The volume is very welcome for many and the best reasons. Doubtless a jealous Orthodox critic, intent on finding heresies, will discover more or less to cavil at or challenge; but these Discourses lift us into an atmosphere too high and serene for polemical controversy, and tend to make the reader's heart cry out after the living God, or lovingly adore him as for the gift of his glorious self to the soul. All the charm of Dr. Channing's glowing and finished style lend themselves to this significant and reverent message from the depths of his heart. Not many books are so thoroughly saturated with religion as this, and it is of such a sort as the world greatly needs to-day." — *Dover Morning Star.*

"To all who are capable of discriminating we recommend it as a work which will enlarge their conceptions of the greatness and preciousness of Christianity, and lead them to deal more reverently with their own nature, and with all questions of duty and destiny." — *Christian Standard.*

"They tell what we would all gladly believe, if we cannot prove it to be true. And they will save those who read them with sympathy from that pride of half-knowledge, which makes the present seeming a barrier to all future revelation." — *Christian Register.*

Sold everywhere. Mailed postpaid by the Publishers,

ROBERTS BROTHERS, BOSTON.